Jean Fullerton is the author of nineteen historical novels. She is a qualified district and queen's nurse who has spent most of her working life in the East End of London, first as a sister in charge of a team, and then as a district nurse tutor. She is also a qualified teacher and spent twelve years lecturing on Community Nursing studies at a London university. She now writes full time.

Find out more at www.jeanfullerton.com

Also by Jean Fullerton

A Child of the East End

Jean Fullerton

CORVUS

First published in paperback in Great Britain in 2022 by Corvus, an imprint of Atlantic Books Ltd.

Copyright © Jean Fullerton, 2022

The moral right of Jean Fullerton to be identified as the author of this work has been asserted by her in accordance with the Copyright, Designs and Patents Act of 1988.

10 9 8 7 6 5 4 3 2 1

A CIP catalogue record for this book is available from the British Library.

Paperback ISBN: 978 1 83895 286 0
E-book ISBN: 978 1 83895 287 7

Printed and bound by CPI Group (UK) Ltd, Croydon, CR0 4YY

Corvus
An imprint of Atlantic Books Ltd
Ormond House
26–27 Boswell Street
London
WC1N 3JZ

www.corvus-books.co.uk

MIX
Paper from
responsible sources
FSC
www.fsc.org   FSC® C171272

*To my husband of forty-five years Revd Kelvin Woolmer,
my three daughters and eight grandchildren*

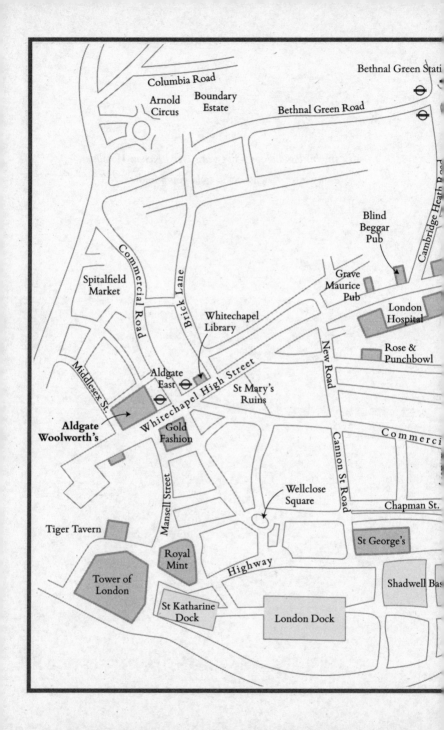

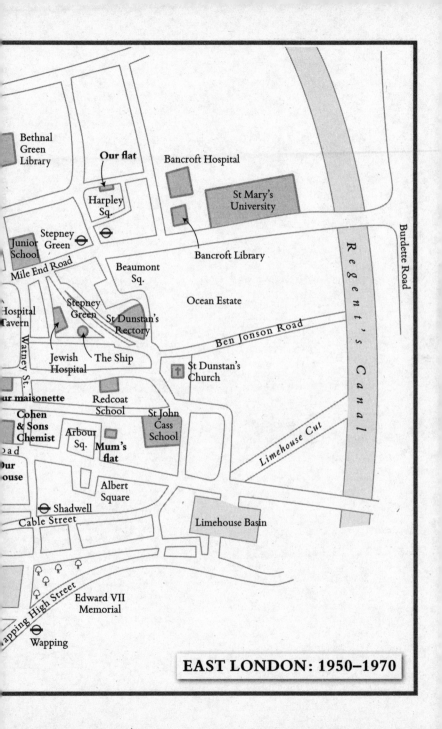

Bethnal Green Library

Our flat

Bancroft Hospital

Harpley Sq.

Bancroft Library

St Mary's University

Stepney Green

Junior School

Mile End Road

Beaumont Sq.

Ocean Estate

Regent's Canal

Burdette Road

Hospital Tavern

Stepney Green

St Dunstan's Rectory

Ben Jonson Road

Watney St.

Jewish Hospital

The Ship

St Dunstan's Church

Our maisonette

Redcoat School

St John Cass School

Limehouse Cut

Cohen & Sons Chemist

Arbour Sq.

Mum's flat

Road

Our House

Albert Square

Shadwell

Limehouse Basin

Cable Street

Wapping High Street

Edward VII Memorial

Wapping

EAST LONDON: 1950–1970

East London: a Place in the Heart, not on a Map

O NE OF MY first East London memories is lying in bed, listening to the low boom of the barges as they nudged each other on the Thames, just half a mile away from our estate. It is a sound my family had listened to for just short of two centuries. Today, I am the last Fullerton to have heard that noise floating on the still night air.

What used to be nothing more than a gravel floodplain has since been transformed into the waterfront of million-pound apartments, chic restaurants and coffee bars known as Canary Wharf. Where a silt marsh once lay, sharp, angular glass towers now stretch into the sky. When I was a child, this part of London looked very different to the way it does now.

It was work that first drew all my ancestors to the East End – to Wapping, Stepney and Bethnal Green – and work revolved around the water. As the dock and its surrounding factories began work at seven, the first front doors in the street started banging just after six, and the sound of dozens of pairs of hobnail boots marching southwards echoed between the rows of houses. East London was alive with industries. The docks – London, St Katharine's and the Royal – were unloading spirits and food daily from all four corners of the globe. The warehouses – now riverside apartments – were bursting at the seams with goods ready to be loaded on to trucks. Further from the docks there were machine factories, food processing plants, woodwork shops and hundreds of small wholesale companies working out of old Victorian houses along Commercial Road.

East London is the oldest suburb of London, springing up in the Middle Ages when craftsmen like boat builders and bakers settled there, and the area dates back to pre-historical times. The Ratcliffe Highway, as it was known for centuries, runs along the same high ground as an Iron Age causeway. If you stand on the Highway, and look south down Wapping Lane towards the river, you can still see the dip away as it goes towards the shore.

Through the sixties, when post-war promises crashed around our ears, followed by the oil crisis and industrial unrest of the seventies, to the nineties and now almost a quarter of the way through the twenty-first century, I've always known my roots. They are embedded in the tangle of streets in the true East End, where I grew up.

I was part of the large, tight-knit network of families in the East End whose very survival often depended on each member pulling together for the good of all. The unwritten rule of East London was that you had a duty to your family. You were loyal to them and they took precedence over everyone else. People who broke that rule were often cold-shouldered. I would call across the street to gloriously rowdy neighbours; I knew the auntie behind every door, who would tend to your scraped knees or give you a mouthful if you stepped out of line. I bore witness to crime from a young age, too. There was always someone who knew someone who could get you what you were after, be it a television or a fur coat.

The East End way of life I was born into had a rhythm that had existed for generations. The men came home on a Friday night and put housekeeping money on the table; their social life centred around the pub, the betting shop and football. Women caught up with each other on street corners and in shop queues; they lived communal lives – helping each other with childcare and pitching in with a hot meal when there was sickness or bereavement in a neighbour's house. Everyone had a part to play and everyone did what was expected of them.

Life was tough. Living conditions were diabolical. Damp walls and an outside toilet were the least of it, as often there was just a single cold tap in the kitchen and no electricity upstairs. Although it's hard to believe now, it wasn't unknown for a family of seven or more to occupy a couple of damp rooms in a house, with smaller children sleeping on truckle beds beside their parents and older children top-to-tail in double beds.

However, these were our streets and they were where we belonged. I grew up through the fifties, when the old Victorian houses were being swept aside to make way for high-rise blocks with indoor toilets and modern kitchens, but even when we were moved into flats and maisonettes on new council estates, the spirit of the old streets remained. Children played on concrete landings instead of cobbles and women gossiped at the top of the stairwell rather than on street corners, but the sense of community was the same.

So what does it mean to be an East Ender?

It means a no-nonsense attitude, an understanding that you have to make your own opportunities, as no one is going to hand you them on a plate. It's knowing that you've come from a long line of survivors who have overcome disadvantage and poverty, scorn and oppression, to make a better life for themselves and their family. It's knowing you belong to a special breed, and that no matter how far you travel or how high you rise in life, the invisible mantle of being an East Ender stays wrapped around you.

Many of the streets I knew as a child have long been swept away and life has distanced me from my old haunts, but that doesn't matter. Being an East Ender is more than coming from a place on the map or even the way you talk. Being an East Ender is in your very marrow and your heart until it beats its last beat.

CHAPTER ONE

Our 'Owse

I N 1954, THE people of Britain had two reasons to rejoice. Firstly, after fourteen long and tedious years, wartime rationing had finally ended. And, secondly, I entered the world – bright and early, on an August bank holiday. Two weeks later, my parents left the hospital with me and took me to my first home: a one-up one-down cottage at 71 Anthony Street.

It was situated on the Chapman Estate, a self-contained area to the south of the renowned Commercial Road, which included the infamous Watney Street Market. There were two churches nearby – the Catholic St Mary's and the C of E Christ Church, something to cater to every spiritual need. The streets on the Chapman Estate had names like Jane, Martha, Richard and our own Anthony Street.

Lined by workers' cottages on both sides, the street had existed since the eighteenth century. It had been built cheaply to house Victorian labourers, and had no foundation, no damp course – and, as I'll get to later, no indoor bathroom.

You entered the fifteen-by-fifteen-foot parlour from the front door, straight off the street. At the back was a small scullery that also served as our kitchen. The cottage had a beaten-earth floor; the lounge was covered by brown lino. There was just enough room to squeeze in a two-seat sofa, a couple of fireside armchairs and a rag rug in front of the cast-iron grate. The single bedroom above could be reached by climbing the narrow wooden stairs that ran up the side of the lounge.

Still, half the housing stock in East London had been destroyed or damaged beyond repair thanks to the Blitz. I know my parents were thankful to have their own home – not least because they had been living cheek by jowl with my grandparents for the past six years in a three-bedroom, mid-terrace home in Ilford. This kind of arrangement was very common. I had several friends at senior school who lived with their grandparents well into the 1970s.

For reasons I'll explain a little further on in my tale, by the time I was born my father's eldest sister Nell had become my mother's father's second wife. Thereby making her both my aunt and my grandmother. The cottage was just a few streets away from the house where my father had been born in 1917, and where his parents and older brother Jimmy still lived. His eldest brother Arthur, his wife and my cousin Edie lived a few doors down from us, and his younger sister, my Aunt Martha, lived around the corner in Planet Street, alongside half a dozen Fullerton cousins. My great-great-grandparents had walked these streets, too, in their day, and even lived in some of the same houses.

Although we had electricity, to save money on a fine day – once the morning chores were done – women would take a chair and sit alongside their front doors to knit, sew or gossip in the street. Today no one would dream of letting their children play unsupervised in the city, but when I was a child the streets and alleyways were our playground.

With very few cars – the only passing traffic was likely to be the milkman – children too young to go to school would play in the street; those not yet walking would be propped up in pushchairs. I remember being one of the toddlers parked outside the front window so I could 'get some fresh air into my lungs' – a worthy sentiment given that the houses had no foundation or damp course, with those beaten-earth floors beneath the lino, so damp and mould were a constant problem.

In fact, other than the coal merchant with his horse-drawn wagon, and the occasional door-to-door salesman, the street was mostly populated by women in flowery wraparound aprons, cleaning their windows with newspaper and gossiping on doorsteps. I remember my mum on her hands and knees scrubbing the paving stones outside our door to wash the obligatory half-circle on the pavement each morning, which signalled to the neighbours that she was a diligent housewife. Another time, I recall two women having a furious row in the middle of the street.

As I've mentioned, there was no indoor bathroom. Instead, there was a brick privy in the triangular yard at the back; with a single cold tap over a deep butler sink, it was barely fit for human habitation. This was fine for me as my mum bathed me in the kitchen sink or, when I wouldn't fit any more, in a zinc bath in front of the fire. As there was only a single cold water tap in the house, she had to boil a kettle or two for the hot water. However, if my parents wanted a bath they had to traipse half a mile to the public bathhouse on the Highway. Because of this, most days they, like everyone else, would make do with a strip wash – that is the removal of just the top half of your clothing and an all-over wash with a flannel at the kitchen sink. It was not uncommon when I was a child to walk into a neighbour's kitchen and find a man in his vest, with his shirt still tucked into his trousers and his braces dangling, washing himself at the sink.

Of course, these old workmen's cottages weren't the only dwellings in the area, and in previous centuries, when Stepney was a village outside the City boundaries, it was a desirable place to live.

Thomas Cromwell had a country mansion in Stepney, and as the centuries passed, rich merchants built fine houses in Stepney Green. Eighteenth-century property investors mimicked the growing western side of London by building squares like Wellclose and Prince's, lined with townhouses.

Fast forward to the twentieth century. The area was already known for its half-derelict, overcrowded houses and tenement buildings long before the Luftwaffe arrived in 1940, so by the time I arrived on the scene the housing shortage was chronic and living conditions in those homes that remained was appalling.

In order to temporarily alleviate the housing shortage caused by the destruction of the Blitz, the council had cleared land throughout the area to put up a couple of dozen prefabricated dwellings – prefabs, as they were commonly known.

There were built by various companies, but all were made from pre-formed concrete and put together like an oversized puzzle to create a standard two- or three-bedroom single-storey design. They were much favoured by the post-war Labour government, who were trying to implement their election promise of better housing against the crippling national debt of the war, as prefabs were both cheap and quick and easy to construct.

As a small child, I remember visiting friends of my mum who lived on a brand-new estate within walking distance of Anthony Street. I recall thinking how bright and modern their home was in comparison to our dingy little cottage. Those council flats were much loved by their occupants, and many protested vehemently when the council later tried to rehouse them in cramped tower blocks.

Seventy years before I was born, in response to unhealthy and overcrowded housing, Octavia Hill, a Victorian feminist and social reformer, set up the East London Dwelling Company. They built two blocks of flats in Stepney Green, one for single occupants and one for families: Dunstan House and Cressy House.

Cressy House, a triangular block of two-room artisan dwellings on the corner of Hannibal Road, was similar in design to the famous Peabody Buildings in Blackfriars Road, and the Rothschild Dwellings in Flower and Dean Street, Spitalfields. They were designed originally for the families of tradesmen – in other words, the respectable working poor – and had communal toilets on each floor rather than one or two for a dozen tenants.

By the late sixties, when I first visited school friends who lived there, they had been modernised to include an inside bathroom and toilets. I had another friend who lived on the Boundary Estate, which was built to replace the notorious Old Nichol rookery in Shoreditch – as featured in *A Child of the Jago*. They, too, had the standard design of two bedrooms, lounge and a small kitchen but, unlike the original Victorian artisan dwellings such as Cressy House and Peabody buildings, homes on the Boundary Estate each had their own bathroom. Like most dwellings of the time, their only form of heating was an open fire in the lounge. It was only in the 1960s that people swapped coal and ash for an electric fire. There are other such philanthropic blocks of flats dotted around in Limehouse and Shadwell, and in the 1930s the council, too, built yellow-brick council houses, examples of which can still be seen along Greenbank in Wapping.

Through the centuries, rich and poor have always lived side by side in East London, often only streets apart. There are still a number of elegant Regency houses in the area, and if you walk along Stepney Green itself, with its double-fronted houses with white steps leading to lacquered front doors, you could be forgiven for thinking you had been transported to a trendy street in Islington or Hackney.

When my parents moved back to Stepney, my mum started going to church – I think it must have been St Paul's along the Highway – and for the first time I met people who didn't live in shared houses or council flats. I remember us visiting one of the older ladies of the parish for tea. Her name is lost to me now, but her husband was a lock keeper on the Limehouse cut and they lived in a large house with several rooms owned by The Port of London, situated by the bascule bridge that sat across the Shadwell basin. The London Docks was a working dock in those days, and I clearly remember staring out of her parlour window in amazement as the bridge rocked back to let a ship sail through.

There are still plenty of Georgian houses in and around Wapping High Street. Of course, by the time I was born, most of these elegant dwellings had become multi-occupancy, with three or four families living on different floors.

In 1958, after four and half years in number 71 Anthony Street, my parents received a letter telling them that, along with the rest of the street, they were going to be rehoused on one of the new council estates. I imagine after four years cooped up in a damp cottage with a single cold water tap in the kitchen and an antiquated outside lavatory, they were beside themselves with joy.

Initially, like many East Enders at that time, my parents were offered a house with a garden in Harold Hill or Dagenham, but my father turned them down. These places are now part of Greater London, but in the 1950s somewhere like Harold Hill was regarded as being the back of beyond. To my father's way of thinking, London was where the work was, so although wide-open fields and an actual house might be tempting, he decided to stay put, and was instead allocated a flat on the fourth storey of a block in Harpley Square, just off Globe Road. It was two miles from our little house on Anthony Street and halfway between Stepney Green and Bethnal Green tube stations.

After living in two damp rooms with an outside bog, the new flat – with a separate bathroom and toilet, a fitted kitchen with hot water, a pantry and an airing cupboard – must have seemed like a palace. It was also at the end of the landing, so we didn't have people walking to and fro past our kitchen window.

Until we were rehoused again some six years later, I had to share a bedroom with my brother. I remember we could choose our own wallpaper. We compromised, with Huckleberry Finn and Yogi Bear on one wall and Disney's Snow White on the other.

There were two slight disadvantages to the family's new home. One was that it had a small balcony, which overlooked the grassy square. Immediately identifying this as a potential hazard for small children, my father designed a wooden frame with chicken wire stretched across it, which he fixed across the space. The second disadvantage was that the flat was up four flights of stairs. There was a lift that you could just about squeeze a pram into, but you'd be lucky to find it working.

The rest of the Fullerton family moved with us to Harpley Square. My Uncle Arthur and his family lived in a second-floor maisonette on the other side of the square while my Grandmother and Uncle Jimmy lived in the two-storey block opposite. Martha and her husband Wag had a two-bedroom flat in a block on the west side; it was conveniently located on the ground floor and I would often knock on their door when I was playing in the square to use their loo.

We would always visit my father's elderly mother, Little Nan, on Sunday mornings. She was as tiny as you'd expect for someone called Little Nan, with a very wrinkled face. She had a full set of dentures, but like Queenie Brogan in my Second World War Ration Book series, she only wore them on Sundays or when the vicar called.

Her flat was comfortably furnished and decorated with bric-a-brac from trips to the seaside, while family photos in ancient frames were displayed on the mantelshelf and sideboard. There was also a fringed chenille table covering draped over the folded table and cotton lace antimacassars on the chairs. Little Nan maintained the old way of keeping her door on the latch, so we would knock and then just walk in. She was always sitting in a large armchair by the hearth with her feet up on a pouffe when we arrived.

My father told me that when he was a child his mother was always on her feet doing something, be it housework or cooking, and when she did sit down, she would have some sewing or knitting in her hands. It's a testament to her hard work and care for her family that hardly a day passed without one or other of her children dropping by to see her. Although I was just nine when she died in 1963, I remember her very well.

Although we had most of our immediate family living just a short walk away across the square, we often ventured further afield and took a bus to Bow to see my Uncle Bob.

Bob had had a kidney removed some time before he married my Aunt Elaine and so despite having a good income they couldn't get a mortgage. Instead, they lived in the converted basement of Elaine's parents' Edwardian townhouse in Bow. Aunt Elaine adopted the sophisticated tailored styles made famous by Jackie Kennedy a decade later, whereas Bobby was pure fifties Italian chic in flannel slacks, polo shirts and loafers. I thought them very modern.

Sometimes we took the long bus journey to Ilford, to visit my mum's father and her stepmother, Nell – known as Big Nan, she was five foot six and broad in the beam. From the bus stop next to Ilford police station, it was a short walk down Ilford Lane to Nell and my grandfather's house.

Although people commuted into London from Ilford each day, back in the sixties it was still very much a town in its own right. There was a busy high street with shops that are still with us today like M&S and Boots. It also had other names that have long since disappeared from town centres, like Woolworth's and C&A – or Coats and 'Ats, as we called it. There were other shops such as Freeman, Hardy and Willis, Hepworths and the grocery store Home and Colonial. In addition, any girl wanting to cut a dash at a wedding would save up her pennies to buy something a little bit special at Mason Riches, which sat on the opposite corner of the road from the police station.

Visiting family was considered a special occasion. We would always dress in our best clothes, and before we set out our parents would remind us not to interrupt, to say please and thank you, and not to touch anything that might break. I always had trouble sticking to the last rule.

Unlike East London, which had predominantly rented accommodation, most of the Edwardian terraced streets in Ilford were owned by those living in them. Although Ilford was not as heavily bombed as East London, it was still on the flight path for the Luftwaffe bombers and so it had suffered its fair share of bombings during the night-time air raids. Because of this, people in Ilford had started selling up and moving away.

Because they worked in Bethnal Green during the war, my mum's family applied to the local air raid precautions authority for a family ticket which allowed them to shelter from the bombing in Bethnal Green station. The station had been constructed as an extension eastwards from Liverpool Street, but although it had been completed, the war had started before the trains started running. Deep beneath the ground, it made the perfect air raid shelter and my mum, her sister Gladys and their stepmother sheltered there each night, along with hundreds of other East Enders.

On 3 March 1943, as people were making their way down the stairs for the night, someone tripped. Other stumbled over them as people behind surged forward; unable to move, people panicked. One hundred and seventy-three people, including sixty-two children, died in the crush. Thankfully, my mum and her family had just got to the bottom of the stairs when it happened so narrowly avoided being part of the disaster, but they were led out the station by rescuers hours later and saw dozens of bodies lined up on the pavement outside.

After that close shave with death, my mum's stepmother persuaded my grandfather to take their savings from the bank, and for the princely sum of £375 they bought a three-bedroom mid-terrace house. 36 Albany Road had two reception rooms, an inside bathroom and a fifty-foot garden. The front parlour, which smelled of dust and polish, held an upright piano. That room was reserved for high days and holidays, so when we visited, we always sat in the back room that overlooked the small garden.

On fine days my brother and I would be let out to run up and down the stretch of lawn, while the adults sat on the raised patio and drank tea. A far cry from scuffing our knees on the gravel of the communal playground or being knocked off the climbing frames by the big boys. However, there was many an afternoon when we had to sit and gaze at the patch of green through the rain running down the French windows.

Honestly, compared to our little flat at the top of a tower block, my grandparents' house was like a palace. There was no heavy footfall on the celling from the tenants above and no raised voices of arguing neighbours coming through the wall as you were sitting watching TV. You could get into your home without climbing over the junk the people in the next flat had left outside their front door or without travelling up in a lift reeking of urine. Instead of the handkerchief-sized hallway of the flat, the house had a proper hall and stairs; but most of all I loved the garden with flowers and would stay out there playing even on the coldest day.

Come rain or shine, when the five o'clock pips sounded we

had to be deathly quiet as the football results were broadcast over the radio and my grandfather would check his Littlewoods pools, saying, 'I'll buy you a house if I win.' He never did.

We always ended the day with Nan picking flowers from her well-tended borders for my mum to take home. Then we'd trundle back to the bus stop to await a number twenty-five to return us to London.

After my brother was born, my father applied to the council for a bigger house – but it took another three years before we were offered a three-bedroom maisonette in Redmans Road on the edge of the newly constructed housing estate, so we packed up our belongings and moved back to Stepney.

Unlike our first council home, which was a top floor two-bedroom flat, the council house my parents were offered was in a newly built block of twenty, arranged over two floors, with a communal stairwell and a rubbish chute at one end. The living area was large, with a proper hallway and a kitchen that looked out on to the landing at the front and was big enough to accommodate a table and four chairs.

The lounge at the back was the width of the maisonette but with a chunk taken out of the floor space for a small outside balcony.

Our new home also had a separate toilet and bathroom, an airing cupboard and a fitted kitchen; with more space for two growing children, it was a great improvement on the flat.

It also meant I had a room of my own. Such joy! Even from an early age, often sparked by something like an image in a book or a television programme, I was always inventing characters and weaving their stories, usually innocent romantic ones, about princes and princesses. Having my own room meant I could hide myself away with my sketch pad and illustrate those tales.

However, you had obligations to fulfil as tenants, one being you had to clean the shared stairwells and passages. Although many of the tenants didn't bother, my mum diligently mopped down the landing and stairs to the floor below with bleach when it was her turn and later, when I was a teenager, it became one of my most hated chores.

The worst thing about the maisonette wasn't hearing the neighbours shouting at each other through the paper-thin walls, or catching your shins on tricycles, scooters and prams left on the landing. It was the communal rubbish chute.

Located halfway down the stairs, the chute had a hinged cast-iron cover with a handle that opened, allowing you to drop your household rubbish down said chute. My mum diligently wrapped all our waste – from potato peelings to sanitary towels – in at least two layers of newspaper, but not everyone one was so conscientious. Putting out our rubbish was another job I was given when I was old enough, and I can't tell you how many times I gagged doing it. In fact, I feel a little queasy writing about it now.

As owning your own home was something the majority of my parents' generation couldn't afford, nearly everyone I knew lived in a council house. For tenants who had suffered decades of neglectful landlords and precarious tenure, council houses gave not only security but also a realistic hope of having faults repaired. The council even decorated a room for you every few years. And if you wanted to move there was a scheme whereby you could swap your council house with that of another tenant by mutual agreement.

There was no shame in living in a council house. When the young couple who lived next door to us scraped the money together to buy a house in Upminster, my father couldn't fathom out why they would. He regarded taking on a mortgage as being a financial millstone around your neck, which today seems bizarre.

However, one group of East London residents still lived in very plush houses indeed: the clergy.

When my family moved to the maisonette in Redmans Road, my mum started going to St Dunstan's Church. The vicar had a daughter of about my age called Cecily, who, unlike every other child in the parish, went to a private school in the City. Deemed by her parents to be an acceptable playmate among the local children, I was invited around to the vicarage to play.

I felt like Pip in *Great Expectations*, walking into Miss Havisham's for the first time, as I passed through the front door of the rectory on White Horse Lane. The large, detached Victorian house had a massive garden surrounding it. Although the servants' rooms on the upper floor had been converted into flats, I've never in my whole life been in such a huge house.

They had a music room with a grand piano; we had a kitchen table that all four of us could barely squeeze around and a lounge that could only accommodate a two-seater sofa and a pair of armchairs. They had classical statues on their mantelpieces; we had knick-knacks with Clacton and Southend stamped on them. They had objects I'd never even seen before – a metronome, a roll-top desk and a double-oven Aga – whereas the furniture in our entire house would have fitted into the vicarage scullery. I had to deposit our household rubbish down a stomach-churning communal shoot. Their gardener put their dustbins out for collection when he'd finished pruning the shrubs.

Street Life

Harpley Square, where we lived had a purpose-built playground with monkey bars, concrete tubes and swings, and logs hammered together to form a climbing structure specifically designed for you to acquire splinters in your hands and knees. Even as an eight year old I had been let out to play with other children in the flats with just the warnings 'don't get into a stranger's car' and 'stay where I can see you'.

By the time I was ten, and in the last year of my junior school, I used to roam far and wide around the streets and parks, running across main roads and scavenging on bomb sites. We climbed over fences into building sites and sometimes even jumped on a bus to Aldgate or Stratford.

There were plenty of parks in our part of London, too. Meath Gardens – or Meefy Gardens, as we called it – was an old Victorian cemetery complete with mock-medieval archways at its entrance; Bethnal Green Park wasn't as big, but it had the library that had been the notorious eighteenth-century Wright's Madhouse so was nicknamed Barmy Park, and if you wanted to stretch your legs a bit then there was Victoria Park, complete with formal gardens, ornamental lake, bandstand and open-air 1930s lido. Unfortunately for us, with sour-faced park-keepers constantly shouting at us to 'keep off the grass', 'mind the ruddy flowers' and 'get down off those trees', you couldn't always just run wild.

We had our favourite games, too. Hopscotch was popular, chalking up the numbers on paving stones if you were in the street, or using a hopscotch grid the council helpfully painted on the gravel of designated play areas. A game called 'two balls' was popular with the girls. We would line up in a row, facing a convenient section of brickwork, and would bounce and catch balls off it while performing variations like over-arm, dropsy, letting the ball bounce on the floor once before catching it ... 'Two balls' had rhymes too, like, *When I was two, I buckled my shoe over the sea to Rye. A bottle of rum to fill my tum and that's the life for me*, each word accompanied by an action in between throwing and catching.

The other game I recall was Gobs. For this you needed five coloured half-inch cubes of chalk. You threw them up and then tried to catch as many as you could on the back of your hand. Any that landed on the ground had to be picked up whilst balancing the others. If they fell off, you lost that round and handed the gobs over to another player.

As we got older, we stopped running around the park, preferring to hang around in groups on street corners, or buying a bottle of Tizer or cream soda and sitting around on the brick-built flowerbeds or one of the odd concrete sculptures that the architects dotted around between their faceless tower blocks.

Truthfully, it wasn't as if there wasn't enough laid on for children, as every church ran a youth club and had Brownies, Cubs, Scouts and Girl Guide packs attached. There were numerous boxing clubs scattered all over the East End, too. Because so many of the local population had Irish ancestry, almost every Catholic church had an Irish dance class attached.

I'll be honest: from about the age of eight or nine, our parents had no idea where we were – if you weren't at school, you were out of the house playing with friends, away from adult scrutiny. It wasn't that they were neglectful, that's just how they had been brought up.

The Language of the Streets

Now in the same way that the Irish people aren't forever saying 'top o' the morning' or Scots pipping in with 'och aye the noo', East Enders don't use rhyming slang all day long.

Rhyming slang can be traced back to street cant from the Regency period used by criminals, but its modern origins stem from costermongers, street traders and those on the shady side of the law communicating with each other without the police or authorities being able to understand.

There are also two types: straightforward rhyming – such as a Godiva meaning a fiver – and double rhyming – such as Barnet, taken from Barnet Fair, meaning hair.

However, although I've never heard anyone say 'apples and pears' in everyday conversation, there are some phrases that my family and others have used for as long as I can remember.

You'll find dozens of sites on the internet which will give you long lists of rhyming slang, most of which are just made up and were never used by true East Enders. Apart from the aforementioned Barnet, phrases I remember my family and others using are as follows:

Having a butcher's = butcher's hook = a look
Plates = plates of meat = feet
Mincers = mince pies = eyes
Porkies = pork pies = lies
China = China plate = mate
Dog and bone = often used complete = phone
Using your loaf = loaf of bread = head
Syrup = syrup of fig = wig
Whistle = whistle and flute = suit
Treacle = treacle tart = sweetheart
Trouble = trouble and strife = wife
Would you Adam and Eve it = believe it (a phrase I have
    used on occasion as an email header to my agent)
And of course, Bristols = Bristol City's = titties

Some were more complicated, such as Aris = from Aristotle = bottle = bottle and glass = arse.

Aside from the rhyming slang, there were other phrases, too, like 'losing your bottle' or 'bottling it', meaning to lose your nerve. My mum's stock reply to any enquiry as to what was for tea would be, 'Shit with sugar on', while my father favoured the one that got Chas and Dave in trouble with the BBC – 'Gercha cowson' – for anything that riled him.

CHAPTER TWO

No One's a Native

ALTHOUGH I OFTEN refer to myself as a native East Ender, the truth is that like almost everyone else in the area, my ancestors originated from somewhere else.

East London has always been a magnet for anyone trying to make their way in the world. Intricate Viking swords, Anglo-Saxon pennies, Norman drinking horns and bits of rusty Flemish armour have all been discovered over the centuries in the mud and silt on both banks of the Thames – a testament to the fact that people from far and wide settled on that part of the river.

The Industrial Revolution brought even more nationalities to the riverside district surrounding the dock: Germans who worked in the sugar industry flocked to St Mary's in Whitechapel, Indians who arrived on East India Company trading ships settled in Blackwall; Chinese citizens were employed to hump coal in Limehouse Basin, exploited for cheap labour. It was sweat and brawn from dozens of nations, most notably Ireland, that built the infrastructure of Victorian Britain which helped this country move into the modern world.

Then came orthodox Jews – the men in long grey coats, trailing beards and homburg hats and the women in sheitel (a wig worn by married women) – fleeing the pogroms in Russia. They were joining their distant cousins from Spain and Portugal who'd arrived a century and a half earlier, escaping Catholic persecution in Iberia.

Jewish culture is deeply embedded in East London to this day. My whole family lived and worked alongside Jewish people. Food such as bagels, matzos and pickled herrings were everyday fare for East Enders. After all, if not from a Jewish baker, where would you get your daily loaf? Yiddish words – nosh (to eat), schmatta (rags), schlep (to travel) and spiel (persuasive talk) – were commonly used by my family and others.

To save them sitting in a cold house all day during the Sabbath, when they were forbidden to work, Jewish families would pay local kids to light their fire and heat up food on Saturdays.

Old Jewish traditions lived on into the mid-sixties when our neighbours, the Greenbergs, who weren't Orthodox Jews, used a traditional matchmaker to introduce their daughter to her future husband. In fact, a small number of very religious Jewish households keep up this tradition today.

As well as anti-Semitism, which expressed itself with complaints that factories were owned by Jews, there was praise for Jewish doctors, like the legendary GP Hannah Billig, known as the Angel of Cable Street for her tireless and life-long work among the poor and sick of East London. Dr Billig tended to my family's health through to the 1950s.

While not frequent, marriage between Christians and Jews happened, as with my Uncle Arthur and Aunt Dora. Dora's cousin in Belgium perished in the gas chamber in Auschwitz and our family had friends and worked alongside people who still bore their concentration camp numbers, tattooed on their wrists, so even as children we had an understanding of the horrors of the holocaust and anti-Semitism.

Following the end of the Second World War, new residents arrived from Malta, the Caribbean and Africa. They were later joined by Greek and Turkish Cypriots, many of whom opened cafés, fish and chip shops and restaurants and added to the mix of cultures.

The slaughter of war wasn't just something that happened to my parents' generation. I knew dozens of both Greek and Turkish Cypriots whose families had moved to East London during the troubles caused by the British withdrawal from Cyprus in the 1960s. One such was a friend of mine from a large Greek Cypriot family. She lived at the eastern end of Wapping High Street, long before there were million-pound houses there, where her mother kept a corner shop. On the wall behind the counter was a picture of two young men in military uniform with gleaming smiles: my friend's two brothers, who were decapitated in a skirmish with their Turkish counterparts. No doubt there were similar photos on Turkish Cypriot walls in East London, too.

I had always had Jewish children and children of colour and mixed heritage in my infant school; my class register in senior school included names such as E'quilant, Riley, Levy,

Papadopoulos, Hussain, Ali, Osman, Conner, Murphy, Greenburg, Stein, Sassoon and Faraqui. There was even a girl called Antoinette Malkovich. We East Enders were multi-ethnic long before the phrase was coined.

And my family were in those waves of desperate people looking for a better life. The first to arrive on these shores on my mum's maternal side was John Assers, clothworker. Fleeing persecution in the Low Countries, he arrived in the late seventeenth century and settled at Spitalfields with his fellow Huguenots silk weavers. Not long after, Allan Fullerton, my umpteen times paternal great-grandfather, fresh from Rothsay in Argyle, stepped off a ship in London Dock and found rooms in Martha Street, where many of the Fullerton family would reside until the slum clearances in the 1960s. Allan's grandson Alexander, had eleven children and I suspect all the Fullertons in East London and Essex, myself included, are his descendants.

My paternal grandmother's family were next to arrive, in the 1860s. They came from Inchigeelagh, in Munster, to escape the Irish Famine, settling in an area in Wapping that was so Irish it's marked on maps of the time as Knockfurgus. They stayed there for a year or two before moving to the Brick Lane area of Whitechapel where, as a child, my grandmother walked the same streets by day that Jack the Ripper prowled by night.

The last to arrive were my mum's paternal side, the Aplins. They pitched up in Limehouse in 1888 from Dorset, where they had been solid yeomen in the small village of Iwerne Minster – they can be traced there right back to the early seventeenth century.

So, like so many East Enders, I am a mongrel: the blood from many different lands and people flows through my veins.

Meet the Family

Raising children, putting food on the table and keeping a roof over your head in East London before the NHS and the Welfare State, women had to be strong-willed and stubborn. However, neither adjective comes anywhere close to describing my Aunt Nell.

Standing just over five foot five tall, with a pair of shoulders like a docker, a jaw that could chisel stone and an eye that could pierce steel, she was the undisputed dictator of the Fullerton family. Sometimes challenged, but never defeated. She wasn't backward in coming forward to tell you where you'd gone wrong and putting you on the right path.

She was fearless, too. I've seen her take a complete stranger to task on the platform at Stratford station when he spat on the floor in front of her, and God have mercy on a stallholder who sold her apples from the back of the barrow! When she was well into her seventies, a rash youngster tried to snatch her handbag in a drive-by robbery. She punched him mid-mugging, sending him and his moped careering off into a lamp-post.

Three years after my Fullerton grandparents welcomed Nell into the world, they were blessed with another daughter, Millie. Two boys, my uncles Arthur and Jimmy, followed in swift succession, before the arrival of my father, George Henry.

Jimmy and my father were choirboys together at St George-in-the-East and went on the church's annual seaside trip to Hastings each year. When my father's voice broke, he could no longer sing in the choir, but Jimmy's voice held true. At family get-togethers the call always went up: 'Give us a song, Jimmy!'

The Hawksmoor church where my father sang as a boy is still there on the Highway, but if you walk inside, you'll have a bit of a shock. Instead of elegant eighteenth-century columns, memorials and church furniture, you'll find an interior straight out of the 1960s. In May 1941, at the height of the Blitz, the church took a direct hit and the subsequent fire destroyed the original interior. However, a Nissen hut was set up in the burnt-out wreckage and St George's continued to conduct services, including my Aunt Martha's wedding in 1943.

Being a quietly spoken, unassuming individual, my father was particularly close to his brother Jimmy, who was a gentle soul and a lifelong church-goer. My father wore a black mourning armband – something you never see today – for over a month after he died.

By the time my father arrived in 1917, the three-up three-down house in Planet Street was getting pretty crowded.

With my grandfather away fighting in the trenches, Nell, who was now twelve, took up the position as second in command in the family, a role she held on tight to for the rest of her life.

My Aunt Martha made her appearance on April Fool's Day three years after my father in 1920. Her husband Charlie was called Wag by all and sundry, because all Charlies are known to be wags – that's to say they're jokers. He was a big-hearted character who smoked like a chimney and talked like Ray Winston and I loved him. His relaxed, unruffled attitude to life was the perfect foil to my Aunt Martha's busy, do-everything-now ways. He did as she asked without batting an eyelid, even re-wallpapering a room within a week because she didn't like the first pattern when it was up.

My grandparents had another daughter and son, Edith and Ernie, after Martha but both children died in infancy. I have no photos of Edith, but there is a poignant one of Ernest with Nell and Millie taken in the backyard.

Finally, in 1928, my grandparents had their last child, Robert Peter, known to the family as 'Mad Bobby'. Being their last child, Bob, according to everyone including Bob himself, was thoroughly spoilt. Unlike his older brothers he always had shoes, and rather than having to help with family chores he was told to clear off and play with his friends so as not get in the way. Also, whereas his three older brothers were unassuming and softly spoken, Bobby was loud and demanding. He earned his nickname Mad Bobby for the many scrapes he got into and he was returned home more than once with bumps and bruises from falling off a wall or getting into a fight with the kids in the next street.

Bobby's lasting contribution to Fullerton family folklore is that he gave his older sister Nell her nickname: The Sheriff.

He was gregarious and exuberant and after he'd completed his National Service in late 1948, Bobby threw himself into the post-war jollity. It was while tripping the light fantastic in one such establishment that he met my Aunt Elaine. She was a grammar school girl and a typist in the Civil Service, so several steps up the social ladder from the Fullertons. But not backward in coming forward, Bobby asked her to dance and, during the course of their first ever turn around the floor, told her he was going to marry her. Undaunted by her initial reluctance, Bobby made good on his word and they married two years later. They too wanted children but after several years of trying, reconciled themselves to being childless.

Bobby would do anything from jump on a stage and dance, to grab a mike and sing, so I think my father envied his outgoing nature. He was also a complete but lovable fraud. According to him, he could do anything from rewire your house to drive a rally car. He maintained that having been stationed in Palestine he could speak Arabic fluently, thereby making him the only squaddie who could move around the Arab quarters unmolested. In truth, he could swear and say a few phrases in Arabic, but any solider stupid enough to venture outside of barracks was usually found in a ditch with their throat cut. But honestly, I defy anyone not to smile when Bobby was in full, completely over-the-top flow.

In the late nineteenth century, there was an animal trader called Jamrach who kept all sorts of wild and exotic beasts in his Wapping warehouse. One day a tiger escaped and pounced on a little boy who happened to be strolling by. Mr Jamrach came out, beat the tiger over the head and rescued the child. However, had it been one of my aunts who had caught the tiger's eye, I'm sure that they would have wrenched the crowbar out of Mr Jamrach's hands and done the job themselves.

CHAPTER THREE

Earning a Crust

U NTIL THE 1960S, there was no point asking an East End child what they wanted to be when they grew up. Boys knew they would be following their fathers into the docks or one of factories that lined the river. Girls would go into one of the clothing factories like their mothers until they married, after which they would spend their days at home. Had my fairy godmother appeared to my teenage self and told me that one day I would make my living as a writer, I would have laughed in her face.

The importance of getting a good job was drilled into you from the moment you went to school. My parents were brought up before the Welfare State, when if you didn't work you didn't eat, as my father learned the hard way when he was out of work for three years in the early 1930. Having to rely on a few shillings of dole money each week haunted him for the rest of his life and shaped his socialist ideology.

Work as a dock labourer was hard and erratic. Until as late as the 1960s, most labouring work in the London Docks was casual. This meant the men would wait outside the dock gates each morning, hoping to be chosen for a day's work. Your employment that day was dependent on a number of factors: how many ships were in, what was to be unloaded and if you were related to the dock master or he knew your family.

All three of my aunts and my mother left school at fourteen and went straight into clothing factories; they were machinists all their lives.

Other than their youngest brother Bobby, whose father-in-law found a place for him in the installation department of the GPO, my father and uncles worked as dock labourers until they managed to get work as decorators a few years before the outbreak of the Second World War.

After they were demobbed, my uncles went back to this profession, and remained in it until they retired. Back in civvy life my father took a job on the assembly line at Ford's Motor Company in Dagenham, which was more lucrative. It was only by a twist of fate that he landed a white-collar job in Ford's drawing office. Had he not, I'm almost certain he would have been an assembly-line worker for the rest of his life.

I have no idea when my father discovered he had artistic talent, but I do know that when he came home after the war, he painted the interior of the family's outside toilet with scenes of the desert, complete with camels and pyramids.

After I was born, he enrolled in art classes at the local adult education institution and as well as the pencil sketches he had always done, he started painting, too. I have one of his early attempts with oils – a picture of me as a five-year-old playing with a handful of bricks.

After his early success at the local evening classes, he decided to enter one of his paintings into the annual Ford Motor Company Art Exhibition. It was a full-size canvas depicting the men and machines on the Dagenham assembly line where he worked. Somewhat to his surprise he won first prize; however, the silver-plated cup and his picture in the papers weren't the real prize. The real prize was my father being offered a chance to leave behind the assembly line and take a job in the technical drawing office in the plant.

With minimal education and after almost twenty years of back-breaking manual labour, my father walked into the sort of white-collar office job he couldn't have dreamed of in a thousand years. Unlike the shop floor, where men worked in shifts, he now had a nine-to-five office job.

It's wrong to think that women have only appeared in the workplace in the last thirty or forty years; working-class women have always worked. This is evidenced by generations of the women in my family listing themselves as seamstresses, dressmakers and clothing machinists in the census. However, as in the case of my mother, this was often home-work or part time so they could undertake all their domestic duties, too.

My mother had gone into a clothing factory as soon as she left school and laboured in one such sweatshop or another until I was born. Even then she took in piecework, often things like collars and cuffs, just to add a few pennies to the housekeeping. She used her solid industrial Singer sewing machine, which was a cast-iron device painted black with faded gold etching.

Originally it would have been operated by a treadle, but in later years had an engine fitted to it. It was in a dark-wood fold-away cabinet which sat in our lounge. And there was no wondering if she was using it because, unlike domestic sewing machines that just putter...putter...putter along, my mum's machine was like a blooming pneumatic drill.

Industrial sewing machine are fast, very fast, and take no prisoners, so having a needle driven through your finger while operating one is a very common injury. Luckily, my finger never got in the way of the needle, but my mum had been injured in this way several times, as had all of my aunts. When I asked my Aunt Nell what you did if you caught your finger under the needle, she said, 'Just pull it out with your teeth and don't get blood on the work.'

When I went to senior school, my mum put aside piecework and returned to the factories during school hours, so she was at home to make the evening meal. Our family's working day would start with Father, who was up first at six-thirtyish to get ready for the day and have his breakfast. I was usually woken half an hour later by Radio 4's seven o'clock news programme blaring out from downstairs. I would lie in bed until my father shouted, 'Get up or you'll be late' up the stairs as he left to catch his train to Langdon. After dragging myself out of bed, I'd get myself washed and dressed for school in the bathroom.

After the usual skirmish with my mum about smartening myself up and wearing too much make-up, I'd set off on the fifteen-minute walk to school. Having packed me off to school at eight-thirtyish, my mum would drop my brother at junior school before going on to her factory.

Of course, when I say 'factory', I mean a filthy prefab shed in the yard of an old Victorian terraced house in New Road. I popped in to see her sometimes to tell her I was going to a friend's home for an hour or so after school, so I remember it well.

I never saw the offices and sales room as they were upstairs on the first floor, but I recall walking through the house to get to the factory at the back. The front parlour was filled with a wide workbench where the pattern-cutters made the templates out of stiff buff board for the various pieces of the garments. The back parlour had another massive table, which almost filled the room. Here, layers of fabric were placed on top of each other and then, using the templates, cut into the pattern shapes with a bandsaw.

There was a disgusting tearoom, full of mould-filled mugs, dirty plates and a sink that looked as if it hadn't been cleaned for a decade.

Passing through the always-open back door you found yourself in the yard. Here, other than the brick-built toilet, which narrowly beat the kitchen for squalor, the whole space was dominated by the prefabricated shed that housed the factory.

My mum and my aunts, who were also machinists, shouted all the time; and it was little wonder as the noise of thirty-plus sewing machines rattling away was deafening.

Although I called it Gold & Son's Gowns in *A Ration Book Dream,* and my character Mattie Brogan worked a treadle-operated sewing machine rather than the electronic machine my mother used, the description of the factory where Mattie worked was based on my mum's place of work. Sadly, unlike my character Mattie, who escapes to work as an ARP warden, my mum spent all her working life bent over an industrial machine in damp, dilapidated factories such as this one.

Power to the People

As far back as the Peasants' Revolt, when Wat Tyler met Richard II on what is now Whitechapel High Street, politics has always been a part of East London.

In fact, East London has been a hotbed of revolutionaries: Carl Marx, Lenin, Trotsky, Joseph Starlin and George Orwell were all residents there at one time or another. At the end of the nineteenth century, political exiles flooded into East London. In the early years of the last century Jubilee Street, not more than a quarter of a mile from our maisonette in Redmans Road, was a centre of revolution, with radical press shops spreading the socialist word far and wide through the *Workers' Friend*.

In the next road over, Peter the Painter, a member of an anarchist group, famously had a shoot-out with the police while Winston Churchill, freshly returned from his adventures in the Boer War, stood by, hoping to have a pot-shot at him.

Clement Attlee, Labour's post-war prime minister who put into being the Welfare State, was Stepney's MP for over thirty years.

Unsurprisingly as one of the poorest working-class areas in the capital, the majority of East Enders were solid Labour Party supporters, and the Fullertons were no exceptions. My Aunt

Nell first got the vote in 1928 under the Equal Franchise Act and told me more than once that she'd never voted anything but Labour ever since. Even Uncle Bob and Aunt Elaine, my most affluent white-collar relatives, voted solidly Labour, even though they confessed to being fans of Mrs Thatcher.

As well as supporting the Labour Party, my family were also involved in the unions. My Aunt Nell joined the Tailors and Garment Workers Union in the 1920s and became the union rep at the garment factory where she was a machinist. My Uncle Bob was a lifelong member of the Union of Post Office Workers, also serving as a shop steward for the Mount Pleasant Post Office until he was promoted to management, after which he joined the Civil Service union.

The most politically involved was my father. I remember clearly sitting on his shoulders as he attended a dockers' strike meeting, in King George's Park next to the River. I could have only been five or six, but I can recall the sea of flat caps and the tassel-fringed banners. He was an idealist and a passionate socialist all his life, and his desire to see social change through workers' power meant that he enthusiastically followed the unions' call for strike action on numerous occasions. His time in the army had solidified his socialist beliefs and his hatred for the upper classes and all management, who he saw as capitalist instruments to keep workers in their place.

It may seem unbelievable today, but with the mass unemployment of the thirties many people in Britain were looking at Adolf Hitler and his Nazi regime as an answer to Great Britain's problem. One of those was Oswald Mosley, an aristocrat and MP who formed the British Fascist League, modelling his black shirts on Hitler's brown shirts, and set about organising rallies and marches. Like Hitler, he believed that there was a worldwide conspiracy by Jews to control the world through banking and stock exchanges. One of Mosley's most notorious stunts in pursuit of political power took place in October 1936 when he tried to march his black shirts through the heart of the East End via Cable Street.

Given that East London had a very high Jewish population, this plan did not go down at all well with the various Jewish and socialist groups in the area. They banded together and vowed to stop Mosley in his tracks.

Somehow my father became caught up in what is now known and celebrated as the Battle of Cable Street. Truthfully, I suspect that rather than taking a stand against the threat to democracy and liberty, he was mainly protesting against the upper-class Mosley, who he saw as part of the ruling class that he hated with a passion. Although my father wasn't in the thick of the fighting – at the front where radicals and members of the Communist Party had barricaded Mosley's path – because Cable Street is quite a narrow thoroughfare, he soon found himself hemmed in by people fleeing the mounted police who were forcing the crowd back.

My Uncle Bob also claimed that he'd been on the barricades at Gardiner's Corner with the anti-fascists repelling Mosley and his black shirts marching down Leman Street during the Battle of Cable Street. He may well have been there, as a number of people, including children, turned out just to see the spectacle. From Bob's description of both the black shirts and the anti-fascist protesters, I have no doubt he was in the vicinity when it all kicked off. However, his assertion that he was in the thick of the fighting has to be taken with a pinch of salt as he was only eight at the time.

Of course, my father's hard-boiled socialist views looked positively Tory compared to some I came across as I got older. The most notable was Iris, a John Cass girl I became friendly with in my sixth year.

She was the eldest daughter of a Jewish mother and Scottish father, both of whom were fanatical communists. So much so that, in support of the glorious USRR, her father drove a Moskvitch car. Some years later I spotted her mother on the six o'clock news laying into a Tory minister with her brolly.

Every Sunday, Iris's parents and other dyed-in-the-wool revolutionaries would plot the overthrow of the West in the Crown pub in Clerkenwell Green. No ordinary pub, the Crown was around the corner from the Marx Memorial Library and, legend has it, is the pub where Stalin first met Lenin. But who knows?

I used to go there with Iris most weekends – goodness only knows why, as not once do I recall a firm-chinned, golden-haired revolutionary strolling through the door. Instead, the place was filled with spotty youths and crusty old men smoking roll-ups and debating who would be first up against the wall come the revolution.

My friend's parents were as much a permanent fixture in the place as the grotty beer-stained bar. Iris's grim-faced mother once tore me off a strip because I didn't recognise Jimmy Reid, the communist agitator from Glasgow Docks.

CHAPTER FOUR

There's Always an Angle

E AST LONDON AND crime have been synonymous with one another for nigh on two hundred years. From the rookeries of Spitalfields and the Old Nichol in Shoreditch to Victorian street gangs through to the Krays – who dominated criminal activity in East London and beyond in the 1960s – crime was a way of life for East Enders when I grew up. I'm not talking about bank robberies or smashing a jeweller's window (although some did). I mean the understanding that in any situation, be it avoiding a bus fare or being given too much change, if you could find a way to exploit it for financial gain, you should. If you didn't…well, you were a mug.

The most common crime – although no one I knew considered it a crime – was pinching something from work for yourself or to sell. It was endemic in the docks and there are plenty of stories of the inventive methods that workers devised to get all sorts through the dock gates. But it didn't have to be a bottle of whiskey from a bonded warehouse, it could be anything: pens or paper from the office, spark plugs from a garage or screwdrivers from the factory. If you worked in an electrical warehouse and you could spirit away a radio or two, that would be a welcome supplement to your wages.

Although he would never have regarded himself as a criminal, my father brought home reams of paper tucked in his briefcase, along with pencils, rubbers and masking tape. And we were never short of buttons or zips, because my mum slipped a couple in her bag now and again ready for when she made the family's clothes.

Children naturally pinched sweets off the counter in the corner shops. If they got lucky and swiped enough they could flog them in the playground. The more adventurous climbed into builders' yards and pinched shovels and small items like screwdrivers or spanners they found lying around. When I was about nine or ten, one kid turned up with a lolly lady's stick he'd pinched from somewhere, although goodness knows what he was going to do with it.

Of course, senior school was an ideal place for sticky fingers, with pupils routinely taking exercise books, pencils, chalk and sharpeners; and some were even more ambitious. There were a couple of boys in my year who were seasoned thieves by the time we were in the third year. They would walk off with hole punches, woodwork tools and even crockery and cutlery from the Home Economics room. During needlework classes, following the example of our mothers, we girls used to slip lace and braid into our blazer pockets.

You didn't regard it as thieving, it was just what you did.

By the time you went into the working world you were pretty quick at spotting a possible scam or something to pinch.

43

My first venture into paid employment was as a Saturday girl in a chemist conveniently situated ten minutes' walk from my home in a parade of shops on Commercial Road almost opposite St Mary's and St Michael's Catholic Church. The job was a fiddle in itself as I was paid off-the-books with cash in hand, rather than being employed officially.

It was a good job and paid well, but even though I had a 50 per cent discount on everything, I had no qualms about slipping the odd mascara or eyeliner into my pocket. In addition, when the shop was quiet, one of my jobs was to replenish the stock with muted-pink envelope-style wallets, the word 'Gossamer' stamped across the front.

The packets of Durex came in boxes of hundreds and were kept in the storeroom at the back of the shop, just by the door that led to the backyard and toilet. It was a location that proved to be useful: on my way to the loo I could grab a couple of packets and shove them down my bra, which saved my boyfriend at the time a great deal of money.

In the days before electronic cash registers and till rolls, my second Saturday job – like so many of my generation – was as a sales assistant in Woolworth's. There I graduated from purloining make-up to having friends drop into the shop to buy things. I would always take a pound or two off when manually ringing up the price, and they would return the favour in the shops where they worked. Of course, there were those who took it further still.

After I'd got to know a few of the girls and they'd judged me to be on the level, I found out that many of them would ring down a shilling or two, keeping a tally in their head until they had a quid, then they'd take the money out of the till and slip it through the gap between their overall buttons, tucking it in the top of their knickers.

The beauty of this was that if the supervisor did a spot check on your till before you had reached the required amount, then you'd have more money than sales, and it would be put down to human error.

Most counters had two tills and the secret was to ring up the sale at the till furthest away from the customer so they couldn't see the price ping up in the window. All the girls were encouraged to do the same, as obviously the more people involved the less likely it was that anyone was going to tell the management; the few who didn't were kept at arm's length.

However, the summer before I moved into the upper sixth, I waved Woolies at Aldgate bye-bye. I had decided to venture into new pastures up West, and trudged up and down Oxford Street looking for a summer job. After hearing 'we don't need anyone, sorry' a couple of times, I wandered into a boutique a few doors down from Bourne & Hollingsworth called Downtown. I asked a young girl who was chewing gum while tidying the rails if I could see the manager. She wiggled out to the back and an extremely tanned man in his mid-thirties stepped out from behind the curtains at the back of the shop.

He was dressed in flares and a fitted round-collar shirt that was open almost to his waist, with a thick gold chain dangling across his hairy chest. As he looked me up and down,

I explained that I was looking for a summer job. He informed me that he didn't have any vacancies in this shop but there were a couple of jobs going at his South Kensington shop so if I wanted to jump on the Tube and pop over, he'd tell them I was coming.

I did just that and after a bit of backwards and forwarding along the street I located the Kensington High Street branch of Downtown, which was immediately opposite the original Biba.

Flowery dresses hung from wall fixtures and there were cubby holes full of folded knitwear. A set of stairs led to the small basement where the shoes and handbags were situated. On the shop floor itself were circular rails full of blouses, shirts and skirts, and as customers drifted around looking at various items, Scott McKenzie warbled advice about wearing flowers in our hair in case we were planning to go to San Francisco any time soon.

I was duly taken on by the bubbly, afro-haired manager who was dressed in a kaftan and beads, with a pair of star-shaped sunglasses perched on her head. I gave her my P45, she set out the working hours, and I turned up the following Monday morning.

There were eight or nine girls who worked full time in the shop, with one Saturday girl who was the sister of one of the long-standing sales assistants. Like Carnaby Street and King's Road, Kensington High Street was the place to be seen, and the almost rich and almost famous would wander up and down it, showing off their style. Although just half an hour on the

District Line from Stepney, Kensington High Street was a world away from council estates and bombsites. Instead of tightly packed terraced houses and high-rise flats, here were elegant townhouses with servants' quarters in the eaves and apartment blocks with doormen to keep out the riffraff.

People lived on their own in bedsits instead of with their families, and the population was transient, without any roots or links with the area. My cockney accent stood out among the plummy tones of the wannabe actresses and models who worked in the shop.

The sixties and early seventies saw a mix of styles, from the block-coloured mini-dresses and the Sassoon bob at the start of the decade to the mod-style tonic suits of the skinheads as the sixties nudged into the seventies, stopping off at the cheesecloth peasant blouses and floaty skirts of the Summer of Love on the way.

As I wouldn't like to look like mutton dressed as lamb – to use one of my mum's favourite phrases – I like to think my style now is classic, but back then, I have to confess, I grabbed every new style that arrived in the store before it was even hooked on the rail.

In addition to the tempting fashions arriving at Downtown every couple of days, I'd also buy clothes from Biba, the go-to shop for anyone who wanted to have the latest look. At the end of every week, clutching my week's wages, I would dash across to the iconic shop in my lunch break. I remember the first week I bought a pair of maroon hipster loon trousers and one of their 'must-have' scoop-neck T-shirts with a tiny drawstring bow at the front. I wore both items so much they practically fell off with wear.

However, after a few weeks of unrestrained clothes shopping, and despite the staff discount, once I'd paid my two-pound-fifty housekeeping each week, I was becoming financially stretched. Thankfully, the girls in the shop decided I could be trusted and they let me in on their little secret.

Like the girls at Woolworth's, the sales assistants at the Kensington High Street branch of Downtown had a little fiddle going on. To be honest, it was absolutely brilliant. The back door of the shop led out into a narrow alleyway that ran behind the parade of shops. The door was neither alarmed nor monitored, so just before your lunch break you selected what you fancied off the rails and dumped it in one of the dustbins that was stored in the alley. When you were sent on your midday break you hurried to the back of the shop to retrieve your clothes from the bin, took them to the dry cleaners next to the station and put them in for a two-hour press, which cost about fifty pence per item. At the end of the day you simply returned to the dry cleaners, paid your money and collected your pilfered togs. As I say, brilliant!

Most of us just took the odd few items each week, and as there was no real stocktaking process and shoplifting was rife, it went unnoticed. However, one day a new girl called Christine joined us and everything changed.

Nothing seemed out of the ordinary until Christine and Jilly – who had started in the shop a few weeks after me – suddenly discovered, with unconvincing wide-eyed gasps of surprise, that they had loads of mutual friends, despite repeatedly stating that they'd never seen each other before. Clearly, they knew each other very well and had come up with a plan. The two of them started shifting clothing out of the back door on an industrial scale.

Worrying that someone at head office would notice the growing discrepancy between the stock on the rails and the money in the till, most of us stopped, but Jilly and Christine had no such qualms.

Thankfully, just as things started to escalate, September came around, so I put in my one week's notice and returned to school. Just in time, as it happens, as two weeks after I left, the police were called in and Christine and Jilly were arrested.

About the same time as I started my final year at school, I was going out with a chap from Bermondsey who had recently got a job in a cigarette and cigar wholesaler at the Elephant and Castle. It didn't take long for us to work out another money-making scheme.

I've never smoked, but when I was a teenager I was very much in the minority, and getting your hands on cheap cigarettes was extremely lucrative. This was in the days of the skinheads, when a bulky sheepskin jacket was the recognised uniform everywhere. It was easy for my boyfriend to conceal a pack of two hundred cigarettes under each arm and anchor them in place by shoving his hands in his pockets. I would meet him for lunch two or three times a week and take them off him to sell in the sixth-form common room. This worked quite nicely for several months until one of the chaps he worked with got rumbled, and he got the sack.

From the age of about sixteen, my school friends and I started going out to public houses, mainly to local ones, like the Ship in Stepney Green or the Horn of Plenty opposite Queen Mary University. Rarely a night went by without someone sidling over to offer you knocked-off bottles of perfume or pairs of tights. I once arrived at a friend's house to find half a dozen discounted record players, still in boxes, stacked up behind the couch.

Having a little sideline going at work or getting the TV for the front room from a man in a pub was just a way of life and no one blinked an eye. After I'd left school I went out with a chap who had a very respectable job in a City firm but if you wanted anything, from a designer coat to a fridge, he knew where he could get it for you.

Above this layer of petty theft, which was carried out by almost everyone I knew, between us and the Krays and Richardsons of this world, there were the local hard men who managed a patch for them. And they were easy to spot in any pub.

Firstly, they, along with a couple of other blokes, usually occupied a booth in prime position at the back of the pub. They were all well groomed and smartly dressed in made-to-measure suits, and you rarely saw them up at the bar – drinks would just appear at their elbows.

One of the pubs where my skinhead boyfriend and I went from time to time was a quiet drinking house off Southwark

Park Road in Bermondsey with wooden floorboards, flock wallpaper and no jukebox. There were always men in cloth caps smoking roll-ups as they checked the racing results, having slipped out for a swift half after supper.

It was also the favourite drinking hole of the local governor, who sat at the back of the narrow public bar surveying the comings and goings with his associates. The lad I was with would always bowl in with his sheepskin slouched open and his polished DMs, hoping to show how tough he was. Naturally, Bermondsey's Big Man just kept on slowly sipping his pint and totally ignored his bluster.

According to James Morton's book *East End Gangland,* my father's cousin Jimmy Fullerton – not to be confused with my mild-mannered Uncle Jimmy – was one such hard man, heading up the Watney Street Gang at the same time as the Krays were the overlords. However, when I put this on a Stepney and Wapping social media chat group I belong to, many people who knew Jimmy personally refuted it, saying he, like many others, was a 'bit of a lad' but no gang leader. Who knows! Perhaps the truth lies somewhere in-between.

But there is honour amongst thieves. I used to hang around with a young man who was a milkman; he overcharged customers but never pensioners 'cos they fought Hitler'. A good friend of mine told me that her father, who worked in a furniture manufacturer, regularly walked out with yards of upholstery fabric which his brother sold in his general goods shop. Despite this, when her uncle noticed that gangs of youngsters were pickpocketing old ladies waiting at the bus stop outside his shop he called the police and allowed them to use his window to observe the goings-on and arrest them.

The first and overriding rule was you didn't diddle your family. A rule my Aunt Millie transgressed with my father in the late forties just after my parents were married. Millie lived in the downstairs room of a house and the woman upstairs was selling her fur coat. My mum wanted it, so my father duly went around to fetch it and was told it was £40. My father was about to go up to pay the neighbour when Millie took the money from him and said she'd take it up later as them upstairs had company. He handed it over, but he just knew that she had added a couple of quid on to the asking price, something he never forgave her for.

CHAPTER FIVE

Food, Glorious Food!

DAILY MEALS WERE different when I was a child. Like most men from our area, my father was a manual worker. Other than a cup of tea before he left, he had his breakfast, which was usually something fried and floating in lard, in the work canteen. My father had acquired a taste for porridge in the army, so that was what I had each morning.

Now, to be honest, I can't stand the stuff and have told my children that if I ever end up as a feeble old woman in a nursing home they are to pin a notice saying 'No Porridge' over my bed. However, when I was a child you ate what was put in front of you or you went hungry.

After breakfast, the working man's next meal was usually consumed at midday. Again, either in the factory dining room or in a greasy-spoon café. That said, as rationing was phased out, men started to take their own food, which their wives had to prepare.

My father was one of them, and armed with his Thermos flask and doorstop-size sandwiches filled with such things as pilchards, ham or cheese packed in his tin, he'd set off at the crack of dawn. The motorbike that they had bought just after my parents got married had disappeared around the time I was born, so he walked the five minutes to Shadwell station and jumped on the old bone-rattling Shoreditch to New Cross line before picking up a District line at Whitechapel that took him to Dagenham East.

While my father set off to earn a crust, my mum's job now I'd arrived was to look after the home. With no refrigerator she had to shop daily, so every day we would head for Watney Street Market to buy the food for our evening meal.

Up until the 1960s, no one turned a hair at the sight of a line of prams with babies in them outside a shop and not a single parent in sight. I'm sure I was one of those unattended infants when I was a toddler. However, as I grew older, I trudged up and down the market alongside my mum as she headed for the butcher or the greengrocer. I can't remember them all, but a few of the shops stand out clearly in my mind even after all these years.

Under the railway bridge at the bottom of the market was Shelton's the haberdasher. The bell above the door tinkled as you stepped inside and you were immediately enveloped in a bygone age. The smell of cloth and polish wafted up, and the clothing folded neatly on shelves behind the counters absorbed the noise and gave the interior a muted quality. If I remember rightly, the men's section, with shirts, cardigans and overalls, was towards the back, while the women's section was to the left, but I can clearly picture the children's area to the right.

Made of light oak and glass, the counter displayed all manner of children's items such as smocked matinee frocks, bibs, vests and knickers, all folded neatly and placed in drawers.

After you'd selected the items you wanted to look at from the display, the shop assistant would slide the drawer out and place the garments on the surface for you to peruse. Having chosen your purchase the assistant either placed it in a paper bag, if it was small enough, or pulled out a long sheet from the roll of brown paper suspended on an iron bracket at the end of the counter and wrapped what you'd bought in a parcel.

Another of my favourite shops was Feildmans, the newsagent on the corner, which always seemed to be packed with people whenever we visited. Not only was it stacked from floor to ceiling with newspapers, magazines and all manner of stationery, but it also stocked books and toys.

However, the shop I remember most vividly was Sainsbury's, which stood halfway down the street on the west side. It had originally been two shops but the wall dividing them had been partially removed so you could walk through from one to the other as you shopped. This was before the time of supermarkets, so depending on whether my mum was in need of dry goods, dairy or general groceries, she had to queue at the appropriate curved glass-fronted counter until it was her turn to be served.

Every purchase had to be asked for and the shop assistant behind the counter would trundle off to fetch your item. When they returned you would then read out the next thing on your shopping list and off they would go again. When everything you'd asked for was weighed, wrapped in paper and tucked into your trolley or basket, you would pay and then move on to queue all over again at the next counter. While things like butter, tea and sugar were pre-wrapped, much of what you bought was weighed out as required. Bacon and ham were sliced for you or the shop assistant would peel off a slice from a pre-cut stack with their bare hands, while cheese was cut into chunks and weighed in much the same way.

My favourite counter was the general groceries one, as running along the front at child's eye-level were a series of boxes in which the loose biscuits were kept. They were sold by the quarter or half pound and were very much a luxury when I was a child, being reserved for weekends. However, along with the custard creams, bourbons, digestives and the pastel-coloured Peak Freans icing-glazed biscuits was another box containing a jumble of them all, the broken biscuits, which my mother always bought for our biscuit barrel on the sideboard.

Of course, there were tins of peas and carrots on the shelf, but as my mum had to make the housekeeping stretch it was cheaper to buy fresh vegetables. I remember as a child shelling peas into a basin at the kitchen table. Fish fingers were introduced in the mid-fifties, but as most housewives didn't have a fridge let alone a freezer I don't remember ever having them as a child.

While my father had a packed lunch, it was unheard of for children to have them – we were expected to eat school dinners, the joy of which I'll talk about later. When we returned from our day's lessons, we were given our tea. This could be something like cheese, sardines on toast or potato cakes, but sometimes it was just a jam sandwich or bread and dripping sprinkled with salt, which makes me heave just thinking about it.

Tea for the adults followed later when the man of the house arrived home. Smaller children were usually tucked up in bed by then, but once they moved into senior school the whole family sat down together. The evening meal could be anything from liver and onion with mash to stuffed pigs' hearts, a particular favourite of mine. This was usually followed by a suet-based pudding of some sort with custard so thick it would stick to your ribs until morning.

I was always given warm milk to drink before being tucked up in bed. My parents plumped for an Ovaltine while they sat on either side of the fireplace listening to the Light Programme and I remember the sound drifting up from below.

By the time we moved into the maisonette, thanks to the purchase of a fridge, the daily shop had moved to a weekly one. Our first call was the butcher's, where we would wait in line until it was our turn to be served. Our butcher – everyone had their preferred one – was between a pub called the Three Cranes and a draper's store just down from Wickhams department store on Mile End Road.

We queued alongside the front of the window, which displayed all the various meats on offer that week. Meats that you never see today, such as shiny-fleshed rabbits with a fluted texture, bleached tripe, quivering mauve liver, pig's trotters with the mud still visible and, hooked up in a neat row above the display, half a dozen pigs' heads.

Inside, the shop smelled of metal and wood: metal from the blood and wood from the sawdust on the floor. As I recall, butchers were always jolly and blood-splattered and they wielded a meat cleaver as expertly as any surgeon. They had a good eye, too, as their party trick would be to slap your meat on a sheet of paper then throw it six feet or so on to their scales. The upright marker on the scales would swing back and forth furiously for a moment until it settled on a weight.

Because of our newly acquired fridge, we took all our meat home with us; but for housewives who didn't – and there were still a great number in the early 1960s – the butcher would write your name on your purchase and keep it in his refrigerator for you to collect later in the week. Having tucked the coming week's meat safely in our bags, we would continue along toward the Waste.

Now some of you old East Enders reading this may know, but for those of you not from around my way, the Waste is the open market that runs along the north side of Whitechapel Road. For centuries, this road was the main route into London from Essex, so the market dates back to the times when carters would sell off any surplus to the locals before taking their produce into the city.

The market is still there, as are the shops, like outstretched arms on either side of Whitechapel underground station. I remember a milliner; Lipman's the grocer, where my Aunt Martha traded her husband's luncheon vouchers for supplies each week; Lyons tea shop; several dress shops and a record store called Wally for Wireless, where youths in drainpipe trousers and girls with sugar-starched petticoats puffing out their brightly coloured skirts hung out.

Now, if butchers were the dare-devil showmen of the Saturday-morning shopping expedition, the stallholders were the cheeky chappies. Many dressed in outlandish waistcoats or hats and each had their own cry and patter, and they often exchanged good-natured banter with each other. Fruit and veg, trimmed, polished and artistically arranged, filled their stalls. There were flowers, too, a splash of colour in contrast to the grey pavements beneath the shoppers' feet and the soot-caked buildings around.

The stallholders juggled potatoes, bicep-bounced apples and whipped away the greenery around a cauliflower with a razor-sharp knife while their eagle eyes darted back and forth looking for customers. But you had to watch them, or you'd end up with yesterday's stock from the back of the display or have an extra weight added to the scales.

Fruit was deposited in a brown paper bag and whirled closed at each corner, but veg was shovelled straight into your shopping bag. Potatoes first, then your greens and lastly tomatoes and lettuce.

Unlike today when you can buy fresh strawberries at Christmas, everything was seasonal. The root vegetables of winter gave way to lettuces and tomatoes some time around Easter, while during a couple of weeks in June you had cherries. Plums and strawberries cropped up in late April and May and were gone by the time the school summer holidays started in July. Apples and oranges were plentiful all year around but tangerines were a special treat for Christmas and a staple in fifties and sixties stockings hung up at the end of the bed.

There were other traders, too. I remember dress stalls selling seconds from local garment factories. Stalls selling underwear, stockings, dress fabric and haberdashery. Stalls selling cooked meat and the Jewish delicacy of salt beef. Bread stalls with bagels and sweet-tasting challah bread as well as crusty rolls and tin loaves.

Costermongers selling household goods – pots and pans, baking trays, casserole dishes, knives and chopping bowls along with teapots, drinking glasses and full dinner sets – were also out in force. They would stack items on a tray then throw it in the air to show the quality of their goods.

'Don't give me a quid,' they would shout, catching the tray of rattling crockery. 'Don't give me fifteen bob,' they added, throwing the tray head height again. 'Just ten bob, ladies and gentlemen. Just ten bob, that's all I'm asking for…'

A stooge – we all knew they were – at the back shouted they'd take it and then others would follow.

By midday, with our heavy bags almost pulling our arms from their sockets, we would return home to offload our burden. Only then, when everything was packed away and all the dusting, tidying and hoovering had been completed, was the family at leisure.

We children were allowed to play; and although my parents would spend the afternoon sitting by the fire watching the television, my mother was never idle. When she wasn't hand sewing a hem or buttons into place she would have a pair of knitting needles in her hands. Although today sewing and knitting rank alongside hobbies such as card-making and needlepoint, when I was a child nearly all jumpers and cardigans were hand knitted.

My mum always had something on the go, and alongside straightforward school woollies she could also whip up a filigree twinset or lacy baby's shawl.

Along with free patterns in women's magazines, there was a wool shop stocking patterns and wool on every high street. You only bought a couple of balls at a time, but to ensure you had the same dyed batch for the whole garment the shopkeeper would 'put some by' for collection later.

As with the other housewifely skills of shopping, cooking and housework, my mum also taught me to knit, something that I continue to do to this day.

School Dinners

As I said previously, the new Welfare State was very interested in child nutrition, so along with daily milk, schools also supplied a hot dinner each day. Having mastered the art of feeding large groups of people during the war in mass feeding centres, ironically named British Restaurants, the government decided the same idea could be used to feed children, and so kitchens were set up in schools.

My junior school in Cephas Street had a single-storey, purpose-built cookhouse by the side gate. Each day, just before midday, a small army of red-faced dinner ladies in hairnets and wearing Bri-Nylon overalls would push a trolley loaded with massive aluminium cooking pots across the playground.

The meals provided didn't pretend to be anything other than basic and although my Aunt Nell called me a fussy eater, in truth, what was dished up on my plate each lunchtime often bore no resemblance to any kind of food I knew. Most days it was a meat pie of some description, mainly shepherd's or steak and kidney, usually with colourless boiled cabbage or turnips and unscraped, half-cooked carrots alongside. Sometimes we had liver and bacon swimming in gravy, but this wasn't often as it meant the dinner ladies had to make an alternative for the Jewish children in the school. Whatever was on the menu, as sure as the sun rises each morning, the meat was invariably half gristle.

There were slices of spam, too, fried in batter, with the obligatory mash and over-boiled vegetables. There was also macaroni cheese – well, I think it was with cheese as it was so sparse it was almost undetectable. It was commonly known as 'dead worms'.

The afters or pudding were usually divided into two categories: milk or suet. The suet variety was usually labelled as jam, treacle or spotted dick. To be honest, it didn't matter as you would have needed to send it to Forensics to detect the conserve or syrup, and your father was more likely to win the pools than you were to find a currant. In any case, whatever it was it was disguised under a sea of thin pale-yellow custard.

The other pudding option was no more appetising. The congealed tray of white something would be milk, tapioca or semolina pudding – all of which I never ate then and haven't since. Of course, whatever the dish, it always complied with the unwritten school dinner rule that, be it mash, gravy or a so-called dessert, it had to have lumps in it.

Friday offered some respite, because in time-honoured tradition there was always fish, but even then it was mostly skin and batter.

Although by the time I got to secondary school there was some recognition of allergies and religious practices, the only dietary concession I remember from my infant and junior schools was to Jewish children, who made up a good proportion of pupils in each class.

Even now, five decades later, the smell of over-boiled cabbage takes me right back to that noisy school hall.

CHAPTER SIX

The Rich Man in his Castle, the Poor Man at his Gate

CLASS IS A much-debated issue in Britain today. Is being upper class about money or is it about who your parents were? Is there even such a thing as class any more or just the cubby holes political pundits put us into, like Workington man or Aldi mum? My parents' generation didn't have to worry about such nuanced divisions: it was all too clear to them where they fitted in society.

My parents' generation had an acute awareness of those who were a few rungs up the social ladder from them. They strove to be counted as hard-working and respectable. It influenced their attitudes and everything they did, from how they dressed to how they spoke. My father railed against it all his life but, try as they might, neither he nor my mum could throw off their deferential attitude to those they judged to be above them – the doctors, vicars and teachers who had authority because they were educated. People in these occupations had a profession that my working-class parents would never have aspired to in a hundred years. To my parents, especially my father, they were experts and there was no arguing with them. Even in the brave new post-war world, the one thing my parents' generation knew was their place.

From birth it was drilled into them that they should be humbly grateful for any largesse bestowed on them by those above.

Even though the pop culture of the 1960s had made being working class fashionable, I still felt the weight of prejudice against coming from the East End on more than one occasion.

The first thing that marked you out, of course, was the way you spoke. You have to remember that although now we're used to listening to television and radio presenters with regional accents, when I was a child they all spoke in the same clipped, upper-class tones as the queen.

I have a cockney accent that could cut glass and it works for me now, but when I attended both junior and senior school the teachers were constantly correcting our pronunciation. To increase their children's chances of getting a job in an office or a bank, some parents paid for them to have elocution lessons.

In my teens I dated a youth whose family lived on the Barbican Estate. His mother was always at pains to impress upon me that they lived in a house owned by the City of London Corporation, not a council house; her main objection to me was that my accent marked me out as common.

It happened again a few years later when I was involved with a young man who lived in a flat at the top of a council block on Churchill Gardens in Pimlico. His mother was a Highland

Scot, a lovely woman who had never lost her lilting accent; but his father, a public-school-educated civil servant, was apt to mimic my accent and correct my pronunciation. Well, at least he did when he wasn't slumped in a chair insensible with drink.

My boyfriend's brother was just as sniffy, and used my accent as an excuse to treat me as a comical Eliza Doolittle.

Now while my family aren't landed gentry and I haven't had a classical Oxbridge education, as long as no one switches to Latin, I like to think I can hold my own in any company. But sometimes, just sometimes, when I open my mouth, I catch someone giving me a second look. Try as I might, I can't help the faint feeling of being judged and found wanting because my accent echoes through me.

Keeping Us on the Straight and Narrow

St Dunstan's and All Saints Church, to give it its full title, is the mother church of Stepney. It was founded in the 900s and still has a rune stone behind the altar from that period. It's also the mariners' church, so anyone born at sea on an English ship can claim it as their parish for the purposes of getting married and receiving parish assistance.

The church on the site today was mainly built in the 1600s but was extensively restored – or damaged, depending on your viewpoint – during the nineteenth century. Although the building we filed into each week was over two hundred years old, the massive stained-glass window behind the altar had been installed just over a decade before after the original had been blown out by a bomb that had obliterated most of nearby Stepney High Street in 1942. The window depicted a very blond and very young Christ on the crucifix, surrounded by the bomb-damaged streets of Stepney.

Like many churches in those day, St Dunstan's had five services on a Sunday, matins and communion three times a week and evensong each night. The church had a very large congregation, plus a Sunday school and youth club, so there was a lot going on.

Back then, the Church of England was very much the Establishment. The clergy were never seen in anything but long black cassocks and were always addressed as Father. They were treated like minor royalty and in contrast to the dropped 'h' and elongated vowels of the cockney accent, all their sermons and homilies were delivered in the precise, plummy tones of the BBC announcer.

Alongside making sure you behaved yourself so you could have a place in C of E Heaven, their task was to preserve the heavenly ordained traditions and social order of this sceptred isle against the Godless permissive society. A doomed endeavour, if ever there was one.

Unlike my father, who was a chronically shy introvert, my mum made friends easily. Although the initial reason for my father joining my mother on her weekly trek to St Dunstan's Church was to get me into Sir John Cass, for reasons I'll explain later, my mum went because she had always been a regular church-goer and she really enjoyed it. Being the gregarious sort that she was, she soon joined the Mothers' Union and made friends. Although I think my father had long since dismissed Christianity and the Church, he continued to attend, as he felt it was a good moral foundation for me and my brother. I also think, as the pews of St Dunstan's were populated by middle-class chief engineers, teachers and local civil servants, that my father like the idea of being counted in their number.

Unlike today, churches were full each Sunday morning when I was a child, but you couldn't just wander in wearing your jeans and receive a warm welcome. Going to church was what respectable office workers and professional people did and so you had to dress accordingly in your Sunday best. This meant suits and ties for men and a smart outfit for women – with a hat plus matching shoes and handbag if you could stretch to it.

Going to church indicated to those around you at work and in your street that you didn't subscribe to all the things looked down upon by the powers that be, like drinking, gambling and swearing.

That's not to say the clergy weren't sincere or genuine in their attempt to minister to us.

But it wasn't just the good old C of E who were active in the East End. In fact, the Roman Catholic Church set up missions, and priests like Father Joe worked tirelessly amongst the seamen and prostitutes. In addition, there were the Nonconformist churches, and, famously, the Salvation Army, which was set up by William Booth in Whitechapel in the 1860s to help relieve the suffering he saw around him. My father's generation of East Enders had a fond regard for the Salvation Army. Although none of my family were in the slightest way religious, they always bought a copy of *War Cry* as a small token of appreciation for what was regarded as a local charity.

CHAPTER SEVEN

Reading, Writing and 'Rithmetic

PHILANTHROPISTS SUCH AS Angela Burdett-Coutts, William Booth and Annie and Frank Besant dedicated their lives to improving the lives of the poor in East London and like many of the Victorian benefactors who worked to alleviate poverty, they identified one of the surest ways of avoiding the workhouse to be education. This is evident by the number of schools set up by wealthy patrons, such as Raine's Grammar School in the eighteenth century and church schools such Greencoat infant, founded in the opening years of the eighteenth century, and Redcoat secondary, founded at roughly the same time. And it didn't end when you left compulsory education; numerous workers' education institutes were established around the turn of the last century, such as Toynbee Hall, set up in the 1880s by Samuel and Henrietta Barnett, which was dedicated to social change and education, and the famous People's Palace, offering culture and education and opened with a much grander flourish by Queen Victoria at about the same time.

In addition, Passmore Edwards Libraries were founded as a place for working people and helped countless thousands of newly arrived immigrants to access opportunities. The most famous of these was Whitechapel Library, founded in the 1890s. Many people, such as historian Jacob Bronowski, artist Mark Gertler and playwrights Arnold Wesker and Bernard Kops, credited the Whitechapel Library with being instrumental in their education.

During the war years, in an effort to help women make the most of their rations, the local government set up housewives' classes. Home Economics instructors would demonstrate cooking techniques to cut down on food waste and save fuel.

East London has always leaned to the left politically. It's therefore unsurprising that after Labour's landslide victory at the Khaki Election in 1945, East London councils extended their range of afternoon and evening educational classes, and I have a very clear memory of sitting alongside my mum scribbling in a colouring book at one such class as a well-spoken woman in a colourful apron explained how to use a pressure cooker.

Although there were a great number of foundation schools in East London, which were set up by wealthy patrons and endowed with money in the form of a trust fund, it wasn't until the 1880s that it became compulsory for all children to attend, and the task of running the schools was handed over to local authorities.

Children went to school because it was the law, and the man from the school board would be after their parents if they didn't. My father and his brothers and sisters when to Cable Street School.

The red-brick Victorian building was brought into existence by the 1870 Education Act, and along with the three Rs – reading, writing and arithmetic – children were taught about God, British history and the Empire, plus skills such as woodwork and sewing, which were thought necessary for them to find a job.

The school day was regimented and strict, with the ever-present threat of being pulled to the front of the class and given six of the best – that's to say, six strokes across the palm of your hand with a three-foot length of cane – for the smallest violation of the rules. The thought of beating children with anything, let alone a cane, is abhorrent to us today but to my father and his generation such punishment was commonplace in the home as well as in school.

Again, rightly regarded as child abuse now, back then no one blinked an eye if a father took off his belt to punish his wayward nipper. And it wasn't just parents who were free to chastise cheeky or naughty children. Anyone – shopkeeper, market trader, neighbour or stranger, or even the local bobby – would, if they felt a child was misbehaving, give them a clip around the ear.

Many children in London were evacuated to the country within days of war being declared, but not my Uncle Bobby. The Fullerton family took the view that if they were going to cop it then 'we might as well go together'. With so many children and teachers absent, the schools in the area amalgamated and Bobby found himself moved to another school. On top of which, with people being bombed out, some families ended up repeatedly changing their address or even moving out of the area, so keeping track of the children who were meant to be in school was nigh on impossible.

In his own words: 'No one took no notice if you went or not, so after a couple of months, I didn't bother.' Having decided he'd had enough of school, Bobby divided his time between scavenging for souvenirs among the rubble and making a general nuisance of himself. According to him, he amassed quite a collection of fragments from German armaments, the most prized trophy being half a blue tailfin from a high-explosive bomb.

Thankfully, by the time I turned up for my first day at school, education had moved on from those draconian Victorian days. The cane was still in regular use in secondary schools but infant and junior schools had dispensed with them decades before. Although we still sat in regimented lines of desks facing a blackboard, brightly coloured posters of nursery character and animals adorned the walls. There was also a map of the world, with large red areas indicating the British Empire, and an ABC chart illustrated with jolly pictures.

Today, children are given taster days and introduced to the new world of school in gentle stages, but back then the first Monday in September and you were in.

Cephas Street Nursery, Infant and Junior School was situated behind Wickhams department store on Mile End Road and, like so many in the area, it was a late-nineteenth-century building with classrooms and a hall on each of its three floors. It butted on to Charrington's brewery on two sides and had an entrance in Cephas Street. It was a bit of a trek from our old house in Anthony Street, but, in anticipation of the move to Bethnal Green, I'd started in its nursery the year before when I was four. However, going to the local junior school wasn't my father's plan for my education at all.

Prior to discovering my mum was pregnant again, it was intended that I should go to Sir John Cass School, which was situated then in Aldgate; in fact, my father had put my name down for the hugely oversubscribed City foundation school before I could walk.

However, as it was a half-hour bus ride away from our new flat, my mum did something she rarely did: she put her foot down. She told my father she wasn't prepared to lug a pram on and off a bus twice a day, so I'd have to go to the local nursery. To be honest, I don't blame her one little bit.

Now, although I was part of a large family, my generation of Fullertons was pretty sparse. On my father's side, apart from my cousin Edie, who was now an adult at work, there was just me and my brother. Although by the time I went to school my mum's sister Gladys had two girls; they lived in Harold Hill, a two-hour journey away on a Green Line country bus.

There is the odd photo of our family visiting people with children but by and large my parents pretty much kept themselves to themselves.

One of the other problems for me was that unlike at home, where I was more or less allowed to run wild, at nursery I was surprised to find out I had to do what 'Miss' said.

At home everything in the toy box had been for my exclusive

use, so the idea that I had to give other children a turn with a dressing-up costume or a toy was a totally new concept to me.

Oddly, I can remember that my coat peg had a picture of a squirrel next to it but other than that my time in the nursery is a bit of a blur. However, a few instances stand out. One was when a child lobbed a large wooden building brick into the Wendy house where I was playing, which resulted in an ambulance being called. The other was when, as part of nature study, I dropped the guinea pig and the school caretaker had to dismantle half the classroom to recapture it. But it wasn't my fault as I'd never held a live animal before.

After a year of playing mums and dads in the Wendy house, painting and scrambling about on the monkey bars and climbing frames, I moved up to infant school to start my education.

In those days schooling was divided into three distinct parts. Your real schooling started at age five in the infants; when you turned seven you went up to the junior school, followed by secondary school once you were eleven.

A typical day in school would go like this. After kissing your mother goodbye at the gate – it was always mothers back then – you set about locating friends. Having done that, you dashed around wildly, screaming and shouting, while the playground attendants, usually older women with sour faces and a fag hanging out of their mouths, bellowed at you to stop. This went on for about fifteen minutes or so until one of the teachers came out and rang a bell.

You stopped whatever you were doing, lined up in your classes and then peeled off in order of seniority and made your way to the classroom. After registration you trooped out to the main hall and sat crossed-legged on the floor until the headmaster and his deputy came in, which was the cue for you to stand up again. In fact, right through to when I left school in 1971, I spent a great deal of my day bobbing up and down as teachers came in and went out of classrooms.

Although my infant school wasn't attached to a church, like all schools at that time the morning assembly was an act of Christian worship. There was a Bible reading followed by a couple of minutes' talk from the headmaster, then we all said the Lord's Prayer and sang some hymns, which, when I hear them sung even now, take me right back to the polished parquet-floored hall crammed with children.

The hall was on one side of the building, with the classrooms overlooking the asphalt playground on the other side. Separating the hall and the classrooms was a corridor. The first- and second-year classes resided on the ground floor, and I remember on fine days carrying my chair through the open door and having lessons outside.

We sat in desks of two and were taught the three Rs, much as my parents must have been taught, by repetition. We recited the alphabet out loud as the teacher pointed to each individual letter then we were required to copy a passage from a card on to a piece of lined paper to perfect our handwriting. Times tables, too, were learned by saying them out loud, although I confess, to this day, I don't know my seven and eight times tables.

Boys, even from quite an early age, were allowed to bore holes in wood with hand drills before twisting screws into them, but this wasn't considered suitable for us girls so we were taught sewing. We started making simple cross-stitch samplers in the same way our grandmothers had, but, as we got better, we progressed to more ambitious projects such as aprons and embroidered antimacassars (which we called chairbacks). And, in my last year at junior school, I even made myself a pair of red polka-dot pyjamas – all by hand.

Halfway through the morning we drank our allocated third of a pint of school milk, before being released from our desks to relieve ourselves and head outside to let off steam during morning play. And believe me, your bladders were busting by then because although you were allowed to put your hand up and ask to go to the lav, permission wasn't automatically granted as there was a suspicion you were skiving off. To be honest, unless you were on the point of wetting yourself, I don't know why you'd want to go into the toilets because not only did the brick block in the corner of the playground smell like the antelope house at London Zoo, it was obviously an overspill facility for the spider breeding programme of the same institution. In the summer you gagged at the smell of sewage and in the winter you were in danger of having your rear frozen to the china. And I say china because other than a six-inch piece of wood bolted on to the front rim of the toilet basin, there was no seat.

Playtime for the boys was largely dashing around kicking a ball or fighting, but us girls had a wider choice of games. Skipping was always popular but this was communal rather than individual. Chanting, Up and Down all the way to London

Town or Teddy Bear Teddy Bear, two girls would turn a long rope while the others jumped in and out for a couple of verses.

Of course sometime, having spent two hours sat at a desk, the girls ran around the playground too, playing tag or galloping, fists raised in front of them, as they pretended to be riding ponies.

Having dashed around shouting at the top of our voices for twenty minutes while the playground assistant pulled fighting children apart and picked injured ones off the floor, the bell summoned us back inside.

Although televisions in the classrooms were still decades away, our teachers did have one media resource they could call on: the BBC Schools programme. Each programme became the introduction to the lesson and came with a supplementary workbook with exercises for you to do after the broadcast. The programmes often used actors to dramatise events and one from my junior school that particularly sticks in my mind was Oliver Cromwell's invasion of Ireland. And let me tell you that the blood-curdling screams of the actors portraying the massacred Catholics kept me staring at the ceiling in fear for many nights after.

Anyhow, after a morning of mastering literacy and numeracy skills, or listening to the school broadcast, the school bell would go again to signify dinnertime. Some children, who were the envy of many of us, lived near to school so they went home for lunch; however, the vast majority of my class – me included – were forced to sufferer school dinners.

Of course, the hall was the site of that other great escape

from academic studies: physical exercise or, as it was universally referred to, PE. This was also a barefooted activity, which we did in our underwear. For boys this meant Y-fronts (in various shades, ranging from white to grey) and a vest, while the girls wore navy knickers and a vest.

PE back then was very much a do-it-yourself type of activity. For the infants, exercise mainly comprised of doing bunny hops back and forth over a bench, forward and backward rolls on rubber mats and catching and throwing balls of different sizes.

This progressed to turning the said benches over and then balancing along the narrow beam and jumping off the low section of the vaulting horse. Naturally, there were always a few children taken to the office with bumps and bruises after PE. However, for the most part, there was no real risk of serious injury until you moved up to the juniors; then PE was quite different.

By the time you reached the age of eight you were judged to be ready for more adventurous forms of keeping fit. The apparatus was introduced.

The apparatus, which every school had, was a large wall-mounted climbing frame. It stayed folded up against the hall wall when not in use, but when it was PE time you dragged the two folded wings open until they were at right angles to the wall and, once they were in place, bolted them to the floor to secure them.

From these wooden frames hung climbing ropes, wooden-runged rope ladders and other bits of equipment considered vital for the development of young people's fitness. To make it even more 'fun', the school benches, which up to now had been reserved for the safe bunny-hopping and balancing exercises, were hooked on to the bars at various heights to create slopes for us to clamber up.

As you can imagine, this gigantic structure afforded children no end of ways to injure themselves; the most spectacular involved a boy having the skin ripped off his toes by the casters as he pulled the structure into place, while another was socked in the face by the knotted end of a swinging rope. Thankfully, mainly due to my lack of enthusiasm for PE lessons, other than the occasional twisted ankle, I avoided serious injury.

In addition, once a week each school year was marched in crocodile formation a mile along Cambridge Heath Road to York Hall. Although it is better known for boxing, York Hall had a swimming pool and Turkish bath, too.

After slipping on our swimsuits and stowing our clothes in the cold, white-tiled changing room, with our towels wrapped around us, we stepped though the equally icy trough of disinfectant before emerging into the echoey, chlorine-laden expanse of the main pool area. There were tiered seating areas on both sides and a three-height diving board and springboard at the far end.

Having left your towel on the first row of seats, those who couldn't swim were relegated to the shallow end where, clinging tightly to grubby plastic floats, they thrashed back and forth from one side of the pool to the other.

Those of us who had mastered the art of keeping afloat were taken to the deep end, where we swam the length of the pool before embarking on activities such as swimming underwater through hoops or rescuing drowning rubber bricks from the bottom of the pool.

The best bit of the morning excursion was after the class, when with wet hair and your damp costume and towel shoved into your swimming bag, you bought a slice of toast and jam to eat on the way back to school.

However, one lesson I and every other girl in my class loved and which the boys universally hated was country dancing. We skipped to rustic reels and square sets that wouldn't have looked out of place in a Regency ballroom, while one of the teachers bashed out the tune on the upright piano in the corner.

Of course, there were variations to the daily routine – Easter and Harvest Festivals, for example – but the highlight of the school year was, of course, Christmas. Festive celebrations started with the annual carol concert. Each class had to practise 'Silent Night' and 'Good King Wenceslas' endlessly for their moment in the spotlight.

Time was set aside for children to draw and paint Christmas cards for their parents and grandparents and to decorate their classrooms with snowmen, paperchains and jolly Santas. On top of this, early in December, a handful of children who were identified as good singers were gathered from each year group to form a school choir. Unsurprisingly, as I'm more or less tone deaf, I was never amongst their blessed number.

On the big day, usually during the last week of term, we were scrubbed to within an inch of our lives by our mothers and then packed off to school in our best clothes. Dire warnings were given to boys not to scuff their shoes or get their cuffs dirty, while we girls were told not to play with our hair or get our white socks grubby in the playground.

Once the register had been taken, we were checked over by our teacher to make sure there were no untucked shirts or missing hair ribbons then marched into the hall, where we sat crossed-legged in class formation on the floor. The audience, which in those days was mainly made up of mothers, would already be seated on the chairs set out at either end of the hall.

When the headmaster, senior staff and the odd special guest such as the vicar walked on the stage, the chattering ceased. As a hush settled over us, the door at the far end of the hall opened and Pete Kemp – I'll talk more about him later – led in the choir, looking like Victorian ghosts in long white gowns. Pete would progress slowly past the parents and then around us seated children while singing the first verse of 'Once in Royal David's City'.

In the time-honoured tradition, the choir joined in with the next verse and finally the rest of us less-harmonious songsters pitched in for the final couple.

As they wended their way around the hall, murmurs of 'Bless their little cotton socks' and ''ow could anyone 'urt 'em' could be heard as mothers dabbed their eyes.

Once the choir had taken their place at the side of the stage, other classes stood up to perform their bit: a story, song or poem. The performances were interspersed with a child from each class faltering their way through a section of the Christmas story.

During 'Away in a Manger', which was always the final

carol, one of the children in the first year would solemnly walk up and lay a plastic baby Jesus in his rightful place amongst the school's Nativity.

Once the performance was over, the headmaster would tell the school how well they'd done then thank all the special guests, teachers and last of all parents for coming, after which we filed out as we'd come in, in class order. Unlike today, there were no mothers taking photos or recording their child's performance, so no record remains of my junior school festivities.

The day of the carol concert was also the day we had the school's Christmas dinner, with its over-boiled cabbage and lumpy mash alongside the seasonal addition of one roast potato and a clump of stuffing. As chicken in those days was much more expensive than beef, we had a couple of slices of fatty lamb or stringy beef.

Now Christmas wouldn't be Christmas without a party, so the day before we broke up for the two-week mid-winter holiday, we had a class party. Mums were asked to supply cakes and sandwiches, while the school provided a slab of red or green jelly in one of the catering-sized metal trays plus large metal jugs filled with very diluted orange squash. Children also had to bring with them their own cup, plate and spoon.

Although I looked forward to all the fun and games, there was one thing about the annual form party I absolutely hated. My father, who during my junior years was hoping to become part of East London's avant-garde creative fraternity, favoured rough cords and baggy sweaters rather than the sharp-cut Italian suits fashionable at that time. His love for this style resulted in my parents dressing me in similarly practical, hardwearing clothes even for special events. This meant that while the other girls in my school arrived at the class Christmas party in flouncy dresses and angora boleros, I pitched up in a plain skirt or dress, with perhaps just a lacy collar as a concession to the fun-filled occasion.

There is one stand-out moment for me from the year before I moved up from the infant to the junior school, and it took place in the summer term: the trip to London Zoo.

One morning I woke up with a raging temperature. But that wasn't the worst of it. To my mum's utter horror, I had turned decidedly yellow. Having dosed me with junior aspirin, she marched me off to the casualty department at Bancroft Hospital half a mile away. After checking my eyes and having me poke my tongue out several time, the doctor diagnosed Yellow Jaundice.

Well, I was certainly yellow, that was for sure, but I know now that jaundice is a symptom not a disease. What I suspect I really had was hepatitis A, a virus commonly found among those who lived in poor and unsanitary conditions.

I wasn't the only one suffering. When my mother went in to tell the school the next day, she found that several children were ill with the same complaint. I suspect we caught it either from the pungent spider-infested toilets or from a less-than-stringent adherence to food safety amongst the fag-smoking dinner ladies.

I was immediately ordered to stay at home and rest. I was also told to cut down on my intake of the colour yellow, so no butter and I wasn't to be given bananas either. But the thing that worried me most was missing out on the trip to the zoo next week. Well, said the doctor, when my mother enquired, as long as my temperature was back to normal and my imitation of a daffodil had faded, I could go.

After asking God each night for me to look less lemon-like, every morning I checked myself in the mirror. Thankfully, by the time the school trip came around, my unusual colour had all but gone, but even so I was packed off on my school trip with butter-less sandwiches, just to be on the safe side. As far as I can remember, it was a brilliant day and although I'd been there dozens of times with my parents, running around with friends made me feel very grown up all of a sudden.

Although he constantly railed against the nebulous 'they' and 'them' – members of the Establishment who keep the working man down – my father was deferential to anyone he regarded as better educated or a professional. He might protest and argue against their ascendancy, but he always bowed to what he considered to be their superior knowledge or understanding.

An early example of this would be the way he dealt with the headmaster in my junior school when he was called in to discuss my progress – or, actually, my lack of it.

Although by the time I left infant school I had pretty much mastered holding the pencil correctly, learned my alphabet and could do a credible job of copying the set texts into my exercise books, my move into junior school revealed a deep-seated problem.

84

I had been surrounded by books at home since I was born and I'd had my own junior library ticket since starting school. My father took me to Bancroft library every Saturday morning, so mastering the complexity of reading wasn't difficult for me. It was only when English lessons moved on to spelling that my problems began.

Despite working hard at memorising the list of words the class was given, I just couldn't recall them properly when it came to the weekly spelling tests. As other children in the class hadn't had the advantage of a book-filled home, and so had to start from scratch when it came to reading and writing, for the first couple of years no one really noticed my slow progress, but by the time I got to my third year, it was clear I was slipping behind.

Having received their summons from the school, my parents arrived in their best clothes to be told by the headmaster that, while I was doing well in all other areas of schooling, my teachers were concerned with my lack of progress in written English. He suggested I might have a condition called 'word blindness'. He was right, as I found out some forty years later when embarking on my first degree, although by then word blindness was more commonly known as dyslexia.

Today children of all abilities and disabilities are schooled together. However, when I was a child, children who didn't progress as expected were sent to special schools. And I don't just mean children with visual and hearing impairments, but children with cognitive impairments, too.

My parents were mortified and feared the worst. However,

the headmaster reassured them that as my reading was up to the expected level, my word blindness was still at an early stage so if I did extra spellings at home, it would solve the problem by the time I sat my 11+.

My father eagerly asked his advice, and the headmaster suggested the best way I could master spelling was to do crossword puzzles. Now, anyone who knows anything about dyslexia will tell you that this is the absolute worst thing to ask a person with this condition to do. For goodness' sake, we struggle enough getting the letters in the right order, let alone trying to fill in missing ones.

I tried but I just couldn't do them; yet still my father insisted I should do crosswords as instructed by the headmaster as he was an educated man.

Perhaps I'm being too hard on my parents and their generation; if you are raised by those whose only escape from grinding poverty or a spell in the workhouse lies in the hands of those richer and better educated, then perhaps you learn not to question.

Although my struggle with spelling and grammar continued, as I worked my way through junior school I started to do quite well at other subjects. Thanks to my mum's tuition, I was streets ahead in my needlework and as I was – according to my father, at least – an artistic child prodigy, I won the art prize each year too. Music was another matter. For some reason, my school taught children in alternate year groups how to play the recorder, and yes, you've guessed it, my year wasn't one of the chosen years, so we had to make do with smashing tambourines, shaking maracas, hitting triangles dangling from string and singing.

Although, as is often the case, our class teachers were jacks of all trades and taught all the various subjects, for music lessons we had a dedicated teacher called Mr Palmer. So, once a week, we trooped into the hall, where our class teacher handed us over to Mr Palmer and then went off for a cigarette in the staffroom.

Somewhere north of sixty and heavily built, the man in charge of opening our minds to the beauty of music looked like he'd walked straight out of a Grimm's fairy tale. If this wasn't enough to terrify us, he spoke like a BBC announcer, which was almost unintelligible to a bunch of East End kids. He wore gold-rimmed glasses with lenses so thick his eyes looked freakishly large, and he barked at us when we went wrong.

He was fine when tickling the ivories during the daily school assembly, but as the council's education department wouldn't pay him for just half an hour's work each day, he was forced to take music classes.

I don't remember most of the songs we sang except one called 'Donkey Riding' in which we had to belt out a lusty *Hey ho and away you go,* at one point. The best song he tried to teach us was 'Camptown Races', not because of the song itself but because of the way he taught it to us. I can still hear his aristocratic accent enunciating the lyrics to a bunch of cockney kids who couldn't understand a word. The whole thing sounded like Prince Charles auditioning for a part as a field hand in *Gone with the Wind*.

However, it was the subjects of History, Geography and Nature Studies that really caught my interest. This was partly due to my weekly trips to the library with my father, where I'd borrow books full of illustrations and photographs that sparked my enthusiasm in these subjects, but also because of the go-to reference books in our house, the Books of Knowledge.

These little gems were a children's encyclopaedia that my father, rather uncharacteristically, bought from a door-to-door salesman. It comprised of a set of mock-leather-bound books with gold lettering. Subjects were listed alphabetically across seven of the volumes, with an eighth volume containing additional facts and the index bringing up the rear.

They were, in fact, a very, very poor man's *Encyclopaedia Britannica,* but they did cover most subjects, albeit in a rather colonial *Boy's Own* sort of way. My father's answer to any question about a country, an animal or a natural phenomena was, 'Look it up in the Books of Knowledge.'

Not only did they have photos and diagrams on almost every page, but every now and again, usually to illustrate something anatomical or botanical, there would be cellophane overlays which you could turn back to reveal different layers of the body or the cross-sections of a flower. I tended to skip the ones about insects and plants, but I spent hours peeling back those about the body. To be honest, on a damp Sunday evening with just *Sing Something Simple* on the radio, the Books of Knowledge were always worth flipping through.

Another class I enjoyed was Drama and although I was useless at acting, I was pretty good at making up the stories to be acted out. In fact, it was storytelling that got me out of the hole my tangle with spelling had got me into.

It also got me into trouble in other ways.

My storytelling abilities are now put to good effect in my East End novels but, unfortunately, when I was at school sometimes I used the power of my imagination in ways that had me branded a liar.

And, truthfully, I was.

I started small by telling my school friends I had a twin sister who couldn't come to school because she had a wooden leg. Next I told them my grandfather was a French prince but he didn't like living in a castle. I almost had everyone believing that my father was offered a job drawing cartoons for Walt Disney. One of my best stories was telling everyone I suddenly couldn't see and having them lead me to the school office. However, my pièce de résistance involved my birthday.

During school assembly, children who had a birthday that day would be called out to the front. After the whole school had sung 'Happy Birthday' to them they could take a sweet from a big jar. Well, with an August birthday, I burned with the injustice of this all through infant school, so when I moved up to the juniors I decided to take matters into my own hands. I would, like the queen, have two birthdays. Therefore, each year in the first week of May, when the headmaster asked if anyone had a birthday, I stood up and marched to the front.

I got away with it for a couple of years, until a teaching assistant who happened to know my mother told her that my fictitious birthday in May was on the same day as her sister's. Well, I tell you, did I get a roasting. Reluctantly, I resigned myself to never again being the dishonest recipient of a sweet from the headmaster's jar.

In addition to my somewhat inventive nature, I was, and still am, an inveterate chatter. I now know it's because I am an active learner, but when I was at school it was seen as lacking in attention. However, if this was the only thing my parents were told at open evening, then I would have been happy.

Unfortunately, it wasn't. My teachers explained that although I was doing well in other areas of study, I was very bad at spelling because I didn't work hard enough. My father, of course, accepted their reason for my lack of progress without question, which led to him giving me a stern lecture when we got home, asking me, 'Do you want to end up working in a factory?' Or telling me, 'You'll never make anything of yourself if you don't get an education.' It always ended with him saying grudgingly, 'I wish I'd had your opportunities.'

Life moved on, as it does, and at the start of my final year in junior school the inevitable question of moving up to senior school loomed large; and with it came the 11+.

The 11+ exam was introduced in the last years of the Second World War and was designed to sift the wheat from the chaff – the wheat being the bright kids who got places at grammar school and the chaff being those who were sent to a secondary modern school.

The thinking behind the separation of children into academic- and competence-based schooling was to ensure

Britain had the brightest and best for the professions and a skilled workforce for industry.

In theory, prior to the 1944 Education Act, working-class children could go to grammar school if they were able to get one of a limited number of scholarship places and if they passed the competitive entrance exam. However, even children who were selected sometimes couldn't take up their place as their parents couldn't afford the cost of the uniform and books.

If their parents did manage to scrape the money together to kit out their child, as in the case of my Aunt Elaine who went to Coborn Girls Grammar in the 1930s, the children often had a terrible time of it as they were regarded by their wealthier fellow pupils as guttersnipes and charity cases.

It was worth putting up with the taunts and bullying because a grammar school education meant opportunities such as university or a career in banking or nursing would be open to you – only grammar school girls could be State Registered Nurses, for example.

However, after the introduction of the Education Act, places at grammar school were funded by the state and open to any child who passed the 11+. Even though the uniform was still expensive, many working-class parents were keen to have their children go there. Naturally, my father was one of them.

The test itself comprised of three main elements: arithmetic, problem-solving and, of course, English, which took the form of an essay on a particular subject.

If I remember correctly, the 11+ was taken in the term after Christmas, which allowed the school to prepare their pupils during the autumn term. It also allowed my father to do the same at home with me. Knowing my spelling was still pretty shocking, he set me five words each evening to learn for the next day and then he would give me a random test at the end of the week. The next-day test wasn't too bad as I could retain the correct order of letters overnight, but the end-of-the-week test was always a complete disaster, which resulted in him telling me I had to 'pull my socks up' and me in tears. He also bought more crossword puzzle books, which, despite my lack of progress, I reluctantly did.

Exams were a way of life for children back then and we had weekly and monthly tests along with additional exams at the end of each term and the end of the year. There were none of these modern ideas about not putting children under pressure to achieve or worrying about them feeling they were failures. No, the results of any tests were read out in front of the whole class, with teachers often adding things like, 'And once again, children, XXX came last.' Your exercise books were marked with black crosses and comments like 'very poor work' or 'bad handwriting'. A lack of progress was seen to be the child's fault for being lazy or inattentive in class. Although junior school children weren't subject to six of the best with the cane, spare the verbal rod and spoil the child was very much the teaching philosophy.

With my father constantly telling me not to 'throw away' my chances of getting to a good school and that I ought to be more 'self-disciplined', I spent much of the time leading up to the test worrying about disappointing him.

Anyhow, the fateful day came. Although it was over half a century ago, I can remember it was a bright, late winter's morning when my class trooped into the room that had been set up for us to take the dreaded 11+.

We had had mock tests to prepare us, so I cracked on with it as soon as we were told to start. I can't remember what order the questions were set, but I know we were asked things like find the length of a side of an object and there were lots of sequence puzzles with shapes and dots where you had to work out which pattern or number came next.

In the English section I could find the right word to fit the sentence from the choice of three but when I had to substitute or add letters to words to make other words I floundered. With my father's expectations weighing on my shoulders, I dipped my pen in the inkwell and did my best.

We were in the kitchen at teatime when my father opened the letter, and I knew immediately that I hadn't passed by the look of disappointment on his face. When he told me I had failed he added, 'I told you this was going to happen if you didn't work harder.'

My mum countered this by saying I'd done my best to which he replied, 'To end up in a dead-end job.'

Disappointed with my failure, my father put plan B into action.

As I said previously, his original plan for me to go to Sir John Cass City Foundation School when I was five had been vetoed by my pregnant mother. However, before I went up into my last year of junior school, our family had moved to the new three-bedroom maisonette back in Stepney.

We were now within walking distance of St Dunstan's Church, which had the Redcoat Church of England School attached to it. The old school would be amalgamated with Sir John Cass senior school in a brand-new building the year after I started senior school.

As with all denominational schools at that time, Redcoat, reserved places for children who lived in the parish and for children of recognised members of St Dunstan's congregation.

As a back-door way of getting me into the prestigious Sir John Cass Redcoat School, as soon as we moved from Bethnal Green back to Stepney my father started to join my mother on her weekly trips to St Dunstan's Church each Sunday. My father was overjoyed, therefore, when the letter arrived saying I had a place at Redcoat School, and his ambition for me to go to university was rekindled.

Once our secondary school fates were sealed, we didn't need to do any more exams so our final weeks at junior school were filled with concerts, class plays and team games. We had our final assembly, and I picked up my annual art prize at the end-of-year prize giving.

A few in the class were moving on to Raine's, the local grammar school, but most were going to Morpeth Secondary School, the nearest one to our junior school. However, some, like me, who lived outside the catchment area, were off to pastures further afield.

Perhaps it was the realisation that, after some six years of being together, in a few short weeks we would be going our separate ways. Maybe it was that we were about to take our first steps into the adult world. Whatever it was, during those last few weeks of term our class suddenly came together.

We signed each other's autograph books with kisses and hearts, and made plans to meet up during the summer. We thanked our teachers with home-made cards and presents and assured them we'd never forget them. On the last day of school we girls hugged each other and, with tears in our eyes, wished each other luck and set off for our new life in senior school.

CHAPTER EIGHT

Workers' Playtime

W HEN I WAS growing up it was still customary for people to work a forty-two-hour week and have just Saturday afternoon and Sundays off. And people packed as much fun as they could into that day and half. Many dance halls and variety theatres were just a bus or tram ride away and all of my family were good ballroom dancers – even champion ones, in the case of my Uncle Arthur and Aunt Dora. In addition, my father and his generation were great cinema and theatre-goers, often going a couple of times a week. And they got more than just a film.

Along with the main feature there was a B picture, often an educational film, sometimes a short cartoon, and Pathé News, which in a time before television was the only way they saw images of people from other parts of the country and the wider world.

My father also loved going to the many music halls dotted around the East End. He saw all the variety greats, such as Max Miller, Arthur Askey, Max Bygraves, Flanagan and Allen, Tommy Trinder and the bizarre sand-dancing trio of Wilson, Keppel & Betty – Google them and you won't believe your eyes! There was street entertainment, too, and acts like the Nancy Boys, who were singers and dancers, would turn up and do their routines on the pavement.

However, by and large, you had to make your own entertainment, which usually meant a singsong in the pub at the end of the working week, something we did every Friday night as a family right through to the 1980s.

Gatherings at home needed a piano and, although he never had a formal lesson, my father taught himself to play by watching his younger sister Martha having lessons on the upright piano in the front parlour. She couldn't play a note but after a couple of runs at it my father could bang out almost any popular tune. I've even heard him play a couple of early Lennon and McCartney songs. Playing an instrument was a vital social skill because, as he explained, 'if you played a piano you were always invited to parties'.

After the war, with secure jobs and good wages, they set about enjoying themselves. Both my uncles Jimmy and Bob bought a car, an almost unaffordable luxury at the time, and Bob added a tent and they spent most weekends at campsites along the Kent and Sussex coast.

If you live anywhere east of the City on the north side of the Thames, it is all but compulsory to be a West Ham supporter. However, although football was practically a religion to many of their contemporaries, my father and uncles only really followed the beautiful game so they could tick off the results on their football pools coupon each Saturday.

It's difficult to imagine in today's world of twenty-four-hour news and instant access via the internet to people, places and events on the other side of the world, but in the first quarter of the twentieth century people looked to their local community for entertainment, whether in public houses, churches or socials clubs. Much of people's recreation at this time centred around work, and trips to the seaside and full-blown Christmas parties were the norm. Employers were regarded as stingy if they skimped on their obligation to provide entertainment for their workforce.

When my father was growing up there was no such thing as an annual holiday, so the work's day out to the seaside was the highlight of the summer. Even when paid holiday started to be commonplace, it was only a week and usually taken when the whole factory shut down.

Areas like Southend, Clacton and Margate were popular holiday destinations, and although today people easily commute from these places into London, before the Second World War it took the best part of a day to reach the coast from East London by train or coach. These seaside trips held such special memories that many East Enders eventually moved there when they retired.

Today, by law, workers are entitled to paid holidays. However, my father and the rest of the Fullertons only had working holidays, when they left the grey London streets once a year and travelled to Kent to strip the hop vines of their lucrative harvest.

I don't know exactly where in Kent they went, but the Fullertons were regular hop pickers at a farm which, according to my Uncle Bobby, was in the Paddock Wood area. As a reliable family they received an invitation each July from the hops farm they'd been to the year before. After which they'd book themselves on one of the many trains running from London Bridge Station to the Kent hop fields.

My Aunt Nell told me that she remembered walking the three miles from their home to London Bridge Station to catch a Kent-bound train at the crack of dawn. Her sister Millie was with her and Arthur, a toddler, was sitting on a pile of suitcases on top of the hand cart. That must have been just before the First World War because, by the time my father did the journey in the 1920s, my grandparents regularly booked a place on a lorry to take them all to the station.

According to my father, his mother kept a 'hopping box', where all the old clothes that were not respectable enough to be seen in were stashed away to wear while working in the fields every summer. My Uncle Bobby remembered my grandmother scouring the jumble sales and second-hand market stalls for wellies to take ''opping'.

The women and children would go to the farms for the whole of August through to mid-September, which meant that the children often missed a couple of weeks of schooling. In usual circumstances this would have had the Council's Truant Officer knocking on your door but, as my Aunt Nell explained, 'there were so many kids gone 'opping they turned a blind eye'.

The work of stripping the vines was done by my grandmother and the older children while, according to my Aunt Martha, she and baby Bobby would play close by. Like most work in those days, you were paid for what you produced, so when you'd filled the large family hopper you'd been given you lugged it off to the tally man who weighed it and marked it off against your name. The daily quantities would be added up at the end of the week and you'd be paid accordingly.

Families would be allocated a hut to live in, which was something akin to a large garden shed. Like many of their neighbours, my grandparents took with them an old pram and a handmade cart loaded with all the family clothes, pots and pans, sheets, blankets and pillows, enamel washing bowls and carbolic soap. Cleaning products were essential as the first job upon arrival was to rid your hut of mouse and bird droppings, mildew and spiders, before you unloaded your gear.

Inside the huts were truckle beds if you were lucky or a straw mattress on the floor if you weren't. My Aunt Martha told me she remembered the sweet smell of the hay they were given to stuff inside the mattresses when they arrived. Even by the lax health and safety standards of the time, the wooden-planked huts were considered no better than tinder boxes, so rather than stoves inside the huts there was a communal cookhouse with a large brick-built stove in front of each row of huts for preparing meals and boiling water. It was where women, like my grandmother, sat at the end of a long day in the fields, drinking tea and chatting.

Men arrived at the weekend to join their families, thereby increasing the trade in the nearby village pubs. Then, after chucking-out time, everyone gathered together between the huts for a singsong.

My grandmother continued to make the annual trip with her younger children through to the mid-1930s, but by then Millie and Arthur were married and Nell, Jimmy and my father had regular jobs so, finally, my grandmother, who was in her mid-forties, called it a day. Although hop picking went on until the early 1960s, none of my aunts and uncles ever returned to the hop fields after the war. I don't blame them. It was hard, physical work and they endured dreadful living conditions for not very much money.

While the family had long since hung up their hopping boots by the time I came along, they had fond memories of their times in Kent. One Friday night, not long after I'd got married, I was sitting with my Aunt Martha and my father in the Duke of Norfolk, near where they lived. Martha's husband Wag was there, too, along with a handful of long-standing friends, and the conversation turned, as it so often did, to the 'old days'. Although by then my family were some of the millions of Brits who flew out to Spain each year to roast themselves in the continental sun, there was no disguising the sense of deep loss in their voices when they talked about the fun and camaraderie of when they went used to 'go 'opping'.

Sometimes at weekends, if we weren't visiting relatives, my family would jump on a District line train heading west for an afternoon walk. We'd get off at Tower Hill to stroll around the Tower of London and although my father would never pay for us to go in, we'd happily climb on the cannons and scoff ice cream instead.

To the west of the Tower there was a large flat area and often on Sundays there would be street performers – escapologists wriggling about in chains surrounded by onlookers or Morris Dancers, complete with hobby horse, skipping about on the cobbles.

Sometimes, instead of jumping back on the bus or train, we would walk home along Wapping High Street with the tall warehouses looming over us on each side.

In the summer we would go further afield, staying on the train until we reached Charring Cross, where we'd amble along the Embankment to Blackfriars station, or we'd head for Trafalgar Square to feed the pigeons before wandering down the Mall. Today Nelson's Column and the grand buildings along Whitehall and the Mall are the beautiful biscuit colour of Portland stone, but back then, because of the use of coal in every house and factory, the familiar sights of the capital, like St Paul's Cathedral, Admiralty Arch and Whitehall, were almost black with centuries of encrusted soot clinging to them.

As my brother and I got older, our family outings went even further afield as we explored the wonders of London. We were already regular visitors to the Bethnal Green Museum, which back then displayed a variety of things, not just toys. However, in line with my father's philosophy of broadening our horizons, we started doing day trips to the South Kensington's museums, too.

Interactive displays in museums were a rarity then and I found the self-opening door in the Science Museum fascinating as I walked back and forth through it, while the massive beam engines in the foyer made me stare as they rocked slowly up and down.

As the skeleton of Dippy the diplodocus was the first thing I saw as I walked in through the door, I was rather expecting the Natural History Museum to fall down when, after so many years, it was replaced with a blue whale because as a child the ancient dinosaur seemed to be holding up the roof.

However, my absolute favourite exhibit was the costume gallery in the V&A. I loved the feathered hats, parasols and crinolines, which fed my passion for all things historical. I used to take a sketch book and pencil with me so I could draw the gorgeous dresses, then, when I got home, I'd paint watercolour pictures using my sketches as inspiration.

Some weekends we'd visit Victoria Park, which was local to us and where a band played every Sunday, but we also visited the Royal Parks in the west of the city, such as Green Park and Regent's Park.

However, we never visited Madame Tussauds or the Planetarium as you had to pay. In fact, until I paid the entrance fee myself, I never went into the Tower of London, the Transport Museum in Covent Garden, Soane's Museum or the Maritime Museum at Greenwich.

One of the few places where we went regularly that my father was happy to put his hand in his pockets for was London Zoo. We went there so often that Guy the gorilla used to wave at us as we passed his cage.

Today, for all the very best reasons, there are hardly any of the large animals at the London site, but when I went as a child there was everything from elephants, rhinos and bears to every species of big cat, as well as hippos, antelopes, monkeys and apes. Although there was an attempt to give the animals more natural surroundings, sadly many of the exhibits, like the lions and tigers, were still housed in the old Victorian cages and spent their days pacing back and forth in those small enclosures.

There were other things, too, that have thankfully been done away with, such as the chimpanzees' tea party, which had man's closest cousins dressed up like children so everyone could laugh at them swinging on the chairs and throwing food about.

The Bactrian camels and Central American squirrel monkeys also had to work for their daily crust, the former by walking up and down a dusty track giving excited children rides while the latter had to perch on juvenile shoulders to have their photo taken.

Of course, back then I didn't know any different so I enjoyed everything from the antic of the penguins at feeding time to having my crusts hoovered up by an elephant's trunk.

While the museums and zoo I explored as a child are still going, there are two attractions that I visited every year which have not survived into the twenty-first century. Both were situated in Battersea Park, which, as part of the 1951 Festival of Britain, was the site of a full-blown funfair, complete with a carousel, roller coaster and swings. And I loved it.

Although the Festival of Britain, with its famous Skylon and Dome of Discovery, was all about modernity, Battersea Funfair, as I knew it, was all about the great British tradition of the travelling fair. All the rides and shies were brightly painted in the customary green, yellow and red swirls. A steam organ piped out old-fashioned tunes at a deafening volume as the merry-go-around slowly spun and the coconut mats provided for the helter-skelter had you scratching the back of your legs when you got off. There was popcorn, candyfloss and ice cream, plus booths selling small bottles of lemonade and cream soda.

It was such a feature of our family days out that my father painted a picture of Battersea Funfair which now hangs on my lounge wall.

The other permanent feature of my childhood, now also for ever confined to history, was Battersea Park's Easter Parade. It didn't take place until the afternoon, but we made sure we arrived early so we could walk along the fairyland walkway, which had lights strung from tree to tree above our heads, and have time for our picnic before the parade began.

That done, we would find a good place by the barriers so we were at the front, ready for when the massive floats, filled with waving children and teenagers, processed slowly by.

Each year there was a theme, such as countries of the world or children's books, which the Rotary Club, Boy Scouts and other such organisations would use to inspire their colourful creations. The displays often had moving parts and I remember that one year there was a stylised pink and cream steam train with pumping pistons, and another float that showed the sleepy dormouse in *Alice in Wonderland* popping up and down in his turquoise teapot.

There were also marching bands blasting out popular songs

and acrobats cartwheeling between the lorries as they crawled by at a snail's speed so we could all get a good look. Although the number of floats varied from year to year, it never took less than an hour for them all to pass.

When the final float had disappeared and the crowds had dispersed, we would gather our things together and walk back across the park to Battersea Park station for our hour-long journey home.

Children eat out in restaurants, pubs and cafés all the time now but, other than a very rare cup of tea and a sandwich in a department store eatery, we never did. Whenever we went out for the day, we would always take a picnic lunch and find a convenient bench upon which to eat it.

It usually consisted of umpteen rounds of sandwiches, cheese or corned beef being favourites, and an apple for after. There was no tin foil or clingfilm, so sandwiches were carefully wrapped in a paper bag. My parents would also bring a Thermos flask filled with tea for themselves and a smaller flask filled with orange squash for us children. It was all packed into a holdall and carried there and back.

Our family trips went on through summer and winter alike. However, if it was either too cold or too wet to wander about town, then we were reduced to doing what children do today, which is watch the box.

My father started renting a television when we were still living in Anthony Street. The screen was the size of a loaf of bread and, of course, back then there was just one channel, and children were allocated set times in the schedule for their programmes.

I vaguely remember a few children's programmes like *Rag, Tag and Bobtail,* stuffed toys on sticks; *Andy Pandy; Bill and Ben the Flowerpot Men,* who spoke utter gibberish; *The Woodentops,* a family of farmers who seemed to go around topless all the time, and *Pinky and Perky,* who I hated and who had silly, high-pitched voices.

Later, when I was more able to understand a story, one of my favourite shows was *Captain Pugwash,* a programme that in recent years was rumoured to have deliberately given its characters rude names such as Seaman Staines and Roger the Cabin Boy. This rumour is apparently untrue, but, in my innocence, such things were lost on me anyway and I thought it was about an inept pirate. Although I enjoyed *Ivor the Engine,* with Jones the Steam, Dai the Station and Mrs Thomas, my favourite by far was *Noggin the Nog.*

This was a Norse tale about Noggin who is married to Nooka of the Nooks. Noggin rules a Viking settlement in the far, far north. There are various characters including a dragon and a wicked uncle called Nogbad the Bad. I absolutely loved it as a child as it fed right into my passion for all things historical, and I still love it, so much so that I've bought my grandchildren the books.

As we moved from the fifties to the sixties, we started getting American cartoons like *Yogi Bear* and *Top Cat.* In response, the British producer Gerry Anderson and his wife Sylvia hit back with puppet shows featuring UK characters.

Firstly *Supercar*, which I can barely remember, and then *Fireball XL5,* with jerky Captain Steve Zodiac and his visible strings, which I can still recall vividly. I could even sing you the theme song, in fact. However, my unquestionable favourite of all the Gerry and Sylvia Anderson animations was *Stingray*. *Stingray* was an underwater craft manned by a very dishy Captain Troy Tempest, modelled on James Garner apparently, and a green-haired woman called Marina, who couldn't speak and belonged to a race that lived in the depths of the ocean.

Looking back now, I can see why those programmes appealed to me so strongly. Unlike children's programmes set in the here-and-now, those shows, be they set in space or in the past, took me to different times and places.

I was a devotee of *Blue Peter,* too, and always made the little craft things, like Christmas decorations and painted Easter eggs, but my favourite how-to-make slot was when the presenter Valerie Singleton made clothes for the resident doll. They ranged from glamourous outfits through to native costumes from around the world, and I made them all for my blonde-haired Suzie doll. Making clothes was a way of life for the women of my family.

Hi-De-Hi

Although my father was reluctant to spend money, he did feel a family holiday was a must – and he and my mum had taken one every year since they married. Their accommodation of choice was typical of the time, a privately run boarding house which offered a clean room, breakfast and an evening meal.

In return, you were expected to be respectable, considerate to other guests and out of the house all day.

Legend has it that it was upon seeing a bedraggled family of four sheltering from the rain because they'd been exiled from their boarding house for the day that Billy Butlin hit on the idea of holiday camps. Possibly, but what I can say is that trying to keep children amused all day in a damp seaside town is no holiday.

My parents carried on with the boarding houses for a couple of years after I was born, but then they discovered Warner's Holiday Camps.

They were designed to cater for all members of the family, all day and in all weathers, from the moment you arrived until you waved them goodbye a week later. As we didn't have a car, we used to travel to the holiday camp on a Grey-Green coach, which picked us and other holidaymakers up from the Old Globe Pub at Mile End for the three-hour journey to our destination.

The purveyors of this twenty-four-hour fun fest were young men and women wearing dazzling white shorts and bright blue blazers. Upon arrival, it was they who directed you to your one-room family chalet, which was in reality nothing more than a wooden shed. These huts were covered with a lick of paint, and contained a single wash basin and the bare minimum of furniture. Children used a pot stored under their bunks if they were caught short at night, whereas adults had to dash to the nearest toilet block in their nightclothes.

The chalets creaked in the slightest of breezes and no matter how much my mother swept our home-away-from-home, there was always sand on the floor. Truthfully, it was pretty basic, but for the thousands of working-class people who had been born and raised in damp, over-crowded houses and who flocked to holiday camps during the fifties and sixties, the accommodation was close to luxury. And as my mum always maintained, 'You only slept in 'em.'

And she was right.

Taking your summer break in a holiday camp was a full-time occupation. The day kicked off bright and early at about seven with the entertainment manager's voice blasting out from one of the many loudspeakers fixed around the site – 'Good morning, campers!' The morning's greeting was followed by a list of the day's activity.

If you think seven's a bit early when you're on your hols, then you're right, but there was a reason for the early start – the dining rooms were already open for breakfast.

Now, if the word 'dining' conjures up an image of white tablecloths, gleaming cutlery and softly spoken staff, forget it. The dining halls in a Warner's Holiday Camp were nothing more than massive canteens, run along the lines of those mass feeding stations known as British Restaurants that had been set up during the Second World War. Although there was a daily fitness class in the ballroom at the crack of dawn, the main programme of fun started each day at nine, which meant the canteen staff aimed to have breakfast for the hundreds of bleary-eyed guests done and dusted by eight-thirty sharp.

Having got yourself up and dressed for the day, you left your sand-strewn accommodation and trooped into the dining halls. Once you'd secured your place at one of the long benches, the waitress, wearing a pink Bri-Nylon overall, would arrive carrying a tiered plate rack that contained a cooked breakfast and porridge. Even if your favourite choice wasn't there, it was wise to accept something, as with dozens of tables to cater for, it might be some time before she returned.

Next, another young waitress in pink Bri-Nylon would arrive pushing a tea trolley and, after plonking a rack of toast on the table, would serve the adults tea or coffee while the younger children would be given watery orange juice.

Being in the country, there was plenty of wildlife to be seen. Unfortunately, much of it was in evidence while you were eating. Given the barn-like nature of the dining rooms, there were always dozens of sparrows perched on the girders above the tables waiting to swoop, which they did if you left a bacon rind or a piece of crust on a plate. They weren't deterred from their scavenging by waving hands or shouts, either. Mice, too, could be seen scurrying around at the edges of the room, setting women shrieking and jumping on to their chairs. And if you were really eagle-eyed, you might spot the occasional cockroach creeping around the bottom of the stainless-steel serving trollies.

However, despite having the odd sparrow dropping a present in the middle of your meal or finding boiled caterpillars in your cabbage, my mum often said the best thing about having a holiday at a holiday camp were the meals, because she didn't have to cook them.

Having washed down your breakfast with a beverage of your choice, it was time to start the serious business of the day – having a good time.

My mum would take me and my brother back to the chalet to make sure we were presentable for the day while my father went to get a paper in the camp shop. Then, when we passed muster, my mum would walk us around to the Warner's Wagtail Children's Club. We were handed into the care of the children's Blue Coats with strict instructions not to 'run around until your breakfast's gone down'. After getting us to repeat where we should meet them when we were finished, my parents would leave. Once relieved of their parental duties for a couple of hours, they had a choice of activities.

For dads there was everything from the five-a-side football challenge through to the pitch and putt tournament, via billiard competitions and judo demonstrations.

Mothers weren't forgotten. For the more athletic there was netball and tennis; flower-arranging or hair-styling demonstrations in the ballroom were laid on for those of a more sedate nature. Of course, these activities started an hour or so later than the men's to allow the women time to do the family washing and tidy their accommodation.

Late morning there would be ballroom-dancing classes in the grand ballroom overseen by the resident dance couple, followed by a pre-midday quiz in one of the smaller venues.

However, if the weather was nice, and given that most factory workers worked a forty-five-hour week inside, most opted for sitting around the pool to read or chat, untroubled by their offspring.

For me, an on-site funfair, playgrounds with climbing frames and swings, a swimming pool and a children's club meant the holiday camp was Heaven on earth. I practically ran to the children's club as soon as we'd unpacked to get my Warner's Wagtail badge, which was the passport to a week of treasure hunts, Punch and Judy shows, team games and general rioting.

We had tennis tournaments, games of rounders, boys and girls were divided off for football and netball respectively, and in-between running around the site terrorising adults dressed as a pirate or a South Seas cannibal, I swam and met my fellow Wagtails in the numerous play parks dotted between the rows of chalets.

Warner's Wagtails had their own song, which we sang at the tops of our voices at the end of each session. I can't remember all the words now but the first line was: *We are Warner's Wagtails, happy all the time,* and for me that pretty much sums it up.

Having rendered the poor unfortunate Blue Coats practically deaf with our screaming all morning, we were packed off to rejoin our parents for lunch. This was again taken in the inappropriately named dining halls and usually consisted of a salad of some sort – egg or spam – with chips, followed by one of the milk- or suet-based puddings so beloved of dinner ladies. In fact, given the unappetising and unimaginative food dished up three times a day, I wouldn't have been at all surprised to find that during the summer holiday school dinner ladies decamped to the seaside to moonlight in Holiday Camp kitchens.

However, as much as I loved the Wagtail Club with its daily swimming, adventure playgrounds and just the wild freedom of being in a place designed for fun, the highlight for me was the weekly children's fancy-dress competition.

Some people brought their children's costumes with them but most, like my mum, made them from scratch while on holiday using a ready supply of colourful crêpe paper available in the camp shop. The trick was trying to make something different. With that in mind, my mum made a great variety of crêpe-paper costumes for me to parade around the hall in and I was everything from Robin Hood to a hula girl, and one year I was even a Beatles fan with pictures of the Fab Four stuck all over my outfit. To be honest, I can't remember ever winning but that never mattered – I just loved dressing up.

The Wagtail Club only operated in the mornings, but after the midday meal we continued with our frivolity and although some sporting activities carried on into the afternoon, most people, weather permitting, found themselves a spot around the pool for the afternoon entertainment.

On the first day there was always a contest to find the king and queen for the week. The king was chosen from the men willing to parade around the pool showing off their muscles, inviting women to test the firmness of their biceps. The winner was decided by who received the loudest clap from the poolside audience.

However, the choosing of the queen was a much more raucous affair. Although there were always a few young women who came forward voluntarily, in order to have a good number of contestants, the male Blue Coats would run around the pool grabbing any young women who took their fancy, dragging and sometimes bodily carrying them to take part in the line-up.

Of course, it was all supposed to be a laugh and a bit of harmless fun, but I can't help thinking that today the whole entertainment team would be up in front of the magistrate on sexual assault charges.

Having crowned the king and queen of the Camp, other competitions such as the Glamorous Grandmother contest, the Ugliest Mug contest – which had men contorting their face so they looked like gargoyles – and the Knobbly Knees competition were held on afternoons throughout the week.

These home-made entertainments were supplemented by displays such a trick archery and gymnastic. In fact, the first time I ever heard of karate was when a martial arts team arrived and proceeded to smash bricks and concrete blocks at the poolside.

Whatever the afternoon entertainment around the pool, you could guarantee that one of the entertainment team would end up being thrown, fully clothed, into the swimming pool.

However, as is the way during the English summer, sometimes you'd wake up to the heavens opening. On such days, as many activities that could be were moved into the ballroom or other indoor venues and for those that had to be scrapped the entertainment team fell back on good old-fashioned bingo, or housey-housey as it was then called.

After the frivolity and fun of the afternoon you had to get ready for the evening. This meant a 'cat's lick' in the chalet sink or a trip to the single-sex bath houses that were dotted around the camp. Here, along with women shaving their legs and armpits in front of the wall mirror, there would be infants being scrubbed clean in one of the half a dozen enamel sinks fixed along one wall. Then, once everyone was clean and the men had splashed Old Spice on their cheeks and combed Brylcreem through their hair, the campers put on their glad rags for the evening meal.

The babies and toddlers would then be tucked into bed. The camp had a babysitting patrol so having tied a towelling nappy – no disposables in those days – to the door to alert the babysitting team that there were children alone in the chalet, the parents left for an evening of non-stop entertainment in the ballroom.

Older children, with strict instructions to stay around the main buildings and not to make too much noise, were given a couple of bob and allowed to roam with their friends in the penny arcades or the teenage club house, usually billed as the Rock Shack or the Cool Place.

Sometimes a few of the junior-age children were allowed this freedom too, but my parents were wary of having their offspring roaming around in the dark so we accompanied them to the ballroom.

To get a table near the dance floor you had to be there early, so as soon as the evening meal was over and while my mum was getting us and herself ready, my father would go on ahead to stake his claim. After we'd arrived, and having been given our bottle of fizz and a packet of crisps with the warning of 'don't drink it all at once', my brother and I would perch in our chairs beside my parents and settle in for the evening's entertainment.

This kicked off with either a family quiz or an adult treasure hunt, which always sent holidaymakers scrambling for half crowns minted in a particular year or running around to find a pair of men's socks, usually frantically stripped off a husband or boyfriend in the quest to be the first to gather all the items. Other things to find might include a set of false teeth, which had people dragging grandparents up to the compère, and the old chestnut, a gentleman with a pair of women's stocking over his arm, which had men dashing across the dance floor holding their wives and girlfriends in their arms.

After this there might be singing from one of the Blue Coat entertainment team, or a slap-stick routine with the camp comic and his sidekick with accompanying cymbal clashes to punctuate the gags.

Many of TV's successful singers and comedians, Des O'Connor and Cliff Richards to name but two, served their apprenticeships in holiday camps during the 1950s and 60s.

My favourite activity was the ballroom dance demonstration given by the resident professional dance couple. The man always wore evening dress with patent dance shoes, but each night his dance partner wore a different dress of shimmering satin dotted with sequins, held wide by layers of frothy net. On Latin-themed nights her dress might have a fringed shawl attached to it or be black and red for the Gay Paris evening. But whatever the theme or colour, the outfits were utterly gorgeous.

Once the early evening entertainment was over, the band would strike up, which was the signal for the holidaymakers to take to the floor. And take to the floor they did.

My mum and father were pretty good dancers and were always on the floor, leaving me and my brother sucking on our drinking straws watching. My father taught me to waltz and foxtrot but sadly by the time I started going to dance halls, the old ballroom dances had been replaced by the twist and the mash potato.

Although for the most part everyone behaved themselves in the ballroom, sometimes drunks – mainly men but occasionally women – would stagger about, careering into people. Usually their friends guided them off the dance floor, but I remember a couple of times when it turned nasty.

On one occasion a man crashed into another and punches were thrown until the families intervened to drag them apart. Another time, when a woman was trying to coax her very drunk husband off the dance floor, he turned and gave her a backhander across the face. But such incidents were rare and for the most part everyone glided round the room having a wonderful time.

Despite our protests, we were always taken back to the chalet and put to bed at nine o'clock. Having kissed us goodnight, my mum would tie a nappy on the door handle and head back to the ballroom, safe in the knowledge that the babysitting patrol would alert her to one of us crying by chalking up our chalet number on a blackboard beside the bandstand.

My family carried on going to holiday camps through to the 1970s, but I bailed out when I was fifteen. When I look back on them now, holiday camps were like a saucy seaside postcard come to life; one big, happy memory of never-ending innocent fun.

Somehow, when I was about ten, my father got wind of a scheme to send local council tenants to boarding houses in Hastings and Folkstone, so in addition to our annual fortnight at the holiday camp we had another week away at the seaside. My father had gone to Hastings in his choirboy days, so we always plumped for this option and I loved it.

As I've already stated, I've been a complete history nut since I was out of nappies so Hastings, with its ramshackle Old Town, cobbled streets and fishermen's huts on the beach, just set my overactive imagination on fire.

If that wasn't enough to have me making up adventure stories, there were smugglers' caves and a ruined castle with a whispering dungeon, and, of course, William the Conqueror and the Norman landings, which feature large in the town's history. I know we were there in 1966 because the whole town was decked out in celebration of the 900th anniversary of the event. By then I'd progressed from the children's library to the adults' and was steadily working my way through the English history section.

The accommodation in Hastings was the complete opposite to the huts we stayed in at the holiday camps as it was a traditional guest house. It was actually in St Leonards, the posh Victorian suburb with its five-storey houses and elegant squares. Our boarding house, the grandly named Warrior Square Hotel, was situated just west of the town and was a very old-fashioned establishment with elderly waitresses in black servant-style dresses, frilly pinnies and white caps serving us our meals in the high-ceilinged dining room.

Other than a black-and-white television in the communal sitting room and a few board games, there was no entertainment, but there was a piano for guests to use so sometimes there was an impromptu singalong.

In contrast to the holiday camps, which were packed with families, our guest house, like many of the hotels at this end of town, was filled with the elderly, who headed for the seafront for a snooze in the sunshine each morning rather than running down to the beach clutching their buckets and spades.

One of the things drummed into me and my brother by our parents was to respect our elders. This meant letting older people have your seat on public transport – I still find it difficult to see children sitting on the Tube while adults stand. We were also told not to interrupt – which also seems to have gone right out of the window – and to behave quietly.

This was a bit of a problem for me as I was a very noisy child who ran everywhere, thumped up and down stairs and burst through doors like I had a banshee on my tail. However, notwithstanding being constantly told to 'stop shouting', 'stop belting about' and 'watch where you're going', the weeks in Hastings, clambering up the cliffs and searching in the rock pools at low tide while my parents snoozed in deckchairs, were wonderful.

Christmas 1950s Style

The highlight of the year was Christmas, which started for us not, as currently seems to be the case, on the first day of September but just a few weeks before the big day.

The countdown started in earnest when, the weekend before Christmas, we would all jump on the good old number 25 bus and head to Oxford Street to see the Christmas lights. First stop would be Selfridges, where I would stare in wonder at the animated window displays full of elves hard at work in Santa's workshop, hammering the wheels on toy trains, nodding reindeer or characters like Snow White with her dwarves or Cinderella with her glass slipper.

Having worked our way along the department store's Christmas montage, we went in for the annual visit to Father Christmas. Naturally his grotto was situated in the toy department. Having duly told him what I wanted for Christmas, I was given my present and then, after I'd had my photograph taken with Santa, we made our way out of the store and back into the street. While I clutched Santa's present, we would stroll towards Tottenham Court Road, admiring the festive shop windows and the Christmas lights shaped like stars and angels strung above us.

Christmas was the only time I ever remember having a meal out as a child. Having taken in the Christmas sights during our walk down Oxford Street, we would head for Woolworth's café, as my father regarded everywhere else as too expensive. The menu, if you can call it that, was usually something like Welsh rarebit, poached or scrambled egg on toast or a couple of fish fingers and mash followed by a cup of sugary tea.

Having replenished ourselves, we continued on to Regent Street. Although our visit into town was a special Christmas trip, when we reached the Clarks shoe shop, we would always go in.

My parents had put me in Start-rite shoes as soon as I started toddling about but then swapped their allegiance to Clarks when I was about three. In fact, other than plimsolls for PE, I never wore another brand of shoe until, according to my mum, I 'ruined my feet' by demanding a pair of pointed-toe kitten heels for my thirteenth birthday.

Although there were Clarks shops in both Stratford and Ilford, the one in Regent Street had a very special feature which my parents always availed themselves of when we were in the West End: an X-ray machine. Of course, today we all know the dangers of being exposed to radiation, but then it wasn't an issue – even pregnant women were X-rayed if there was a query about the baby's position right up until the late fifties – so X-raying children's feet to see how well their shoes fitted was seen as a selling point rather than a health hazard.

After my parents had been reassured my tootsies were fine or, if my feet had grown, had dug deep in their pockets for another pair of shoes, we continued on until we reached Hamleys toyshop, where again we would stare at the toys displayed in the window for twenty minutes or so before heading back to the number 25 bus stop at Oxford Circus.

We could have carried on down Regent's Street and caught a number 15 from the Haymarket, but thanks to the strip clubs, prostitutes and their clients hanging around the area, Piccadilly Circus wasn't a place you'd want to stroll through with your children in those days.

With our annual visit to Father Christmas done, the next task was to put up the tree and decorations.

When I was very small and we lived in Anthony Street we had a foot-high artificial Christmas tree with painted glass baubles so old they'd be worth a small fortune now. Most people at that time had real trees for the festive season, so I had hoped that our move to a more spacious two-bedroom flat in Bethnal Green would mean we would too. Sadly not. My mum maintained that the dropped pine needles were too much trouble so instead a new, three-foot-tall artificial tree was bought along with new tinsel and decorations.

And so, on the Sunday before Christmas, we'd unfold the tree's rigid branches and weave neon-coloured tinsel between the green plastic leaves and haphazardly hang the old glass balls, newer baubles and bells at the tips of the branches alongside home-made ornaments that my brother and I had created out of tinfoil. We had a thing called rain, too, which you never see now but which was basically shredded silver paper that we used to throw over the whole thing. The final touch was the fairy, which was as old as the original antique trinkets it presided over.

Unlike today's tastefully designed, colour-themed trees, ours was a riot of pinks, reds, silvers and golds. Coloured fairy lights, which inevitably wouldn't work until you'd tightened each bulb in its plastic socket, added to the overall effect.

Rather than having separate chalk statues of Joseph, Mary and the baby Jesus, our family's nativity scene was a single solid piece made of plastic, much in the same way a keepsake you'd purchase at the seaside would be. Even so, we unwrapped it from its protective newspaper packaging with the same reverence as if it had been fashioned by Michelangelo.

The tissue-paper garlands that had been so carefully collapsed down the previous year came out of the cupboard, along with the concertina bells and balls, which were suspended from the light in the middle of the lounge. Greetings cards from friends and family would be hooked over string that had been pinned to the wall for the final touch of festive cheer.

Back then larger companies like Ford, where my father worked for over twenty years, put on children's Christmas parties for their employees, which my brother and I went to each year. There were hundreds of children and always a very jolly Santa, who gave us brilliant presents. I remember one year I was given a farm complete with farmhouse, barn, stable and yard plus pairs of animals, including two rats that lived in the barn.

When we were too old for that the company organised trips to West End pantomimes. I remember seeing Norman Wisdom in *Cinderella,* Des O'Connor in *Aladdin* and Frank Ifield in *Babes in the Wood*.

Once we'd broken up from school at the end of the winter term, Christmas really began. Presents sent by post or given to our parents for my brother and me would start to find their way under the Christmas tree.

On Christmas Eve we would be told to hang our socks up at the end of the bed and warned that Father Christmas wouldn't come if we didn't go to sleep.

We rose first thing to find a couple of tangerines, a bar of chocolate and possibly a comic stuffed into our socks.

Like all children I would dash into the lounge to see the additional presents that had been left their overnight. We weren't allowed to just rip off the paper, so we worked our way methodically through half a dozen small, colourfully wrapped parcels, making a note of who had given them to us so we could write thank-you letters later. After that we were allowed to open our big present. And it was just one. For me it would be something like a new paint box, a post office set or a small loom with skeins of wool and a shuttle; for my brother Andrew it was often a corgi car or a brightly coloured train. Sometimes, as money was always tight, our parents would come up with another way of giving us what we'd asked for. One year, when the must-have present was a bride doll, my mum took one of my dolls and made a wedding dress for her.

As I got older, I was often told that my new winter coat or boots were my Christmas present with just a box of toiletries or a hairbrush set to 'open on the day'. I can't complain too much as one year my father bought my mum an iron and another year it was a new set of saucepans. The saucepans came in a large box which my brother and I played in for hours.

Because there were no buses running on the day itself, my parents, my brother and I spent the day at home, so after the initial excitement of discovering what was under the tree the day settled down a bit.

When we lived in the flat in Harpley Square, while my mum prepared the dinner, my father, my brother and I would walk across the road to visit my grandmother, who lived opposite us. We'd stay for a cup of tea and give her our present. In return, Andrew and I were given a bar of chocolate each as our Christmas treat.

When we moved back to Stepney and into the maisonette, we swapped our grandmother for God and started going to church on Christmas morning instead. Having wished Jesus a happy birthday, we'd return home and while my mum peeled spuds, chopped carrots and cut a cross in the Brussels, my brother and I would watch television.

Although the rest of the Fullerton family were a sociable lot, either having a singsong together in the local pub on Christmas Eve or meeting for a pre-Christmas-dinner drink then going around to have a 'knees-up' with friends and neighbours, my parents never took part in such activities.

Once we'd moved back to Stepney, Christmas Day started in the time-honoured way with us children jumping out of bed at some ungodly hour and dashing down to see what was under the tree. After carefully unwrapping out presents so our mum could refold the paper for next year, we were hustled into breakfast, usually about eight-ish. Having hoovered up our cornflakes or Coco Pops, we were sent upstairs to put on our new Christmas clothes. Then, with my brother and me flanking our parents and my mum wearing her best hat, we would troop off to church for the nine-thirty Christmas service. After sitting through a monotonous service on hard pews, we wished our fellow parishioners Merry Christmas and returned home just after midday and played with our presents.

Although we usually ate all our meals in the kitchen, as it was a special day, my father pulled out the side leaves of the dining table in the lounge. After protecting the surface with a blanket, my mum would cover it with a tablecloth and, usually around one o'clock, in the afternoon we would all sit down for dinner.

My parents had a small Christmas pudding for dessert but my brother and I had jelly with tinned fruit in. For a treat, we'd open a tin of Nestle's cream to have with it. Ice cream wasn't an option as until my parents bought a fridge with a small freezer compartment at the top in the late 1970s we had no way of keeping it.

After Christmas lunch had been cleared away, from three o'clock and after some grumbling from my father about the fact that the country should kick them out, we sat down to watch the queen's speech followed by the Christmas film. Although commercial television started in the mid-1950s, for many years the BBC pretty much had the monopoly on Christmas viewing, but as ITV grew in popularity there was intense competition between the two channels to capture the

Christmas afternoon audience. Each year everyone eagerly awaited the Christmas and New Year edition of the *Radio Times* and the *TV Times* to see what would be on and to plan their seasonal viewing.

Also, as many families still gathered together around the piano after their Christmas dinner back then, about a week before the big day women's magazines would have a pull-out feature containing the words of the old-time songs, like 'You Made me Love You' and 'Down at the Old Bull and Bush'.

At about five in the afternoon my mum would return to the kitchen to make a plate of tinned salmon or tongue sandwiches for tea. Although we drank tea at most meals, because it was Christmas my father bought a couple of bottles of cream soda, lemonade and Tizer at the off-licence as a special tea-time treat. We were also allowed to eat in front of the TV, after which the Christmas cake, with its spikey snow-effect icing and a snowman and wiry fir tree as decoration, would be cut and we'd each have a slice for pudding.

The day finished very much as every other day did, with us children going to bed about eight o'clock while my parents sat in their respective chairs in the lounge below.

To be honest, other than the presents and the dinner, Christmas Day was pretty much like a typical Sunday in our house, but it didn't matter because the next day was Boxing Day.

Being a tyrant and a total dictator, Aunt Nell insisted that the whole family came to her for Boxing Day dinner and if you missed it you were in the doghouse with everyone in the family until at least Easter.

Of course, that wasn't because the rest of the family missed seeing your cheery face, rather it was because they didn't see why you shouldn't suffer all day under Nell's command if they had to.

Wrapped up against the mid-winter elements and wearing our new Christmas clothes, my parents, brother and I, carrying bags of presents, would trudge along to Stepney station for the hour-long journey to Ilford.

Unlike the rest of the Fullerton family, and despite my father working for Ford, we didn't have a car, so by the time we arrived at my Aunt Nell's house everyone else would already be there and the Christmas spirit was flowing. I always remember the smell of roast meat hitting you in the face as you walked in.

Having exchanged tales of how easy or otherwise everyone's journey had been, we dutifully placed our presents with the others at the foot of the artificial tree in the backroom. Then my parents tried to find themselves a perch while us children sat on the floor.

My granddad would pop a bottle top off a pale ale for my father while my mum would say no to the gin, brandy or Advocaat snowball her sisters-in-law were drinking in favour of a small, sweet sherry.

After a brief respite and a couple of sips of her drink, my mum would announce she was going to help Aunt Nell in the kitchen. I suspect this wasn't just to give her stepmother a hand with the monumental task of getting a hot dinner ready for almost twenty people, but to escape from her less-than-friendly sisters-in-law.

While we awaited the call to take our seats at the table, my granddad would warm up the valves on the gramophone. Billy Cotton's Christmas concert would blare out and the whole Fullerton family would start singing along until Nell shouted through the five-minute warning.

Drinks were thrown back as the aunts dashed off to 'spend a penny' before settling down in their allotted seats. Even though the dividing doors separating the two downstairs rooms had been thrown open, it was still a bit of a squash, to say the least. The dining-room table had been pulled out to its full length and the kitchen table added on at the end but even then, with fifteen and five children (me and my brother, my mum's sister's children, our cousins Tina and Susan, and the teenage daughter of my dad's eldest brother, Edie) seated around the table, you spent your dinner knocking elbows with your neighbour.

Although today the joint of meat is often carved at the table and vegetables are set out in tureens so you can serve yourself, every meal I ever had as a child arrived in front of me already dished up on a plate. As always, I was warned that if I didn't eat it all there would be no afters and I was also reminded that 'there are children in Africa and China who'd be glad of that dinner'. To my parents' generation, wasting food was the blackest of all mortal sins. Those of us raised by parents who lived through wartime rationing and shortages still have trouble throwing food away today.

With the adults' glasses replenished with alcohol and us children with lemonade, the Fullerton family, under the watchful eyes of Aunt Nell, sat down to munch our way through the mountain of food set before us.

Having forced down the last slither of meat and a final chunk of parsnip, the gravy-smeared plates would be whisked away and the afters bought in. In keeping with the season, it was another Christmas pudding – larger and home-made this time rather than the little one that had graced our table the day before.

To shrieks of 'watch your hair' and 'don't burn yourself', my granddad would light a spoonful of brandy and tip it over the pudding. Everyone oohed and aahed as the spirit evaporated, then the pudding was portioned out. Thankfully, there was trifle for us children, but I still earned a tight-lipped rebuke from my Aunt Nell for being a 'fussy eater' for leaving the custard layer.

As the last of the bowls were ferried to the kitchen, the furniture was returned to its rightful place. And while the men were left to get on with the washing-up, everyone who'd avoided being co-opted into helping with the dishes poured themselves another drink.

After what seemed like for ever, the chores would be done, everyone would come back into the main room and Nell took up her position beside the tree.

While the adults unwrapped their toiletries, aftershave, socks and embroidered handkerchiefs, we children ripped the paper off our knitted hats, scarves and mittens, along with children's annuals and colouring books.

After the adults had expressed delight at their gifts and the children had given the particular aunt or uncle a kiss on the cheek for theirs, all the torn paper, bits of Sellotape and discarded labels were gathered up. Once the room was tidy it was time for my favourite part of Boxing Day, which was when the Fullerton family stood up to do their 'turn'.

My father, who was the only one who could play the piano, would take his seat and start banging out the wartime tunes and everyone would join in. Somewhere in the proceedings Aunt Nell would give her solo rendition of the old sentimental ballad 'When I Leave the World Behind'. There would be a few more songs then Jimmy, the undisputed singer in the family, would be called upon to perform a couple of old favourites, which took us up to Boxing Day tea.

The women would head off into Nell's twelve-by-nine kitchen, where they'd all get in each other's way while they buttered bread for sandwiches and plated up cold meat. One of my aunts would be delegated to lay the table in the lounge ready for the spread being prepared in the kitchen, while another would be in charge of making the tea. The Christmas cake and mince pies were ferried in along with pastel-coloured fancies for the children.

Finally, all the plates of food, accompanying relishes and side dishes like pickled onions and gherkins would be laid on the cloth-covered table, and everyone was told to help themselves, which they did en masse.

My parents usually made their excuses and left soon after tea, saying they wanted to get the children home before it got too late. Of course, I never wanted to go as I was having too much fun, but my father always insisted. Truthfully, I think my brother and I were the excuse really.

As everyone had been drinking steadily since midday, by the evening the family were very merry. Even with his family my father wasn't at ease or very social, so to avoid making a fool of himself by playing what he considered to be silly games, we left. My mum didn't object either as having very little in common with her much brasher sisters-in-laws, she was happy to put on her coat and hat as soon as my father suggested it.

Having dutifully thanked everyone for our presents and kissed them goodbye, my brother and I were bundled up against the elements for the journey home, leaving the rest of the family to drink and make merry into the wee small hours before, in pre-breathalyser days, getting in their cars and driving home.

Of course, on Boxing Day 1962 we couldn't get to the family Christmas celebrations at all. In fact, we couldn't get out of our street.

We lived in the two-bedroom flat in Bethnal Green at that time, so my brother and I shared a room. When my father came in to wake us up, he told us there'd been a bit of snow overnight. Excited at this rare sight, I jumped out of bed and looked out to see a blanket of white covering the square. Well, not just the square, even the cars in the street had snow over their bonnets and the low wall surrounding the play area had disappeared completely.

My mum wasn't too sure about venturing out, but my father said it would be fine as it was early and the snow was bound to melt enough for us to get to the station. Usually, given that snow rarely settled in the centre of London, he would have been right, but when we stepped out of the lift door and saw that there was thick snow even in the sheltered area of the stairwell, we should have realised this was something more than the usual light sprinkling of snow.

One of the things you notice when living on an estate of high-rise flats is the way the air is funnelled between them. Lift shafts let out ghostly shrieks and gusts of wind trapped between the buildings whirl around seeking an escape, so when we stepped out from the shelter of our block, the blizzard – which is what it was – nearly knocked us off our feet.

There was a thick drift of snow almost stretching to the second-floor balcony of the block of flats opposite and only the red dome of the post box on the corner was visible. We set off towards the station, but after struggling to move the wheels of the pushchair through two foot of snow, my mum put her foot down and said we weren't going.

While my mum manhandled the pram and my brother and I back into the lift, my father went to the phone box at the end of the street to ring his sister with the news she would be four less for Christmas dinner. It was just as well we stayed at home as the weather only got worse and it turned out to be the first day of what we now know became the 'Winter of 1963', the coldest winter in two hundred years. The snow and extreme temperatures continued on through to the start of March.

All around the country people and animals suffered. There were reports of frozen birds dropping from the trees while ice covered rivers and even the sea. Hundreds of people had to be dug out of remote farms and cottages and the entire transport system ground to a halt. Even in East London, where usually any snow brave enough to fall on our part of capital was turned to slush with an hour, we had five-foot snowdrifts stacked against tower blocks and imprisoning people in their terraced houses.

We got off lightly as apart from a week off school and a trip to the shops feeling more like an expedition to the Arctic, for me, as an eight year old, it was like a magical winter wonderland, with snowmen on every corner.

CHAPTER NINE

Sickness and Health

M Y GREAT-GRANDMOTHER, born in 1841, lived until she was over eighty. Even so, for my parents and others of their generation, health was often regarded as the luck of the draw.

A chesty cough was treated with a home-made mustard plaster or Vicks rubbed into your skin or stuffed up your nose to help your breath. A sore throat was prescribed lemon juice and honey.

Mass inoculation against polio was introduced soon after I was born, but I still remember older children hobbling about on withered legs at school as a result of catching the disease.

If you were unwell, your first course of action was to try one of the old remedies, like rubbing a wedding ring on your eyelid to get rid of a stye or pouring warmed olive oil in your ear to unblock it. One such folk remedy was to 'sweat it out'. This harked back to the misconceived belief that illness was caused when the body's 'humours' were out of kilter. Traditionally there were several ways of rectifying this: purging, bleeding and sweating. Thankfully, by the time I arrived the first two

Christening Day, August 1954. In the backyard.

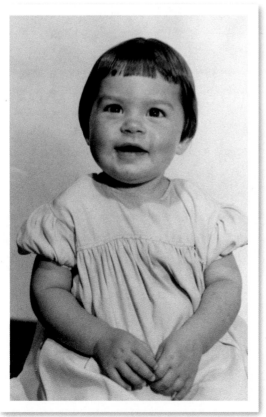

The winner of St Paul's annual baby contest, 1955.

The whole Fullerton family, 1960.

Christmas trip to see the Oxford Street lights and Santa.

Me at 3-ish with my parents.

71 Anthony Street.

Hi-de-hi: The fancy dress competition

August summer holiday at Clacton. Note the warm jumpers!

Off to nursery in a pretend uniform, blazer badge included.

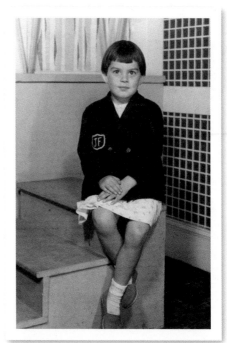

The festive bunfight at my Aunt Nell's in Ilford. She's standing guard at the back.

When flares were fashionable
the first time around…

Hastings clifftop, July 1976.

All set to protect
London, July 1976.

Overleaf: The next
Mary Quant

Community Staff
Nurse Fullerton at
Lord Lister Clinic,
1998.

had gone out of fashion. However, when I was four and a half and my mum was in hospital having my brother, I remember my father and I caught flu. Instead of trying to cool my temperature, he dosed me up with junior aspirin and then stoked up the fire, turning our front room into a furnace. Thankfully the doctor arrived and persuaded him to lower the temperature, or I might have had febrile convulsions.

If folk remedies didn't set you right, your first port of call was the pharmacy, called the chemist by my parents. Here you could buy all manner of remedies, such as blood-strengthening pills for 'women's problems', liver salts for dyspepsia and indigestion and kaolin and morphine for the trots.

Unlike today, when for safety and quality control purposes all tablets come in bubble-wrap packs, when I was young the pharmacist, who was always a man, counted them out from a big bottle.

The two dispensing pharmacists who worked where I had my first job did this with the use of a triangular pill counter before slipping them into a smaller bottle with a handwritten label stuck on it. You could also ask your pharmacist to make you up 'something' for whatever ailed you, such as a chesty cough or a gippy stomach, or even something to rub on your aching bunions.

However, if one of the potions the local pharmacist cooked up didn't put you back on your feet, then you had no other choice: you were reluctantly forced to present yourself at your general practitioner.

I say reluctantly because whether it was a hangover from

the time when you had to scrape together sixpence before the doctor would treat you I don't know, but I do know that my parents and others of their generation had a god-like reverence for doctors, bordering on fear.

If the doctor said you were to do or take something, then you did it without question. No matter how long you had to wait in the waiting room or how rude the doctor was when you finally saw them – and they were habitually rude and bullying – no one ever complained. The doctor we had growing up looked as if he'd been around since Queen Victoria's coronation. His consulting room looked like someone had emptied several wastepaper bins on his desk and cabinet. He always wore a morning coat and bow tie as if he'd dropped into the surgery on his way to the opera. Even with his half-rimmed glasses perched on the end of his nose, he had to hold a thermometer six inches from his spectacles to read it, so God help a mother who brought in a child in with a rash!

Unlike today, you couldn't just take your custom elsewhere: your GP had to agree to you moving, and as the NHS paid them a fee for every patient on their books this was not easily done. We were only able to change to a doctor who had been born in the twentieth century when our old one finally retired.

A perfect illustration of my parents' forelock-tugging attitude to the medical profession happened a few years before my father died. I went to see the cardiac consultant with him to have a better understanding of my father's heart condition and treatment. I questioned the doctor about each drug my father was on and if there was any other treatment available, such as this new pacemaker device I'd heard about. On leaving the consultation room I was roundly told off by my father as '[the consultant] knows more than we do, so it's not for us question'.

This attitude meant that doctors had carte blanche to try any new drug or procedure they thought fit. Patient consent was presumed, and if it didn't work out as expected the doctors just chalked it up to experience.

Even as late as the 1980s when I was a nurse working on a hospital ward, elderly patients had total faith in the doctors treating them and agreed to anything they suggested – sometimes totally inappropriate treatment that would lead to their health deteriorating rather than improving.

One of the things my grandparents' generation had lived in fear of was the workhouse – and with good reason as several of my not too distant ancestors spent time within their dreary walls. Although by the 1960s Bancroft Hospital was part of the London Hospital, older members of my family still referred to it as the workhouse, which indeed it had been.

There was an obligation on children to care for their elderly parents when they were too old or frail to look after themselves. As male mortality was some five to ten years less than female in the 1960 and 70s, in the majority of cases it meant shifting your household around to accommodate your widowed mother or mother-in-law. This duty tended to fall to the oldest son or daughter.

My paternal grandfather had died a year before I was born, but as my Uncle Jimmy and Aunt Marie still lived at home with his parents my grandmother was able to stay put.

Even when the whole family were rehoused to Harpley Square my Uncle Jimmy lived in the one-bedroom flat above my grandmother's ground-floor flat and popped in to see her every morning before he went to work and took an evening meal down to her each day.

Mindful of their duty, my Aunt Martha, who lived opposite, went across the road twice a week to clean my grandmother's flat, and Nell dropped by frequently after work.

When I was a child this way of caring for your elderly parents was the norm rather than the exception, and at least half of my school friends had either their grandmother or their grandfather – and sometimes both – living with them.

It's tempting to be nostalgic about the 1950s and 60s and to think that we were more compassionate in our care of the elderly, but you have to remember that life and aspirations were very different then. Firstly, with life expectancy for both sexes hovering around seventy mark in the 1950s, anyone aged sixty plus was elderly. Unlike today's pensioners, who hope to enjoy their years of retirement, many of my grandmother's generation had only their state pension to keep body and soul together.

However, today many women have careers and fit raising a family around that, whereas the majority of women of my parents' generation saw their primary job as looking after the home and family.

Although during the Second World War women took on all sorts of roles and jobs, the government actively encouraged them to return to their domestic duties of caring for home and family after the war, which meant they were more available to care for elderly parents, too.

Another factor was that many illnesses that you have a good chance of surviving today, such as strokes and heart attacks, would have carried you off in the 1950s, 60s and well into the 70s. If they didn't take you immediately then the next wave of winter flu or pneumonia would probably have the Grim Reaper knocking on the door.

My grandmother died at eighty but was caring for herself in her little flat, with minimal daily input from her family, right up until the end. My husband's grandmother, who lived with his family, was ninety-three when she died in the 1970s and had been doing the family washing just the week before. Neither would have survived that long had they become bedbound for any length of time in their sixties.

Of course, if you had no family to care for you in your twilight years you were reliant on the kindness of neighbours. One such couple were the elderly brother and sister who lived in the flat directly beneath ours on the ground floor in Harpley Square, Jack and Edith Carp (although my mum never addressed them by their first names).

They must have been in their seventies and my mum regularly visited and got them odd bits of shopping. Their flat had a musky smell of polish and dust and their front room fascinated me. Edith Carp was stick thin, with fluffy white hair piled high into a bun. I never saw her in anything but long skirts and high-necked blouses, while Jack always wore a black suit and tie.

The Carps belonged to one of the more affluent families living around London Docks. Their father had been a manager in one of the many bonded warehouses along Wapping High Street. Edith had lost a fiancé during the First World War and never married, pouring her energies into good works instead. Jack had been an official in the Port of London. They had been stalwart members of St George-in-the-East so knew my Uncle Jimmy, who also attended church there. He too popped over and did little jobs for them and he arranged for the vicar from nearby St John's to visit. I don't know why they were seeing out their twilight years in our tower block, when they obviously came from a well-to-do background, but living in their little council flat, they were like Edwardian flotsam and jetsam washed up on a modern post-war shore.

Their flat was a treasure trove of Royal Doulton figurines, Staffordshire shepherdesses and Venetian glass, and as I was a child that would touch what I shouldn't, my mum always kept a worried eye on me when we visited. Sadly, after a lifetime together, Jack died, leaving Edith, who was extremely frail, to soldier on alone. She did for a while but after a fall she was taken away to the geriatric ward in Bancroft Hospital.

In those days, under the all-encompassing Welfare Department at the council, there was no such thing as patient choice. If the man from the council said you had to be taken into a home to be cared for, you went. Even four decades later, when I was working as a district nurse, the elderly patients on my caseload had a terror of being 'put away'.

However, the main things that took a toll on people's

health are the same things that do today – drinking, smoking and poor diet – although my father's generation were largely ignorant of the effects of all three.

Apart from the immediate effects of poor nutrition like rickets, poor health in childhood lays the foundation to poor health in adulthood. Although potatoes and vegetables like turnip, carrots and cabbage were available, fruit was very expensive and often limited to apples, pears and oranges. Tangerines and dates were considered Christmas treats and fruit like strawberries, cherries and gooseberries, which you hardly ever see now, were only in the shops for a week or two a year. Blueberries, raspberries, kiwi fruit and mangoes were unknown to us. However, the food stuff – if you can call it that – which had the most detrimental impact on health was the widespread use of saturated fats.

When I was a child, lard – great big white blocks of it – was used to fry everything from bread to fish. Between suet pasty, roast potatoes and cooked breakfast, housewives got through pounds of it each week. It could be seen swilling around on the plate after most meals, ready to be mopped up by a bit of bread, and it was often left in the pan to solidify between uses. Bread and beef dripping, with a liberal sprinkling of salt, was a cheap teatime offering for school children. Sugar, too, was added to everything, from two or three heaped spoonfuls in tea to sprinkling it on a slice of buttered bread as a treat.

Alcohol mainly impacted on the health of the male population, as the pubs and many licensed working men's clubs were the hub of social activity.

My parents weren't drinkers and only had the odd tipple at Christmas and whilst on holiday. In fact, they were a bit sniffy about those in the family and any neighbours who propped up a bar. However, my Aunt Martha and her husband Wag would wander into the public house at the corner of Harpley Square three or four times a week and could be found with a drink in hand, having a singsong to celebrate the end of the working week each and every Friday.

In the 1960s, my Uncle Bob and Aunt Elaine even had a glitzy cocktail bar fitted in their upstairs front lounge, complete with fairy lights, rainbow-coloured glasses, cocktail shakers and a row of optics suspended on the wall. There were novelty stirrers and a hula girl on a spring who shimmied if you nudged her. They were also regulars in the London night clubs like the Bagatelle and Ciro's, drinking to all hours, and, by my Aunt Elaine's own admission, they often had a lost day after a heavy night on the town.

For young men, being able to hold your drink was a sign of manliness, so sinking six to eight pints on a Saturday night was commonplace. Add a couple of pints on Saturday and Sunday lunchtimes and the odd midweek pint or two, and you can see by modern standards many men drank way too much.

When I was a child and right through to the 1980s the public house was the preserve of men, so the majority of women didn't drink on the same scale. Aside from the occasional half a milk stout favoured by my grandmother, women I knew drank brandy and orange or a G&T if they were feeling sophisticated, or a snowball and lemonade, but only when they were out.

Women wouldn't dream of walking into a pub alone and a couple of women having a drink by themselves were assumed by the male drinkers to be asking to be picked up. With a few exceptions it wasn't until the 1960s and 70s, when young women started going to clubs and pubs with their friends en masse, that they started to match their male counterparts glass for glass, but more of that later.

Of course, one of the biggest health risks associated with alcohol for women was domestic violence and it was commonplace to see women sporting black eyes and bruised faces – thankfully, not in my immediate family. Having said that, my Aunt Millie lost a baby after a beating by her first husband, and I have it on good authority from my Aunt Martha that my grandfather gave my Aunt Nell a back-hander if she annoyed or crossed him.

The risks of smoking first started to be explored in the 1930, but during the Second World War the population were encouraged to smoke as a means of calming their nerves. The women of my family smoked packet cigarettes whereas the men favoured roll-ups. People smoked everywhere: on buses, trains, in pubs and restaurants. It wasn't unknown to have an appointment with your GP and find him puffing away in his surgery.

Cigarettes were bought in packets of five or ten, plus some newsagents would sell them individually to kids. Tobacco was sold in half-an-ounce pouches and needed to be accompanied by a pack of cigarette paper, as other than the headmaster at my junior school, I can't remember anyone I knew smoking a pipe. Like the vast majority of people before the Second World War, all my family smoked and had done since their early teens.

It was a pity.

Although they didn't know it when my family started puffing away at twelve or thirteen, heart disease was to kill all four Fullerton brothers; and in light of current medical knowledge, it's obvious my family has a predisposition for it.

Actually, I'm not telling you the whole truth because my Uncle Jimmy never smoked a cigarette in his life. He was the last one to marry, tying the knot at the age of thirty-eight. His new wife, Marie, was the Pearly Queen of Finsbury, and she had a constant wheeze. Hardly surprising given she smoked like a chimney and worked for the Kensington's Cigarette company, who gave their employees a weekly cigarette allowance.

Sadly, my Uncle Jim died on holiday in Devon when I was twelve. He'd never held a cigarette between his lips but living with someone who received free packets of fags each week and smoked continuously had finally taken its toll: his death certificate stated the cause of death as a heart attack. My Uncle Bobby, a lifelong smoker, developed an aortic aneurysm in his early sixties, which he survived, and had a massive stroke in his seventies, which he didn't, the contributing factor for both being smoking.

However, I felt the family's scourge of heart disease most keenly when I was a teenager and my father started to get pains in his left arm and occasionally across his chest. He was in his early fifties at the time and over the course of the next ten years coronary heart disease tightened its grip on him. He became breathless on excursions then developed cramps in his calves, an indication that the furred-up arteries within couldn't cope with the muscles' demands for oxygen. To compensate, his heart sped up, putting further strain on the whole system. Unsurprisingly, it finally culminated in a heart attack, which had him hospitalised for several weeks. He survived, but it debilitated him further. More scares followed, including a series of mini strokes, which had him back in hospital, and his health deteriorated further until, at the age of fifty-eight, he had to take early retirement as he was no longer fit to work.

Of course, today there's routine screening to discover problems early and monitor them. In addition, there's a whole spectrum of drugs available that, although they can't cure or prevent the onset of coronary heart disease, can at least mitigate some of the effects. Strangely, and fortunately for me, the family gene for heart problems seems to have missed all the women of the family, as all my aunts were well over eighty when they died of other causes.

However, women had other health issues unique to their sex that they had to grapple with.

CHAPTER TEN

A Mother's Burden

UNTIL THE START of the last century the infant mortality rate in the poorest areas of London, including the East End, was so high that only one in four infants reached their fifth birthday. Alongside this sobering statistic sat another equally grim one. In 1900, five years before my grandmother had her first child, for every thousand live births, fifty women died during or soon after childbirth. Because of this, in the previous century, women in the final stages of pregnancy often prepared their shroud alongside the layette for their new baby.

Although there were many charities working among the poor of East London who tried to improve the lot of mothers and infants, most women of that time relied on family and friends to help them through pregnancy and childbirth. There was no pre-natal or post-natal care to speak of, and certainly no way of knowing if you were having twins or if the baby was breach or miss-aligned before the onset of labour.

After I had an episiotomy with my first daughter, I asked my Aunt Nell what happened if women tore during labour, to which she replied, 'Hoped it healed.'

Although contraceptive sheaths had been around for two centuries, using them had long been associated with prostitution, so in my grandparents' time the arrival of children year after year was seen as just part of married life. It was only after the Second World War, when servicemen had been given endless lectures about venereal disease and had easy access to condoms, that this method of contraception became more acceptable. Within the space of a decade the average family dropped to 2.4 children but, even then, attitudes towards contraception could be very old fashioned.

My Aunt Elaine recounted a conversation she had with my mother in the sixties when less-intrusive methods of contraception, like diaphragms and spermicidal pessaries, were becoming available. Elaine had asked my mum if she wanted to get a diaphragm or cap, and offered to go with her to the family planning clinic. To which my mum replied, 'I trust my husband.' By that my mum meant that she knew women who had taken matters into their own hands as their husbands wouldn't.

Although women had very little control over their fertility, they were often blamed for pregnancy. Sex was regarded as a husband's right and a wife's duty, which left women somewhere between a rock and a hard place as far as pregnancy was concerned.

In many working-class people's minds large families and poverty went hand in hand, illustrated by the fact that when my brother was born my Aunt Nell told my father, 'Two's enough.'

As a district nurse in East London, I visited many elderly women and heard a few stories about what married life was like before contraception was widespread. One told me after the birth of her second child she just 'shut up shop'; another told me after four children in four years she 'let 'im in the back door'.

Abortion only became legal in 1967; before this woman had to take matters into their own hands. This often meant paying for a backstreet abortion, which if you could afford it might be at a private clinic or else in someone's front room. Others used a disinfectant douche or the old favourite of a hot bath and gin, a remedy a few of my friends resorted to, with little effect.

But fertility wasn't the only area of health that caused women to worry in the first half of the twentieth century. Having safely been delivered of your new baby you then had to travel the rocky and dangerous road of raising your infant.

I don't think we can fully understand the constant fear hanging over my grandparents' generation of disease and infection that today would just have a child at home from school for a few days, but could easily put them in an early grave a century ago. I have done countless talks thoroughly East London and Essex and at the end I often have people come up to me and tell me their family stories of life in East London at the turn of the last century. I've heard how their parents skipped a couple of meals to scrape the pennies together to call the doctor or how a child was lost because they waited too long to fetch him.

Although vaccination against diphtheria – the disease that had killed my father's brother Ernie – had been introduced in the 1930s, it had to be paid for and not every general practitioner offered it. Thankfully, with the introduction of the NHS in 1948 things improved rapidly, and by the time I arrived in the 1950s rates of infant and maternal mortality had plummeted. The introduction of penicillin, too, revolutionised maternal and child health, reducing the dangers of puerperal disease, or childbed fever as it was referred to back then. A greater understanding of and better treatment for pre-eclampsia and both pre- and post-partum haemorrhages further reduced mortality.

In addition, as I mentioned earlier, the new Welfare State took a great deal of interest in the diet and welfare of us baby boomers, so the Health Service ran mothers' classes at clinics ensuring they were rearing the next generation properly.

The NHS also monitored children closely to ensure they had enough fresh air and advised on the right foods, so the scourge of rickets didn't rear its ugly head again. When I was a baby my mum took me to the clinic every week to have me weighed and measured and to pick up my allocation of free orange juice and rose-hip syrup. The latter was a vitamin supplement which children were given daily. It tasted like liquid sugar and probably dissolved the enamel as it passed over your teeth.

Putting the whole nine year old lighting an open fire issue aside, before the advent of child safety locks on medication or household cleaners, poisoning was also common, with children drinking bleach and taking pills thinking they were sweets, but again my parents took care to keep all such things out of reach of me and my brother. They also made sure we kept up to date with all our inoculations in our infant years and that we were given milk to drink at meals so we had calcium for strong bones. We had regular trips to the dentist, too, in what could only be described as a chrome-and-white chamber of horrors that smelled like the under-sink cupboard.

Unlike the fast, electric-powered drills used today, the dentist's drill when I was a child was a metal-armed contraption that loomed over you with a slow belt-driver that turned the drill bit.

All dentists then were employed by the NHS and the one we visited looked like the brother of the Child Catcher from *Chitty Chitty Bang Bang*. He had very little sympathy with children's reluctance to submit to his ministrations and would miss the whole painkilling cocaine part if he thought he could get away with it. However, if you behaved yourself, he'd let you pick a sweet from the jar, obviously with an eye to future business.

Once at school our hearing and vision were regularly checked, and we were also examined by the legendary Nitty Nora the Bug Explorer, the school nurse, who having extracted a metal comb from a jar of blue disinfectant would part your hair to look for wildlife crawling across your bonce.

Any child found to have ringworm, a fungal infection, fared far worse: they had their hair clipped close to their skull and their head painted with violet-coloured antiseptic. And God forbid if the school nurse found you had head lice: you were sent off to the council's sanitising department to be fumigated.

Thanks to my mum's constant battle against germs with her dishcloth and bleach, I was spared that shame.

If the nurse found something else that needed specialist attention, such as glue ear or scabies, you were referred on. Thankfully, when I was referred to the local health clinic my condition wasn't as serious as either of those ailments; instead, I was suffering from the common or garden verruca.

Today we know that although you have to prevent cross infection, most warts, which is what a verruca is, will resolve themselves given time. However, when I was at school, the treatment was weekly visits to a chiropodist to have them dug out. Week after week, my mum and I trudged along Vallance Road to the single-storey clinic and week after week, after half an hour of the soles of my feet being scraped and slashed, I hobbled home. Fortunately, after a month or so, they disappeared and my torture was ended.

Having been raised at a time when medicine, a trip to the doctors and even operations like the removal of tonsils had parents digging deep into their pockets to cover the cost, my parent took advantage of everything the NHS had to offer. However, although my mother always used the back gas rings so we wouldn't burn ourselves by grabbing a saucepan handle and we had a fireguard secured around our coal-filled grate, some accidents couldn't be avoided and one such incident has left its mark on me, literally.

Jumping on the bed was strictly forbidden but unbeknown to my mum, who was preparing the dinner in the kitchen, one day I was trampolining on my bed. Somehow, I tipped forward and smacked my nose on the headboard. Naturally it hurt, but thinking it was no more than other bumps and scrapes I'd had before, I did what all children do and went to find Mum. I wandered into the kitchen and as I did Mum screamed.

Grabbing a flannel, she drenched it with cold water and slapped it on my face. Telling me to hold it there and to follow her, she scooped up my brother on the way out of the door. Dropping him off with a neighbour, she ran me – and I mean ran – to the casualty department ten minutes away, where I was immediately whisked into a cubicle.

To everyone's amazement, I hadn't broken anything but instead I had managed to split the flesh across the bridge of my nose. When I'd casually walked into the kitchen thinking I had little more than a bruise and announced I'd banged my nose, my face was, in fact, completely covered with blood, hence my mum's panicked reaction.

Today the wound would have been glued or stitched with dissolvable stitches; back then there was only black silk, and even though it's sixty-plus years ago I can still remember lying there looking up while the doctor stitched my nose, and I also remember a few weeks later sitting motionless while those stitches were removed. Although I still carry the scar, the doctor on duty that day did an excellent job as you'd have to have pretty good eyesight to see it.

That wasn't my last visit to Bancroft Hospital as a child but the next time it was done in a more orderly way. Just before I turned seven, I was taken into the children's ward to have my tonsils out. It was my first time away from home overnight, but after my parents dropped me off I can't remember them visiting for the whole time I was in hospital. And it wasn't because they didn't, I'm certain they did, but the prevailing wisdom at that time was that if parents visited for more than an hour a day, it upset the children too much. Unbelievable, I know, but true!

What I do remember from my time there is being in a four-bedded unit with two other girls and a boy, all in for tonsillectomies. I can also recall the blooming needle in my right thigh for my pre-med injection. However, the overriding memory of my five-day hospital stay is the rocking horse in the playroom.

Now, I've done hundreds of talks over the past decade to a variety of women's groups, conferences and on cruise ships, and when I tell them about my life-long love of history I always say it started when, as a child of five or six, I watched Roger Moore as Ivanhoe galloping over the hill on his white charger – and that's absolutely true. Although I can't remember my parents visiting me during my stay in hospital, I do remember spending hours imagining I was riding over the rolling hills beside Ivanhoe on that wooden rocking horse.

Of course, raising children isn't just about their physical development but their intellectual development, too. Although the Victorian adage of 'children should be seen and not heard' had faded by the time I was born, it was still regarded as folly for parents to pick up a crying baby. Mothers who didn't follow a strict regime for mealtimes, enforce an afternoon nap and a rigid bedtime were thought at best foolish, at worst to be condemning their offspring to an undisciplined future.

During the war, various publishing companies supplied cheap paperbacks to the troops. Woefully aware of his lack of schooling, my father set about educating himself while on active duty. He was a particular fan of Penguin Books' distinctive black-and-yellow-covered Teach Yourself books, notably the ones dealing with philosophical or political subjects.

Having tried to make up for his lack of education through books, my father applied the same method to the task of raising a child. A few years before I was born, a revolution in childcare swept across the Atlantic in the form of Dr Spock's *The Common Sense Book of Babies and Childcare*. While others, notably my Aunt Nell, regarded it as 'a load of rubbish', my father, with his unquestioning belief in experts, swallowed the paediatrician's childrearing philosophy hook, line and sinker.

This put him in conflict with the prevailing ideas around childrearing, and one illustration of this occurred when I was about three. My parents and grandparents had left me unattended in my grandfather's car for ten minutes or so – yes, people did that in those days. When they returned, they found I'd somehow managed to pull all the padding from inside the parcel shelf of my grandfather's Hillman Minx. My mum recalled wondering where I'd got the candyfloss from as she approached!

Nell was all for giving me a smack on the back of the legs, but my father refused and told her it was natural for children to want to explore. Undaunted, he continued to apply this new way of thinking to my upbringing. There was a constant supply of books, too, which were read to me. He took on board the idea that children learn through experimental play and hands-on discovery, so I was given plasticine – the scourge of my mother's rugs and furniture – to squeeze and model between my chubby little fingers. However, one of his ideas went badly awry when he decided to make me a sandpit in the backyard. Having hammered together the planks he then filled it with sand. Unfortunately, working on the assumption that anything labelled sand would be fine, he filled it with the builders' variety. All seemed well and I was left to explore with my bucket and spade. However, after an hour or so when my mum came out to check on me, she found I'd turned a vivid shade of orange from the untreated sand.

My father had greater success with more conventional methods, providing me with coloured pencils as soon as I could hold them and cut-up rolls of old wallpaper and card for me to scribble on.

The health visitor also supplied endless pamphlets on raising a happy, healthy child, but having read that most vitamins found in vegetables were dissolved while being cooked, my father insisted that I drink the cooled water the cabbage was boiled in.

Out of sight

However, aside from the dentist's drill, the verruca clinic and my busted nose, the illness that overshadowed my childhood wasn't anything penicillin could cure.

I never meet my mum's mother or even knew she was called Emma Hopgood. In fact, my mum barely remembered her and was told by her father and stepmother that she was dead.

My grandparents married in 1923, and my mum was born three years later, followed by her sister Gladys two years after that. My grandmother suffered post-natal depression each time (although it wasn't recognised as such). However, when Gladys was two or three, my grandmother was engulfed in a bout of depression that saw her hospitalised in the Claybury Lunatic Asylum, never to emerge again.

At that time divorce carried a massive stigma and was almost unheard of in working-class families, although under the Matrimonial Causes Act of 1937 you could be granted a divorce if your spouse was proved to have incurable insanity.

My grandfather met my dad's eldest sister Nell sometime before the war and married her quietly, moving her into the family home. They told my mum and everyone else that Emma had died. The sad truth was that Emma wasn't dead but a long-term resident of a mental institution at Woodford Bridge.

My mum had lived almost the whole of her life grieving for her mother, when in fact she was alive and just a just a forty-minute tube journey away. By the time my mum discovered the truth it was too late: Emma had died.

As you can imagine, this had a profound impact on her. When we were clearing out her effects after she died, we discovered letters she'd written to her mother and little sketches of her and her mother together holding hands. My mum was a devout Christian and, after she discovered what had happened, she told me on several occasions that she felt her mother's presence beside her in church.

I do know that following her mother's departure from the family home, my mum's life became terribly unstable. Although my father always maintained that Jim Aplin was a neglectful father and blamed him for my mum's mental health issues, the truth wasn't quite as black and white.

Needing to keep a roof over their heads, my grandfather worked long hours at the Electricity Board, which meant my mum and her sister Gladys were cared for during the week by their aunts, who still lived in Bow, and returned home for the weekends. This in turn disrupted my mum's schooling, which in turn affected her education, but more importantly it affected her feelings of security and confidence.

It's recognised today that parental loss in early life and/or an unstable home setting is a recipe for emotional and mental health problems, but in the first half of the twentieth century no such consideration was given to children.

Becoming a mother resurrected her grief of having her own mother snatched away from her when she was young, so although it wasn't recognised in the early fifties, I now realise that she suffered from post-natal depression about six months after I was born. She seemed to have recovered from this, but following the birth of my brother, Andrew, four years later, her post-natal depression returned and she was admitted into hospital.

Although they helped where they could, the Fullertons

also started whispering amongst themselves that my mum was going the same way as her mother. In the early part of the twentieth century, our understanding of mental health had hardly advanced since Victorian times. Conditions such as anxiety, depression and phobias, which are understood and treatable today, were all lumped under the same banner of insanity.

Thankfully, after a spell in hospital, my mother returned home and life went back to normal in our two-bedroom council flat. Well, not quite normal because, although I didn't know it at the time, my mum's first spell as an in-patient was just a foretaste of what was to come.

CHAPTER ELEVEN

Becoming Me

WHEN I LOOK back, I view my school years in two halves. The first being when I was very much the child my parents made me and the second when I found my own identity. And that started the first day I pitched up at senior school.

How can I best describe Redcoat Church of England Secondary School?

Well, it was a bit like St Trinian's but, unlike almost every other senior school in the area by then, without any kind of uniform. However, it did have something very much better: boys.

Except for those girls with older siblings in the school who knew the score, most of us arrived all squeaky clean in pleated skirts and knitted jumpers. Those of us with bobs had our hair held off our faces with Alice bands, while girls with long hair wore plaits secured by ribboned bows. Not to be outdone, the boys, no doubt after having had their mothers licking their hands to flatten their hair, wore grey trousers, white shirts and clip-on ties. Both genders wore a stiff new winter coat purposely bought too big so we would 'grow into it'.

We couldn't have been marked out more clearly as first years if we'd had it tattooed on our foreheads.

The new girls huddled together in the playground, our eyes wide with wonder as we watched the older students milling around us in their miniskirts, psychedelic dresses and pointed-toe kitten-heeled slingbacks.

This was when the Beatles were riding high in the charts and when Carnaby Street and King's Road were giving the sixties generation their iconic look. Although Mary Quant's creations were way beyond our purses, the local factories were making knock-off copies of the latest styles as fast as their machinist could sew them, so they were cheaply available on every clothing stall in the markets.

After twenty minutes or so of being gaped at like we were a newly discovered species, our torture ended when the school bell rang. We headed for the door and trooped up a short flight of stairs into the school.

Unlike my junior school built in the early 1890s, Redcoat Church of England Secondary School started life in the early 1700s as St Dunstan's Church charity school. Over the years it had grown from a single classroom in a hotchpotch of different levels. As far as I remember, you entered the school by the main front steps where the classrooms were. The school hall had a stage at one end and the dreaded PE apparatus bolted to one wall. The headmaster, Mr Jarvis, had his office on this level until a pupil set fire to it and it was relocated to an attic room. The staircases to the classrooms and to the girls' playground were to the right of the stage. There was also a passageway to the side annexe that housed the music room, and on the top floor was the grandly named art studio.

The middle floor had originally been one big room but it was now divided into classrooms by concertinaed wooden panels with windows along the top which were high enough to maximise the light but too high for pupils to peer through unless you were standing on a desk. As the doors were fixed to the floor where the panels hinged, they rattled every time someone crashed into them. They also had small, compass-drilled holes that were just large enough to poke the drinking straw from your school milk through and squirt the pupils in the next room.

After being informed which class we had been allocated, we were directed to our room. My teacher was a Miss Barnaby who, being a fag paper over five foot, I towered over.

We sat at school desks deeply etched with the names of those pupils who had gone before us, facing the teacher's desk and the blackboard, which was balanced on an easel at the front.

We were issued with ink pens, which were in effect just an eight-inch length of dowel with a cheap nib attached. Ink was poured into the porcelain inkwell set into our desk from a large bottle, which gave any number of options for disaster, as the navy stains on the floorboards testified.

As well as being our form teacher, Miss Barnaby also took us for geography. A keen rock climber, she would insert tales of her exploits of dangling from rocks all over Europe in-between information about oxbow lake formation and sedimentation.

The desks were set out in three rows, with the girls choosing the right-hand side of the room and the boys mainly choosing the left. There were about thirty of us streamed into class 1A, so those of us without a friend from our primary schools had to mingle in the middle.

Not wanting to be marked out as a teacher's pet on the first day, I plumped for the desk at the back of class alongside Brenda Murray. She, like me, was a talker and the teacher often sent a piece of chalk flying our way because we were chattering. On more than one occasion we also found ourselves lining up outside the headmaster's office awaiting six of the best.

Unlike junior school, where your class teacher taught all the subjects, we now had a different teacher for each. Sometimes, such as with maths or English, the teacher came to you, whereas for art and music it was you who went to them. This was a gift, as we quickly worked out that once you'd been ticked off the afternoon register, you could bunk off without getting caught. If, however, you decided to grace the school with your presence, it gave you ample opportunity to chat to friends as you dawdled to your next lesson.

I have to say, the change in the lesson structure did me a great favour because although my spelling was still poor, I was now being marked overwhelmingly on the content of my writing, which meant my marks massively improved.

However, that aside, to be honest, it's a wonder I learned anything at school that year because by the time we'd been there a few months, my friends and I used to meet before going into school to decide if we fancied it that day and if not we'd bunk off.

But on that first day, after giving us our weekly timetable and handing us our exercise books so we could take them home and cover them with spare wallpaper, it was time for morning break. We dutifully filed out of the classroom and down the stairs to the girls' playground.

Well, when I say playground, I really mean a yard surrounded by nine-foot-high walls. There was a large plane tree with a peeling green bench around its trunk in the centre of the yard and a brick-built toilet block against the far wall. There was also a door leading to the more spacious boys' playground on the other side of the wall. From time to time boys, minus their trousers and with a look of sheer terror on their faces, would be shoved through the door, while their friends could be heard whooping and laughing on the other side of the wall.

In theory, at each break-time the female teacher who'd drawn the short straw would be on duty to keep us in order. However, the truth was that they preferred to loiter at the top of the stairs smoking a surreptitious cigarette while the third- and fourth-year smokers did the same in the gut-wrenchingly disgusting toilets.

There was no sixth form and no more than a hundred and twenty children in the school, so even though it was half the size of a netball pitch, the girls' playground wasn't particularly crowded.

The worldly wise, miniskirted fourth-year girls with mascaraed eyes and pink lips commandeered the disused stairs leading up to the music-room annexe at the side of the school. Huddled together they would pore over magazines like *Seventeen* and *Jackie* and read out the rude bits of *Up the Junction* and *Forever Amber*. Trying to copy them, a cluster of the third years congregated close by, leaving the rest of us to mill around aimlessly.

Feeling lost in an alien world, the first years, myself included, drifted over to the far corner and tried not to look like the fresh meat we were, but to no avail because Nora Dodds sniffed us out.

A small dark-haired girl with a pinched face, she and her two sidekicks homed in on us from the start, asking if our clothes were second hand, did we still wet the bed and criticising our mothers for dressing us like little children.

Her aim was to make you cry so she and her friends could laugh at you for being a baby. It was a close-run thing some days but she never quite managed to reduce me to tears, although not for want of trying. Bad though it was for me, for my poor friend Audrey Saunders it was ten times worse.

Audrey's parents had also sent her to Redcoat as a way of getting her into Sir John Cass when the two schools amalgamated the following year, so finding we had other things in common too, we gravitated towards each other during the first week or so in school.

Considering her father was a van driver and they lived in a rented flat above a shop that was filled with cats and was an utter tip, her parents were very picky about who she mixed with. However, her mother, who worked as a library assistant, found me acceptable.

Like me, Audrey's parents had high hopes of her going to college and university and we became very close friends, so much so that when I married a decade later, she was my chief bridesmaid. However, unlike me, who refused to wear long white socks after the first week, Audrey's parents wouldn't let her swap to stockings like the rest of us. The socks, coupled with the solid lace-up shoes she wore, gave Nora Dodds plenty of ammunition.

Anyhow, after a couple of weeks we'd found our feet and new friends as we started our move towards adulthood.

Mostly the lessons in our first year were very much as you'd expect: English, Maths, History, and so on. However, there were a few that have stuck in my mind. Music was part of the curriculum throughout my school years and in Redcoat our weekly music lesson comprised of an hour of communal singing under the auspices of an elderly teacher. With white hair piled high in a cottage-loaf-shaped nest on the top of her head, and half-rimmed glasses dangling on a chain around her neck, she looked as if she'd just stepped out of an Oscar Wilde play. I can't remember her name, but Miss Prism would have fitted perfectly as she had that delicate air of an Edwardian spinster about her.

The lesson comprised of us all lining up in a loose choir formation, with the boys at the back and the girls at the front. Someone would give out the much-thumbed songbooks and she would take her place at the piano. With her grey bird's nest wobbling on her head, she'd belt out a couple of choruses of such gems as 'Greensleeves' and 'Early One Morning' to 'warm the old vocals' before we moved on to a new song.

Now, when I say new, I don't mean the Stones' 'I Can't Get no Satisfaction' or the Animals' 'We Gotta Get out of This Place', a sentiment the whole class could go with. No, I mean new as in something the troops sang in the trenches half a century before, like 'If You Were the Only Girl in the World', a lovely song and one of my mother's favourites, but really...

Like with my junior school music lessons, I've forgotten most of what we sang, but there was one she obviously loved as we sang it regularly – 'Riding Down from Bangor', an American Vaudeville refrain from the 1870s. It's basically a ditty about a fella on a train journey taking advantage of a young woman in a long tunnel which leaves one of her earrings dangling in his beard. Hardly the sort of thing a bunch of twelve year olds should be singing but she loved it, often playing the final chorus with a naughty twinkle in her eye.

Other than the music room with the upright piano and the art room on the top floor, the school had no other specialist classrooms so for cookery lessons we girls, and it was only the girls in those days, had to traipse half a mile away to an adult education institute in Salmon Lane. None of us were very keen on wasting a whole afternoon trying to whip ingredients into something resembling food, but there was one very big, fat, silver lining to our weekly trek and that was having pie and mash for lunch in Hazard's pie and mash shop.

Brenda and I, along with a couple of other girls, would pile into the steamy shop at the top end of the long lane that ran from Limehouse to St Dunstan's graveyard. With its white-tiled walls, wooden benches running down the left-hand side of the shop and steaming vats of stewed eels behind the counter on the right, I image Hazards hadn't changed much in the past half a century. I don't suppose the menu had either. Thank goodness, because, believe me, stewed eels or a steak pie served with lumpy mashed potatoes smothered in gravy is the nectar of the gods. To be totally accurate, the pale gravy was in fact liquor – a parsley sauce made from the water used to boil the eels, which gave it a unique flavour and a green tinge.

Having stuffed our faces, we then headed off for an afternoon of Home Economics around the corner. Whether it's timetabled as Cookery, Home Economics or Food Technology, the room where such lessons are held always has a lovely smell of baking hanging over it. Such was the room we all trooped into once a week with our ingredients jiggling about in our school bags.

The old women who taught us looked like a poor relation of our music teacher, with the same mess of grey hair pinned on the top of her head. Her usual black dress looked very much like what a cook would have worn whilst whipping up culinary delights for 'them upstairs'. Over her domestic service attire was a wraparound apron, which was starched white instead of the flowery ones our mums wore. However, the fashion element that sticks most in my mind is how her long, knitted drawers always peeked out from beneath her hemline.

As it was expected that our main occupation in life would be as wives and mothers, we had lessons about household budgeting, cuts of meat, seasonal vegetables and laundry, as well as rolling up our sleeves to make actual food.

As meat was too expensive to chance us ruining it, we budding housewives started with simple things like shortcrust pastry for jam tarts, progressing on to fairy cakes and mince pies as we approached Christmas.

We cleaned the local chemist out of citric acid the week we made lemonade and the baker of live yeast when baking Chelsea buns was on the curriculum. I have to say, they were great lessons, not least because you could muck about with friends and chatter. Someone always got flour-bombed for a laugh and there was the weekly excitement of wondering if we'd all go up in flames because someone forgot to set a timer.

Physical education was very much a part of school life when I was young but along with the hell that was the PE apparatus, senior school had a new level of torture, Fairlop.

Now, if you went to school anywhere in the Borough of Tower Hamlets at that time I suspect you're probably shuddering already. However, for those who never had that joy, let me explain. Fairlop was an outdoor sports facility a short walk from Fairlop Central Line station.

To be fair, for children who lived in flats with very little access to open spaces it was a much-needed facility, but that didn't make me hate the weekly trips there any less.

While most of the boys had played football in one form or another since they were able to walk, at secondary school they were now taught rugby by beefy, shouty instructors. For us girls, along with the usual netball, we had a chance to have a go at hockey. Our attempts at the sport so beloved by our strapping gym mistress resulted in bleeding shins and bruised ankles every week. On one occasion a pupil was hospitalised for three days after being cracked over the head with a stick.

In the summer these team games changed to tennis and cricket. However, the sport – if you can call it that – equally loathed by both sexes was cross-country running. What person in their right mind would think it fun to trudge through mud in all weathers just to arrive back where they started? To compound the sheer hell of it, you were sent out on your run to nowhere in a pair of flimsy shorts and an Aertex top.

In later years, after we joined with John Cass, we had the luxury of a coach to take us to Fairlop, but in my first year at Redcoat the whole school would troop up to Stepney Green station once a week for the forty-minute journey to the activity centre.

I've never liked sport since being dragged weekly to Fairlop for a whole year, which is a pity as it has many physical and mental health benefits, but dreary winter afternoons spent ankle-deep in mud and drenched to the skin, running around the perimeter of the sports field, pretty much inoculated me against exercise.

Of course, as a Church of England school it wasn't just your physical well-being the school promoted, it also cared for your soul. So, every Thursday, we trooped around the corner to St Dunstan's Church for a service. Like a handful of other children in the school, I was a regular Sunday attendee so the echoey interior and high-vaulted ceiling were familiar to me. I was also used to the unyielding pews, but those who weren't and shuffled about or chattered earned themselves a hard look from their form teachers.

There was an expectation that you were confirmed as soon as you were deemed old enough, so some of the pupils in the third and fourth year, along with many of the teachers, would go up for communion while the rest of us sat in the pews. It was usually taken by the curate, but on high days and holidays it might be led by Father Young the rector, who also visited the school from time to time to take morning assembly and assist with prize giving.

Today, even a cursory glance around Redcoat's decrepit building – with its nonextant curriculum and pupils going into the working world without a single qualification – would have had Ofsted put it straight into special measures, but back in the early sixties there was no such thing as monitoring teachers' performance or students' achievements. Unless your parents were like my father and recognised the importance of education, you were just sent to the local school be it good, bad or indifferent.

I can't say I can remember learning anything in my one year as a pupil in Redcoat, but it was certainly an experience. However, one thing about that year did have a lasting effect. It was whilst at Redcoat that I read *Katherine* by Anya Seton. It changed my life and is the reason why, decades later, I started writing historical romantic fiction.

Brand Spanking New

I knew when I started at Redcoat that the following year I would be starting again in the new school we'd seen rise from its foundation over the past two years on our way to church.

I had a taste of what was to come when my parents and I were invited in for an induction day and my first ever uniform fitting before the school opened for the autumn term. With our eyes stretched wide in astonishment and led by a teacher wearing a flowing black academic gown and mortarboard, we were given a tour around the soon-to-be-opened school. And was it any wonder? After the dingy, overcrowded classrooms of the old Redcoat school, the new Sir John Cass Foundation and Redcoat School was like a palace.

Having been shown the separate Woodwork and Metalwork block, we were led across the playground into the main school building. The school was arranged over four floors. The Art, Needlework and Home Economics rooms were on the top floor, with the Science labs and Commerce suite – a room full of typewriters where girls would take classes in typing – on the floor below. The first and second floors were taken up with classrooms and they contained the usual rows of desks facing a blackboard.

Having gazed in wonder at the up-to-date equipment and the spacious provision for our learning, we were taken along the corridor past the staffroom, school office, headmaster's office and sixth-form lounge to the PE and Music block. There was a large music room with tiered seating, an acoustic ceiling and a stage where various instruments were on display, including a full set of drums. Having gazed goggle-eyed at this cultural marvel we were led across to the other side of the block where, wonder upon wonder, there was a half-size swimming pool. There was also a purpose-built gymnasium with windows set high in the lofty walls, fixed nets on the wall and floor-markings for netball and basketball. Unfortunately, it also had the dreaded PE apparatus fixed to the wall.

Having completed the tour with my father repeatedly saying, 'I 'ope you know how lucky you are' and, 'I wish I'd had your opportunities', we were ushered into the main hall where row upon row of tables displaying various bits of school uniform had been set up along each side of the room.

One table was laden with navy blazers, others were piled high with pleated skirts and boys' trousers. There was white and navy PE kit, too, plus diagonal-striped ties, dull brown woodwork aprons for boys and white ones for girls ready to master their housekeeping and cookery skills. The girls were also given a hat that looked like something a 1960s air hostess would wear to greet passengers boarding a plane, which we were supposed to wear but never did.

Legend has it that Sir John Cass, an eighteenth-century city trader and businessman, founded and endowed a school for the poor boys of the City on his deathbed, staining the quill in his hand with blood as he signed his will. The school crest had an arm sticking out the top clutching a red feather to commemorate this, and each February on Founder's Day we were given a red feather to wear in our lapels.

Although the school name has recently been changed because of Sir John Cass's association with the eighteenth-century slave trade, generations of poor City children continue to benefit from his largesse to this day, as I believe the foundation he endowed still supplements the school's income.

A week or so after being kitted out in my new clobber, I pitched up along with six hundred children for our first day in our new state-of-the-art school. The Redcoat kids were outnumbered by our Cass counterparts three to one, so we stuck together at first but soon started to mingle with the Cass crowd. The integration of the two schools was helped by the fact we were restreamed into classes for individual subjects, so during the day we mixed with a different set of classmates every hour or so.

We were put into houses, too, which were named after City landmarks. I was in Cathedral, which was represented by the colour red and a cross. Audrey was in Tower, which was blue with a Tudor rose; Mint was yellow and Mansion House green.

The old Redcoat school was just a five-minute walk away and many of the pupils who attended lived nearby. The children who had been to Cass, situated just inside the eastern border of the City, came from further afield and their catchment area took in the poorest areas around Aldgate, the west end of the Highway and Cable Street. Their intake also included children whose fathers were Beefeaters and who lived in the Tower of London. There was a great mix of ethnicities and religions, too.

Along with a sizeable proportion of Jewish classmates, I had had children of colour in my class ever since infant school, mainly Indian but also Black, Chinese and mixed-race students.

However, despite the new faces and the new building, some things remained very much the same, including morning assembly. Each morning we would troop into the main hall, the lower years at the front, the fourth and fifth years at the back and the sixth form in the gallery above, for our act of worship.

Mr Barrell, who had been Cass's headmaster and who had pipped Redcoat's head Mr Jarvis to the top job, led the assemblies, usually flanked by Miss Dutton, the ginger-haired, tight-faced deputy head, and the heads of departments. Although they'd dispensed with their mortarboards, they all still wore their uniform of black academic gowns.

We would sing the usual hymns and say the usual prayers before trooping back out to our first lesson.

Many of my old Redcoat friends were in the same lessons as me and after a week or so of finding our feet, Audrey Saunders and I started to make new friends from Cass, one of whom was Iris Sinclair.

Through no fault of her own, Iris was a bully's dream. Born prematurely at six months, she had only just survived. Unaware at that time of the damage it could do to premature babies' eyes, she was put into an incubator and given concentrated oxygen to help her developing lungs. The oxygen therapy affected her sight and made her eyes slightly more bulbous than normal, prompting many of the boys to nickname her Marty – after Marty Feldman the comedian with the same problem. Of course, she didn't help herself either because, as the saying goes, she wanted to know the inside and out of a cat's arse. Anyway, us more swottish members of 2A formed ourselves into a loose alliance. After the sartorial freedom of Redcoat, I absolutely loathed the frumpy navy blue school uniform I was now forced to wear so I also joined the dolly-bird collective by hitching up my skirt and plastering on the make-up, including false eyelashes. To be honest, nearly ever girl from the second year up did the same. Even those whose parents had forbidden them to wear make-up could be seen in the bogs each morning putting it on and then scrubbing it off again at the end of school. And the sound of Miss Dutton, the acerbic deputy head, shouting 'Roll that skirt down' echoed daily along the corridors.

Of course, as Cass and Redcoat was a co-ed school, all this pre-school titivating wasn't just for the fun of it. The joining of the two schools meant there was a whole new crop of boys for us all to impress.

However, my life as Jean Fullerton really started when I moved into the fourth year of school.

The year before, we had been streamed into three cohorts for our GCEs, as they were called in those days. Although we would all continue to take English and Maths, we had a choice between Commerce, where the third-floor typing pool came into its own; Science, for those who weren't squeamish and wanted to burn things; and the arts, which broadly speaking was History, Geography, Sociology and Economics, with a bit of Art, Cookery and Needlework thrown in.

As I didn't want to dissect frogs, Science was out. Similarly, Commerce was not an option – given my issues with spelling, there was no way on God's earth I had a chance of earning my living using the written word (yes, I get the irony). So that left the arts stream, which suited me perfectly as it included my favourite subject, History, which was closely followed by Geography and Sociology.

A sizeable number of the girls, but no boys, opted for Commerce, which along with typing offered shorthand, bookkeeping and office skills. Most of my old Redcoat classmates chose this route, with the exception of my friend Audrey, who wanted to be a nurse. The majority of boys chose the science pathway. This left a more or less equal number of boys and girls to take the arts route. As you could only take two out of three of the creative options, I chose Art, which I'd been doing since I could hold a pencil, and Needlework, because I was already making some of my own clothes, plus I hated cooking and still do.

Although a few of the Redcoat teachers had moved to the new school with us, the vast majority of staff were from Cass and it was they who took us forward to our all-important state exams.

I found a kindred spirit in Miss Drake, my History teacher, not only because, like me, she loved the subject but also because she couldn't spell either so she dictated work to the class instead of writing it on the blackboard. Perhaps because of this, too, she didn't use the chalk-and-talk method like most teachers but instead set projects alongside essays for homework.

We had Erik the Viking as our Geography teacher, so-called because he was over six foot tall with a bushy ginger beard. He was an enthusiast for all things animal, vegetable and mineral. Over the four years he taught us O and A level Geography, he took us on marvellous, funny and unforgettable field trips to places such as the Devil's Punch Bowl in Surrey, Offa's Dyke and the Peak District. I say unforgettable because on the first, a visit to the Devils' Punch Bowl, whilst sorting out my Georgian shop fronts from my mock Tudors, I was upbraided by 'angry of Hindhead', a tweedy woman with a moustache, for littering when I inadvertently dropped a paper bag while surveying the High Street.

Two days in to our visit to Offa's Dyke, I twisted my ankle when I put my foot down a rabbit hole and had to spend the rest of the week in the accompanying van, which allowed me to see Ross-on-Wye, Herefordshire, and a couple of castles instead of just endless hills.

And our trip to the Peak District in the upper sixth was notable because I got so drunk that I forgot to zip up the tent flap before I crawled into my sleeping bag. I woke in a puddle the next morning because it had rained all night.

For Maths we had Miss Akeley, a stick of a woman with mousy hair and thick glasses, who tried very hard but who could never manage to control the class. We had an Anglican nun – yes, there were still a few back then – whose name I forget, for Biology. The two art teachers were like Jack Sprat and his wife, as one was a dumpy woman with bright red hair and the other was tall and slim and, much to Miss Dutton's disapproval, wore the shortest miniskirts imaginable. Our cookery teacher was a red-faced woman who bellowed at us constantly and ordered us about as if we were kitchen maids in a Victorian stately home. Once, asked by Iris Sinclair what she should do with the blackened over-cooked cake she'd just rescued from the oven, minutes away from total incineration, she told her to throw it out of the window. Iris took her at her word. Thankfully it missed the school caretaker, who was sweeping up leaves in the playground four floors below.

One of my favourite teachers was Mrs Davies, who took us for needlework. She was a motherly Welsh woman who was constantly mislaying her glasses, and even though I used the professional methods my mum had taught me – creating inward nips instead of outward-facing notches and sewing fabric on the machine without tacking it first as you were supposed to do – she never marked me down.

We girls had a PE teacher who had muscles on top of muscles and spent a great deal of time blowing her whistle, while the boys had a completely bonkers Welshman whose sarcastic comments to any pupil his wild-eyed stare alighted on were legendary.

We had two teachers for English. One of them, Mr Owen, was the head of the English department. With a full head of steel-grey hair and always immaculately dressed, he was very much the old-fashioned schoolmaster. He was also paralysed down his left side, much like someone who had suffered a stroke. Rumour had it that as a young man in the 1930s he'd been an officer in the India army and had been ambushed while on patrol. The platoon he was with had been slaughtered and he'd been left for dead, having sustained a blow to the head.

Although his left hand and arm were withered, he was able to shuffle around fast enough and to administer a hefty six of the best to any pupil stupid enough to step out of line. Although he clearly came from a privileged upper-class background, he was tireless in his attempts to ensure the children in his charge had all the opportunities possible.

However, the teacher I remember most vividly from those days was the other English teacher, Mr Casey.

Although he seemed much older than us, I don't think he was much more than twenty-five or twenty-six when I met him. Tall, slim and with a crewcut, he had more than a bit of singer Joe Brown about him. And he could certainly keep charge – so much so that you made damn certain you'd been to the loo before his class, because a raised hand would always bring forth a sarcastic or belittling remark.

He was passionate about literature and during his lessons, along with the set texts such as *Lord of the Flies* and Leslie Thomas's *This Time Next Week,* we read Thomas Hardy – which I hated – Dickens – which I loved – and many others. He was particularly keen on literature about working people and their lives, and he opened up a whole world of stories and authors to me, for which I'll always be grateful.

Naturally, for our GCEs we had to study Shakespeare. Luckily for us our set text wasn't *Titus Andronicus* but *Romeo and Juliet,* which was much more likely to engage a bunch of fourteen year olds raging with teenage hormones. Mr Casey even took the whole class to see the 1968 film of the same to help us get to grips with the language.

He was also passionate about us writing our own stories and rather than the mind-numbing titles like 'A Day in the Life of a Postage Stamp' or 'What I Would do to Help Old People', we had 'You Open Your Front Door and Walk into…' or 'I Opened My Eyes and Saw…'

However, although Mr Casey was a good teacher, I dreaded his lessons, which were nothing short of torture for me. The main reason for this was that on Monday mornings in English we were given twenty spellings to learn for our double lesson on Friday.

I would go away and try to memorise them, but every Friday it was the same. I'd troop in and, head bowed, I'd write the words down as he shouted them out, before swapping my paper with the person next to me for marking.

Try as I might, it was a rare week if I got into double figures. If my demoralising score wasn't enough for me to bear, I had to suffer Mr Casey's unique way of giving out the results. The whole class had to stand up and as he shouted out your score – starting at the highest – you sat back down. Unsurprisingly, almost always I was either the last or very nearly the last one standing. A mocking or sarcastic comment like 'And once again Fullerton is bringing up the rear' would be followed by sniggers.

I am luckier than many of my generation who have dyslexia as it only affects my written work not my reading or comprehension, but I'm sure generations of children with more complex dyslexia were just shoved into the D stream and left to get on with it.

One day, after suffering this post-spelling-test ordeal for week after week, I finally cracked and burst into tears. I sat there blubbing through the remaining five or ten minutes of the lesson and when the class was dismissed Mr Casey asked me to stay. He apologised and after that, although I still had to endure the same ritual each week as he called out the scores, he never again commented on my performance.

Much to my surprise – and his, no doubt – I did pass my English GCE, probably because I always scored high for composition, comprehension and vocabulary. But I decided to cut my losses and although I loved books and literature, I didn't opt to take English at A level.

I never forgot Mr Casey, though, or what he did, so I named the heroine of my first-ever published novel, *No Cure for Love,* Ellen O'Casey as a sort of two fingers to him for the years of humiliation I suffered in his class.

When I started my fifth year of secondary school, we were plunged into our GCE exams. Well, that's to say we should have been had it not been for someone in Tower Hamlets Council's education department having the bright idea that rather than sitting the tried-and-tested and universally recognised Ordinary Level General Certificate of Education, we should take the untried Certificate of Secondary Education – CSEs – instead.

The argument for the new exams was that because they included coursework as well as a final exam it better reflected a child's ability. That may have been true as the GCSEs that replaced the GCEs in the 1980s also included this element of assessment.

In truth, the CSE was an attempt to make the attainment records for children in secondary modern schools look better, as even the poorest academic pupils could pass at a level four. But the most damning thing about them was that even if you passed at the top level it was the equivalent of a C, which was the lowest pass mark for an O level GCE. No matter how hard a secondary modern pupil worked or how intelligent they were, they could never compete with their grammar school or privately educated contemporaries with their solid GCE A and B passes.

Although in those days the actual grade wasn't displayed on the certificate – so in theory John Smith's grade one CSE could be the equivalent of John Brown's GCE pass – colleges and employers knew CSEs had been developed for the less academic, so those holding them were disadvantaged.

However, I didn't have a choice so I duly sat the six subjects offered in my art option stream. Apart from French, where I got a grade four, despite leaving most of my paper blank and managing only three phrases in the oral exam (thus proving the CSEs weren't exactly academically rigorous), I passed the rest at grade one. I also got an O level in art as, being considered an arty-farty subject, it wasn't included in the CSE exams. Because the school obviously didn't agree with the tin-pot dictators in the education department, when we moved up to the sixth form, we were given the option of retaking our subjects at O level. Naturally, we took up their offer, but it meant that for the next two years we were retaking O levels alongside out A level studies.

However, the exam debacle wasn't the only thing to mark our final term in the fifth year. Once our exams were completed, I had to face the prospect of losing many of my old Redcoat friends who, having turned sixteen, were heading off to the world of work.

We all wept and hugged each other as we said goodbye on that last day before the four classes of a hundred-plus pupils of our fifth year distilled down to the swots, like me, who were moving up to the sixth form in September.

As I'd always been good at art and had been making all my own clothes since I was fourteen, I had decided that being a fashion designer was the career for me. So when my exam results dropped on the doormat one morning, showing I'd done quite well, my father started talking about me going to art college after my A levels, which had always been his dream.

Of course, he added that I shouldn't rest on my laurels and I'd have to work hard, plus the usual 'you don't know how lucky you are' and 'I wish I'd had your opportunities', which after years of the same now just bounced off me.

My return to school in September that year was very different from previous years because instead of trooping into a classroom and sitting at our desks, this time we assembled in the sixth-form common room for registration.

Like the staffroom, our lounge was situated on the main corridor between the four-storey classroom block and the main hall. It was opposite the office of both the headmaster, who didn't teach and who we only saw for punishments, and the headmistress, and was furnished with easy chairs and a coffee table. It also had a small kitchen, and at the far end of the room there were lockers where we could store our books and bags.

Our promotion to school seniors meant other changes, too, notably not wearing school uniform like the rest of the school. There was a still a dress code, but it was more relaxed. The boys could wear black or grey trousers and white or light-blue shirts with their school tie, while the girls could wear a grey skirt of any design and a light-blue top, be it blouse or jumper. In addition, instead of the navy mac or blazer, we could wear any jacket or topcoat to and from school. There was an added bonus in that now, instead of having to sit with the rest of the school for morning assembly, we were allowed to sit in the first-floor gallery at the back of the hall.

The other change was that as many of our friends had left at the end of the previous school year, those of us who remained numbered only a dozen or so. Combined with the upper sixth this meant the sixth form consisted of no more than thirty students, all of whom were focused on getting their exams.

Naturally, as the newbies in this untried world of the sixth form, we stuck together, but with a comfy lounge at our disposal we soon found ourselves chatting with the upper-sixth students and drinking coke together during the private study gaps in our individual timetables.

The dozen or so upper-sixth girls were led by the prissy goody-two-shoes Brenda. She was also the head girl and unlike us, in our short dresses and tight-fitting tops, Brenda favoured a more secretarial look, which was indeed her career goal.

She always handed her homework in on time and instead of larking about in the common room, she and her handful of followers, clutching their workbooks to their chests, headed off to the library. With light-brown hair tied back in a ponytail and a fresh-faced complexion, she could have walked straight out of a 1950s bobby-socks teen movie.

She tried to establish her ascendancy over us as soon as we walked in on our first day but we gang of new sixth-formers were no longer easy meat so we told her to sling her hook, or words to that effect.

After years of being ruled by the school bell for as long as we could remember, the sixth form was a little strange at first as we were left to our own devices. Also, as we didn't have to be at school, we couldn't be truants so we could come and go pretty much as we liked. However, those of us who had opted to stay on past school-leaving age were now focused on getting good A level grades, so after the first week of sitting around doing nothing we all knuckled down to work. The teachers treated us as adults and we mostly rose to the challenge.

While university was murmured about, most of us were considering other options. I had my sights on the London School of Fashion to train in fashion and costume design. As by the end of the 1960s many of the grammar-school-only professions were starting to open up to us secondary-modern types, Audrey was intent on becoming a State Registered Nurse. A few others who'd moved up with us were looking at trainee posts in banking or commerce. I'm not sure what Iris Sinclair planned to do when she left school as her ambitions seemed to change weekly. This was hardly surprising as we were given the opportunity to visit different workplaces such as banks, shops and factories, where we were told what careers might be available to youngsters with a good education.

CHAPTER TWELVE

Joining the Workforce

B ACK IN THE late sixties and early seventies you could get your National Insurance number and leave school to start work at the end of the term before your sixteenth birthday. Predictably, as soon as it arrived my father announced that as I could now legally work I should get a Saturday job as he would no longer be giving me pocket money or paying for my clothes.

So, feeling like Oliver Twist asking for more, and dressed in my best coat and longest miniskirt, I trudged up and down Whitechapel market and other local shopping areas after school for a week enquiring in all the shops to see if they needed a Saturday girl.

After a couple of days of fruitless searching, I walked into Cohen & Sons, a chemist that stood in the middle of a row of shops on Commercial Road, almost opposite St Mary's and St Michael's Church.

The counter ran the length of the shop and on the right were displays of cough pastilles, make-up and razor blades. On the left of the room, there were glass cabinets filled with everything from hair dye to shaving foam, while at the far end were tins of formula milk and boxes of Cow & Gate baby food stacked high. Above the boxes was a window covered with mirrored strips that allowed the pharmacist to see into the shop but prevented customers from seeing into the dispensing room.

There was a rotating display of brushes, combs, slides and Alice bands and another stacked with greeting cards.

As I stopped beside the set of scales that were jammed up against the display of baby items, the owner came out from the dispensing area behind. With his long face and dark hair, the man in front of me could have been a stage stand-in for Michael Winters of the variety double act Mike and Bernie Winters.

Like most of the chemists, doctors and health professionals in East London at the time, the pharmacy's owner, Michael Cohen, was Jewish. He later told me he was actually the '& Son' in the name above the door. His father had bought the chemist in the 1930s when Mr Cohen Senior felt it was wise to leave Germany and join his brother, an optician, in England.

I gave my little spiel about how I was studying for my GSEs. Mr Cohen waved away my newly issued P46 and told me in addition to Saturdays they needed someone from five to seven two evenings a week. If I was interested, I could start right away.

Was I interested?

Blooming right I was, especially when I heard it paid three-pound ten shillings a week, which was a whole two pounds more than my pocket money. Having found out what time he wanted me to start, I practically skipped home and told my parents the news.

I duly arrived at eight-thirty on Saturday morning and was given a pink overall. Mr Cohen introduced me to his grumpy, overweight South African pharmacy assistant Leo, who barely acknowledged me, and the chemist's full-time shop assistant. At eighteen, Angela, apart from being very pretty, had that most prized of all things – a boyfriend. What's more, although she'd walked out of school with not even Pitman stage-one typing to her name, with a long blonde fringe that skimmed her eyelashes, and make-up that wouldn't have looked out of place on the front cover of *Cosmopolitan,* she epitomised the dolly-bird look that my school friends and I aspired to.

She also went to pubs and clubs, stayed out until late with friends and always dressed in the latest fashion. However, as well as being, to my innocent eyes, a sophisticated girl about town, she was also very friendly and put up with my blunders and general gormlessness on that first Saturday. When the door finally closed at the end of the day and we'd tidied away, Michael came out and handed me a brown envelope with my name on it.

Even though it was half a century ago I can still remember the thrill of opening my first wage packet. I spent it on rubbish, of course, but that's what you do when you're fifteen. Anyhow, after a couple of weeks I'd pretty much got the hang of where everything was in the shop and I'd also learned how to ignore Leo's sarcastic comments.

Angela and Michael had a low-level flirting thing going on which I found embarrassing, but when I asked her if she felt awkward with some of Michael's more suggestive comments she simply shrugged and said, 'That's just men.'

During the summer holidays I was asked if I could cover Angela's holiday as well as do the odd extra day here and there. I jumped at the chance, and with money in my pocket I decided to match Angela's swinging-sixties style.

I set about copying the helpful step-by-step make-up guides in *Jackie* and *Seventeen* to achieve the perfect Carnaby Street look. I started colouring my hair, too, beginning with Hint of a Tint's Copper before moving on to Nice'n'Easy's Burgundy.

Of course, my parents weren't impressed; while my mum just rolled her eyes, my father muttered sourly about 'looking like a dog's dinner'. It was water off a duck's back.

By the time I started working in the chemist, the block colours and geometric style of Mary Quant had been softened by the flowing flowery prints and beads of the Summer of Love hippy.

Although miniskirts were still very much *the* skirt length, the mid-calf and the longer maxi were also on trend. Often hotpants were worn under long flowing skirts left open at the front, and blouses were flowery and floaty rather than square cut and shirt-like. Short, Regency-style dresses, with puffy sleeves and lacy trimmings were popular with matching bloomers beneath.

When I wasn't actually working, I was hunched over my mum's sewing machine making myself hotpants, cheesecloth blouses and psychedelic hippy dresses. To add to my cutting-edge look I bought a pair of platform shoes, a wide floppy hat and a pair of octagonal, metal-framed sunglass. And of course, you couldn't be a real child of the Love and Peace generation without a bell dangling from a chain around your neck.

Working in the chemist, I learned how to ring up the till and how to take a packet of Dr White's from where they were kept behind the counter and put them discreetly in a bag without any of the other customers seeing them.

I soon got to know our regulars. The woman who bought Strawberry Kiss in the Born Blonde range every four weeks, the one who always asked for Bristow's Lanolin Shampoo because she had dry, unmanageable hair. There were more intimate purchases, too. The first time a woman asked me for a packet of 'French you-know-whats', I was completely flummoxed and had to ask Angela for help. Sliding out the top drawer under the till, she took out a pack of Durex and popped it in alongside the woman's other purchases.

Unsurprisingly, there were some regular male customers wanting to buy 'something for the weekend', too. One man who sticks in my mind came in every Friday night and bought two packets. I remember him because he was always in his bike leathers and wore a crash helmet, and although he was probably only in his early forties, as a wet-behind-the-ear teenager, I couldn't believe people of that age had sex.

Sadly, my well-paid job in the chemist lasted about eight or nine months before Mr Cohen took on another full-time shop assistant and I was no longer needed. I was pretty annoyed about this for a couple of reasons. Firstly, it deprived me of my three-pound ten shillings a week and secondly, I no longer had a non-stop supply of contraceptives. However, there was nothing for it but to find another Saturday job and my boyfriend would have to start digging deep in his pocket to buy his packets of threes.

So with my National Insurance number in my hand, I went to apply for a job at the company where almost every woman of my age had a Saturday job – Woolworth's. As there were Woolworth's stores in Bethnal Green, Stratford and East Ham, I had a few to choose from, but in the end I plumped for the one at Aldgate as it was just a bus ride away on the 6D.

It's hard for youngsters to imagine today, but during the 1960s you could start a job on Monday and if by lunchtime you'd decided you didn't like it, you could go back to the Labour Exchange the next day and they'd find you another.

It's true! I've done it.

CVs hadn't been invented at this time, and with hundreds of vacancies advertised in newspapers or pinned on the boards in the Labour Exchanges, it was easy to find work. If you walked into most shops and said you were looking for a job, you'd be taken to the manager there and then.

And that's what I did.

Dolling myself up in one of my new creations hot off my mum's sewing machine, I marched into the Woolworth's store in Aldgate after school one day. I collared one of the supervisors and told her I wanted to apply for a job as a Saturday girl. She took me to upstairs to the shop's office, where a pinch-faced manager in a cheap suit got me to fill in an application form.

Balancing on a wobbly table in the waiting area, I worked my way through the questions and then handed the form back. After giving it a cursory glance, the manager told me to come back next Saturday at eight-thirty and if my reference had been returned by then I could start.

It was, so I did.

The store famously advertised that it sold everything and it really did.

As you walked into Aldgate Woolworth's the first thing you could see was the records department, set out on the left-hand side of the store. The popular LPs were stacked on racks, while the singles and EPs were slotted in shelves behind the counter, above which was a board displaying the current top-ten singles and album charts.

Heading deeper into the store, you found the hardware section, which had with pots of paint artistically stacked into pyramids with bottles of turps, white spirit and paintbrushes displayed nearby. Packets of nails and screws of various sizes and types were set out on the counter alongside hammers, screw-drivers, files and hand drills, and on the wall behind the counter, wallpapers in designs exclusive to Woolworth's were papered up in strips for customers to see how they'd look on a wall.

Beyond that, the shop opened out and you were in the food section, where you could get most of your day-to-day groceries such as tea, butter and loose biscuits (including broken ones), all of which were sold by weight. In addition, you could have a pound of cheese cut from the block (with finger impressions in the side where the assistant had grasped it) or half a dozen rashers of bacon, which the assistant thumbed through to count the slices before peeling them away from the pile.

At the back of the shop was the homeware department, which stocked crockery, cutlery, kettles, pressure cookers, saucepans and Pyrex dishes. The whole right-hand side of the store was devoted to clothing, with the children's items, including the store's Ladybird range, next to womens-wear, which sold underwear, stockings and overalls. After which was the men's clothing, again mainly underwear, socks and workwear, such as dungarees, rough shirts and stout boots.

Finally, opposite the hardware department, was a small café which was sectioned off from the surrounding area with metal screens.

Everything else, like light fittings, toys, cosmetics, jewellery, books and the massive sweet counter were set out in the middle of the store.

Having donned my insipid green Bri-Nylon overall and with the floorboards squeaking under my feet, I followed the supervisor on to the shop floor for my first shift as a Saturday girl in Woolworth's. I was paired with a bubbly, round-faced girl called Alma who would show me the ropes. We'd been allocated to the toiletries section, which was in the middle of the store in front of the dangling plastic chandeliers of the lighting department, but unlike the chemist shop I'd been working in, I wasn't so much behind the counter as in the middle of it. Around me were packets of kirby grips, cellophane bags of hairnets and boxes of hair dye, all set out between glass dividers that were clipped together by metal joiners at the corners. There was a till at each end and as they were very like the one I'd used in the chemist's, I was soon ringing up sales and shovelling items into brown paper bags as if I'd been working there for months rather than hours.

Saturday was the main shopping day back then and although the store was situated on Aldgate's one-way system, Middlesex Street Market was only a few streets behind us and the side streets behind were crammed with shops and houses, so there were plenty of customers. In addition, old tenements like Rothschild's House at the back of Whitechapel High Street still housed thousands of families and the Boundary Estate was just a ten-minute walk away.

Tills then only rang up the total amount so if the customer bought several items, you had to calculate the cost – in pre-decimal pounds, shillings and pence – in your head. Although maths isn't my strong suit, as most of the goods on our counter were pennies rather than pounds, I very rarely resorted to the notepad and pencil in my pocket.

Another necessary skill when using the old tills was being able to stretch your fingers wide enough to reach all the round buttons needed to make the bell ring and the enamelled numbers displaying the total amount pop up in the till's window.

A couple of times a day, sniffy girls with leather satchels who'd been singled out for special duties would wander over to your counter. Their job was to extract all the pound and ten-shilling notes – you rarely got given a fiver – and take them back to the office. Sometimes one of the supervisors would descend on you and do a spot check on your till to make sure you weren't dipping your fingers in it.

The shop also had half a dozen male floorwalkers who prowled about keeping their eyes on customers and assistants alike, but they were easy to spot as they wandered around pretending to browse. On my first day, the other Saturday girls warned me to avoid getting too close to them if I didn't want to have my bum squeezed.

One of the floorwalkers, a lanky, spotty individual with greasy hair and particularly bad breath, often lurked around the back stairs. If you weren't quick he would back you threateningly into a corner and breathe halitosis over you. Of course, there was no such thing as sexual harass-ment or a complaints procedure, and if you tried to complain about a male member of staff having wandering hands you found yourself stuck in the paint department for weeks on end.

One of our big sellers on the toiletries counter was 4711 cologne, which was sold in quarter pint bottles. Some avid customers would buy two or three at a time. Another was tablets of rouge sold in small, round cardboard boxes. Like in the chemist's, 5 or 10 per cent hydrogen peroxide was a big seller, along with the accompanying blonde hair dye. Twinkie perms and rollers were also popular, as was the newly introduced 'Mum' deodorant.

Between taking money from customers, when the super-visor wasn't looking we Saturday girls would muck about and generally have a laugh.

Cut Adrift

I found out that the London College of Fashion in Oxford Street had two intakes for their Foundation course, so although I was too late for the September entrance I could apply in January. I would need to earn a crust until then, but with a postcard advertising for staff in every shop window and the Wanted columns in newspapers brimming over with jobs, I wasn't the slightest bit worried.

My friend Iris, whose parents were die-hard communists, was also a Saturday girl like the rest of us, but rather than working in a shop her job was in Islington Library. At that time, the library put on concerts, poetry readings and other events, many of which we would go to.

Although I'd never considered working in a library before, now, as I had three months until I hoped to start on the road to becoming the next Mary Quant, I trotted along to Tower Hamlets' main library in Bancroft Road. The building now houses Tower Hamlets' records and archives, but to me it will always be the place where I first learned to love books, as it was this library that my father used to take me to every Saturday when I was growing up.

When I pitched up looking for a job it was exactly the same as I remembered it from my childhood visits. The expansive marble foyer led to the children's library at the back of the building, while the elegant sweep of stairs took you up to the first floor where the adult and reference libraries were housed alongside the main office. In the stairwell, a painting of Abraham about to slaughter Isaac as he lay trussed up on a stone loomed over you as you progressed upwards. I remember it always gave me nightmares as a child.

After filling in a form and supplying references, I was told there was a job as an assistant at Whitechapel Library and I could start the following Monday.

In short, Whitechapel Library, which had opened just a few years after Jack the Ripper's bloody spree in the streets surrounding it, was the beating heart of education for the poor and marginalised in East London. It was situated alongside the Whitechapel Art Gallery, with one of the entrances from Aldgate East Station between the two buildings. Almost directly opposite were the remnants of Whitechapel's bombed parish church of St Mary's, the original white chapel. A stone's throw away around the corner was Brick Lane, which then was still a predominantly poor Jewish neighbourhood, and Wentworth Street Market was a short walk away in the other direction.

As you entered the library, its Victorian origins were apparent in the majolica green and cream tiles on the wall and the herringbone block-wood floor, plus a tiled scene of a brewer's dray being pulled by two horses which the librarian had rescued from a local public house before it was demolished. To your right was a marble staircase with wrought-iron balustrade leading up to the reference library and the staff- and storerooms.

The librarian in charge, Mr Levine, was a rounded kindly man in his late fifties with thinning grey hair. He had worked at the library for the past twenty years and had been instrumental in saving a vast collection of Hebrew literature that was now housed in a specialist area at the back of the library. In response to the steady influx of people arriving in East London from the Indian subcontinent, he'd built up a collection of books in Urdu, Punjabi and Hindi, which were also housed in a separate section.

There was one trained librarian to every three assistants and after a few days of being shown what my duties consisted of, I settled into the quiet routine of the library day. Well, I say quiet. Before the area was populated with fashionable coffee bars, world-class curry houses and art galleries, Spitalfields was knee-deep in meth drinkers, who could be seen staggering about the streets or lying unconscious on pavements at all hours. Almost every day one would career into the library, shouting and breathing stale spirits over everyone before the security guard was called to show them out.

Back then, you could only have a library membership if you lived in the same borough. However, being just a quarter of a mile from the City boundaries, with its office blocks and banks, Whitechapel Library introduced a new rule allowing borrowers to use their work address to join the library. Lunchtime was therefore busy, with City types in charcoal jackets, striped trousers and bowler hats browsing for the latest *Times* recommendation alongside cloth-capped stallholders searching for a meaty crime novel.

We had other regulars, too, mainly old Jewish ladies who would come in and hoover up half a dozen Mills & Boon books, only to bring them back a few days later and replace them with another six. And oh my goodness, when a new Netta Muskett was due out there was almost a war to reserve it first.

Another duty I loved being asked to do was an evening stint at the small library in Wapping, which had very limited opening times, or being sent as cover to Cable Street library. This was mainly because of Mr Grossman, the chief librarian.

He was a slight man with a head like a light bulb. His hair was brilliantined and he had a clipped moustache and thick-lensed spectacles. He'd arrived in East London as a baby, strapped to his mother's back, after his family fled the Russian pogroms. He and his family, who spoke no English, lived in one room in Old Montague Street and attended the local synagogue. He was another Whitechapel Library self-educator, so much so that from his unpromising beginnings he had risen to head librarian in charge of the new library situated next to Stepney Town Hall. He was a lifelong socialist who, unlike my Uncle Bobby, really had been in the thick of the fighting during the Battle of Cable Street and carried a scar on his forehead to prove it. He'd taken in Kindertransport children during the war, and as his poor eyesight prevented him from being called up, he'd been an air-raid warden, setting up a small library in his shelter. He'd also been one of the first on the scene after the original Cable Street Library was bombed to help salvage books.

In East London libraries today you often see an area set aside for children to do homework, but back then it was unusual. Due to his own childhood experiences, no doubt,

Mr Grossman set up an area in the library for that very purpose. Today he would have been called an activist as he was a well-known figure in the Jewish community.

Having lived in the area all his life, he was full of stories about Stepney, Whitechapel and Wapping, which had me enthralled, and he was always kind, letting us have an extra ten minutes or so for lunch if the library wasn't busy.

Bob-tails, Bow ties and Sticky-up Ears

I'd vaguely heard of Bunny Girls before I met Suzie, a fellow library assistant who had also just left school. She was blonde, only just skimmed five foot, and was the result of a wartime romance between her mother and a GI.

Suzie's father was a career soldier in the American Army and she and her older brother had actually been born in Texas. She also held an American and an English passport, which made her the closest thing to an international traveller I'd ever known.

Now, like me, Suzie had career ambitions, but not as the next hot fashion designer. No, she had her eye on something a little more unconventional, which I got roped into too.

The library was open through to eight o'clock in the evening, so the library assistants did a variety of nine o'clock and one o'clock starts each week. One day I was sitting in the staffroom munching through my packed lunch when Suzie, who was on the later shift, arrived for work. After hanging up her coat, she produced a copy of the *Evening News* from her handbag.

Turning to the back of the paper she showed me a Playboy Club advertisement. They were looking for Bunny Girls and she asked me if I'd go with her to the auditions. I was a bit taken aback – being a sex object in a satin corset and pointed ears hadn't been a career choice she'd mentioned before – but I thought: Why not? It'll be a laugh if nothing else.

Of course, I couldn't just pitch up and sit there while she wiggled back and forth upon the stage; I had to take part, too.

The auditions were in the Playboy Club on Park Lane, so the following week, with our swimsuits and highest heels in our handbags, we met up at Bethnal Green and jumped on the Central line to Marble Arch.

Feeling a little overwhelmed by all the glass, marble and chrome on display, we made our way over to the club's reception desk where two Bunny Girls, towering over us, took our names and directed us to a small ante-room. There were dozens of girls stripping off and squeezing into microscopic swimwear, so, finding a corner, we delved into our handbags and retrieved our costumes, a black all-in-one swimsuit in my case and a tiger-print bikini in Suzie's. Having changed, we clutched our clothes to us and wandered through to the satin-curtained and mirrored club where another couple of Bunny Girls told us to make ourselves comfortable until we were called.

We found ourselves a couple of chairs to the side of the stage and, with Suzie becoming increasingly nervous, watched as a dozen or so Bunny Girl hopefuls paraded one at a time across the stage.

At the end of their audition each girl would present herself to the three judges, to be directed either to the next stage of the audition or back to the changing room.

We sat there for about half an hour watching this parade of girls of all shapes, sizes and colours, mostly in bikinis, as they presented themselves to the judges, finally our names were called.

Leaving our clothes on our chairs we took our place at the side of the stage while the first couple of girls in our batch strutted their stuff. Then it was Suzie's turn.

She tottered back and forth across the stage in her high heels, stopping and turning as directed by the judges. She stood there for a moment while the judges conferred, then she was called forward.

With a look of eager anticipation on her face, she jumped down from the stage to join them. Her bright expression fell as they spoke to her, then she skulked back to where we'd been sitting to retrieve her clothes.

I stepped on to the stage and, feeling very embarrassed to be parading about in my swimsuit in front of three complete strangers, did the same as Suzie, ending with a bit of a whirl in the centre of the stage.

The judges conferred again, then called me forward. Not wanting to end up flat on my face, I stepped carefully off the stage and stood in front of them.

'Jean Fullerton?' asked the woman sitting at the end with the clipboard.

I nodded.

'Well, Jean, I'm pleased to tell you that we think you might just have the makings of a Bunny Girl,' she said. 'So if you'd like to make your way to the table at the back, you can fill in an application form.'

'But I just came here with my friend,' I replied. 'Sorry.'

Feeling my cheeks aflame and my heart thumping in my chest, I grabbed my clothes and dashed back to the changing room.

I was already hooking up my bra by the time Suzie joined me in the changing room.

'I know,' she said, as tears formed in her eyes. 'I'm really upset, too, about not being picked.'

For the sake of our friendship, as I pulled on my loon pants, I didn't reply.

My time working at the library was a happy one, not least because, seeing books pass before my eyes all day as I took them back in and stamped them out, I discovered a plethora of new authors. However, my aim was still to become a student at the London College of Fashion in January. And after a tour of the college's many departments and an interview, I was offered a place. When I told my father I would be starting there after Christmas, he broke the news that I would have to continue to give him my four-pounds-fifty-a-week housekeeping. I was shattered.

The course was full time, so I would only be able to work at weekends, and the most a Saturday job paid was three pounds fifty, which meant not only would I not have enough to pay him, but I'd have less than nothing to live on.

I did argue my case, saying he'd always talked about me going to college, to which he replied with his stock responses: I hadn't worked hard enough at school and I'd squandered my chances by going out all the time.

After reluctantly declining the place at the London College of Fashion, I stayed at the library through Christmas and the New Year. Meanwhile, I pondered what to do and scoured the fashion industry job columns of the local and evening newspapers. There were row upon row of ads for trainee and experienced machinists, but I wanted to design clothes, not sit at a bench all day making them. Unfortunately, all the other jobs in clothing manufacturing wanted experience, which I obviously didn't have.

There was one ad for an apprentice with the world-famous costumiers Bermans & Nathans at their North London workshop, which would have combined my two loves – fashion and history – perfectly. I applied for it but, again, even though I was offered the post, the pay was just six pounds a week. Once I deducted my weekly housekeeping I'd be left with one pound fifty for everything else, including my fare to and from work. Sadly, I had to turn the job down.

Thoroughly fed-up with life in general, and my father in particular, one lunchtime I crossed Aldgate's one-way system and headed to the Star Agency. It was situated at the top end of Leman Street and supplied staff to the clothing and tailoring trade.

Marching through the door with all the self-belief and bravado that only an eighteen year old can muster, I told the woman with orange hair behind the desk that I could draw, I made all my own clothes and I wanted a job in fashion. Looking up at me through the lenses of her cat-wing glasses, she smiled and said, 'That's lucky because I've just had a job for a design sketcher come in that might suit you perfectly.'

And so began my career in the fashion industry.

Carroty-haired Mrs Lewinski was right. The job on the index card she pulled out of the box on her desk was indeed perfect and was, in fact, based in a factory visible through the window of the employment agency.

My interview was the next day, so the following morning I arrived at Gold Fashions and was shown into the general manager's office on the second floor. He asked me a couple of questions and waved aside my GCE certificates as being irrelevant. He explained that Gold Fashions was a family-run business, that the pay was a full eight pounds fifty a week, then said he'd take me to meet the company's designer, Mr Sherman.

The creative talent at Gold Fashions had an office on the top floor next to the sample machinists' room. Mr Sherman sat behind a workbench that was covered with sketches and bits of fabric. Behind him was a corkboard with drawings of individual details like collars and cuffs, while next to the bench was a dressmaker's dummy modelling a dress minus its sleeves.

Sitting at the bench opposite him, perched on a high stool, was his pattern cutter, who was slicing off a length of card from the roll propped up under the window.

Mr Sherman was a fleshy man in his mid-forties, dressed in a roll-neck jumper and slacks, with a festoon of curls and perfectly manicured nails. He was about six foot tall, but with a small head, size-seven shoes and an expansive waist, he looked a bit like a whipping top. He looked me up and down, then thrust a sketch pad at me.

'Draw this,' he demanded, pointing to an image in the open copy of *Harper's* in front of him.

Picking up a pencil, I did and slid it back.

Satisfied I could actually draw, he then asked me to identify various swatches of fabric, which I did, after which he explained what the job entailed. In a nutshell, a sketcher is a general dogsbody who runs errands and assists the designer, but they are also required to do detailed drawings of each design in the company's style book along with notes on how much fabric, lining and interlining each garment requires. They also have to add information about any buttons, trim, lace and zips needed, ready for the design to go into mass production.

I took the job there and then. After working my week's notice at the library – as people were mainly paid weekly no one ever gave a month – I started at Gold Fashions straight away.

The company was housed in a three-storey building in Buckle Street. On the ground floor was the warehouse, which was always filled with row upon row of wheeled rails packed with cellophane-covered garments that were waiting to be sent out to shops and department stores all over the country. A couple of older men worked there under the direction of the stock controller, Albert. Albert spent his days with a pencil gripped between his uneven teeth as he counted dresses.

On the floor above was the stock room, which had floor-to-ceiling metal racks. Resting on these were industrial-sized rolls of fabric ranging from floaty chiffon to coarse tweed and stopping at crimplene and crêpe along the way. The huge bundles of material muted the noise and filled the whole area with the smell of newly milled cloth.

At the far end of the first floor was another set of shelves. These held boxes of zips of all sizes, buttons and reels of trim. This floor was overseen by Fred, who wore a buff-coloured overall and chain-smoked.

The second floor was the factory proper, where fifty or so machinists bent over their noisy machines. There was no tacking or pining; the women just put two edges together and guided the fabric beneath the machine's foot at it ran through at breakneck speed. An experienced machinist could knock out a dress every forty-five minutes to an hour before throwing it into the bin. The overlockers would then take a garment from the bin to finish the seams before sending it on to the woman operating the hemmer. Once the garment was finished, it would be thrown in a hopper for the pressers.

This breed of stout-armed women, who usually wore just their overall over their underwear as the work was so hot, would flatten the seams and iron out the creases in a haze of steam before putting the item of clothing on a hanger ready to be taken to the floor below for packaging.

Gold Fashions was owned by Jacob Goldstein, who despite being in his mid-sixties was still very active in the business, as was his wife Ruth, who was the general manager. Their two sons, Bernie and David, ran sales and distribution respectively, while David's wife Margot was the accountant.

Gillian Goldstein, the couple's only daughter, called herself a designer; however, it didn't take me long to realise that all her ideas were lifted off the pages of glossy magazines.

Although his initial response to me was cool, once I was installed in my place on the bench next to his pattern cutter, Mr Sherman was very friendly. He had a mincing walk and, to be honest, when I first met him I was convinced he was gay. However, you shouldn't judge a book by its cover as he had a wife who he adored and who he was constantly making dresses for. They had two children and lived in Golders Green. Having trained at St Martin's School of Art, unlike Gillian, he was a bona fide designer, and had worked in a minor couture house in Mayfair before joining Gold Fashions fifteen years previously.

His pattern cutter left about a month after I arrived and was replaced by a very bubbly young woman in her early thirties called Rosa. She was from Oporto in Portugal and an architect by trade, but she explained that designing a building so all the flat pieces fitted together to make a three-dimensional structure was exactly the same as constructing a garment, and truthfully she was right.

Another member of our merry band was Joan, the head sample machinist, who ran the small workshop of five in the room next to ours. She was a smartly dressed woman in her late forties and was, as the saying goes, well preserved. Like so many talented people, Mr Sherman suffered from self-doubt and could sometimes become almost tearful with anxiety. When this happened, we called for Joan. She would send us out of the room with the flick of an eye and then mother him back to his usual cheerfulness.

She was fiercely protective of him, too, as Rosa and I found to our cost when she bawled us out one day for repeating a sneering remark Mr Sherman had made.

However, despite these odd wobbles, and although I was very much the junior in the triumvirate, it was a happy office to work in. It was very instructive, too.

I'd been making my own clothes from patterns for almost six years by then, but Rosa showed me how to create and construct an original design, and she often gave me complex assignments like making collars and cuffs, moving darts or dividing the panels of a skirt into six or eight.

Mr Sherman always wanted to know what was going on in the factory and Rosa and I were more than happy to bring snippets of gossip back to the office, especially if it was something about Gillian. Actually, it was easy to oblige him on that score as she was always getting into a dispute with her father and brother Bernie, usually about the cost of her designs.

Machinists get paid by piecework, so the more garments they make in the day the more they get paid at the end of the week. The garments bundled up by the cutters were stacked on a bench and when the machinist finished one bundle, after getting the foreman to mark it up in the tally book, she'd collect another. However, not all bundles are created equal.

A straightforward three-panel skirt with a zip and a waistband would take an experienced machinist twenty minutes to run up. If it had six panels, two pockets with flaps and a button-fasten front, on the other hand, it would take her considerably longer.

As well as being the chief sample machinist and Mr Sherman's unofficial therapist, Joan was also the shop steward for the National Union of Tailors and Garment Workers. Before every new design went into production, she had to negotiate with the Goldsteins the rate for each garment.

It was often just pennies either way, between Joan and the Goldsteins, but you'd be surprised how much you could save in a run of a hundred dresses by losing just a couple of buttons or trimming the width of a skirt. Similarly, an over-complicated design that took longer to make cost the machinists money too, and Joan wasn't having that.

However, Gillian's designs, with all their trim and complicated patterns, often brought her father out of his office and to the cutting floor to tell her to alter her design to bring down the cost.

Even I, novice though I was, knew that just because you can draw something doesn't mean it can actually be made. However, her saviour on some of her more outlandish designs was her pattern cutter, Morris. Having started as an apprentice tailor at thirteen in his uncle's business, Morris had literally been in the business man and boy.

Stooped, balding and with hands gnarled from decades spent clutching shears, he looked ancient but was probably only in his early sixties. He could make even Gillian's clunky designs look as if they could grace a Paris catwalk. He was a master.

However, sometimes even he was defeated, such as the time she wanted to put three circular holes edged with diamante trim next to each other across the yoke of an evening dress. Of course, it could be done on a hand-made couture dress, but it's much trickier when you're trying to knock out two dozen a day on an industrial sewing machine.

Along the corridor from our workshop was Mr Gold's spacious office. Decorated with sofas and mirrors, it was where they held meetings and saw buyers. When they had a whole new collection to show, they would hire a couple of models who would commandeer the loo at the end of the corridor for their changing room and parade back and forth in Gold Fashions' latest styles.

However, if a buyer came in at some other time or there was a new style that needed to be looked at before deciding if it should go into production, then I was called upon.

I was a perfect twelve back then, so I'd head off to the toilet and return wearing whatever item had been selected. Although you might think I'd be thrilled at my chance to be a model, as back in the sixties and seventies that was one of the careers many girls aspired to, trotting about in front of the Goldsteins was not a pleasurable experience.

Mr Goldstein senior was all right, but his son Bernie was a very different matter. Invariably he'd brush his fingers across my breasts and bottom under the pretence of looking at the collar, buttons or the lay of the skirt from behind.

I lacked the confidence to speak up, for fear of him getting angry and handing me my cards. I'd like to think he wouldn't get away with it today, but sadly I'm sure there are still plenty of Bernies around intimidating young and inexperienced girls.

Other than these occasions, I enjoyed my time at Gold Fashions and was excited that I was starting the career I'd always dreamed of. However, it wasn't to last.

Despite the fact my father's aggressive socialist politics had been a constant topic of conversation when I was growing up, as a fashion-crazy teenager I was completely oblivious to the struggle between the Government and the unions that was raging during the early seventies. Unfortunately, my political ignorance couldn't last and after working happily alongside Mr Sherman and Rosa for almost a year, everything changed when Edward Heath announced just before the Christmas of 1973 that in response to the ongoing dispute with the National Union of Mineworkers the Government was introducing a three-day week.

To truly understand Thatcher's Britain of the 1980s you have to have lived as a working adult through the decay and strife of the 1970s. Dwindling coal reserves due to the miners' strikes and the effects of an ongoing oil crisis meant that electricity was also in short supply and so the government introduced that three-day week, which mean business could open only on three consecutive days. When they were open, they also had to operate shorter days.

This isn't the place to document and discuss the political wrangling between the Government and the National Union of Mineworkers, which would finally sweep the Conservatives back into power in 1979 after 1978's Winter of Discontent, but as a self-obsessed teenager even I noticed the daily newspapers' headlines of strikes, go-slows and mass picketing. Nor could I fail to notice that instead of being a hive of activity come six p.m. on a Wednesday night, Gold Fashions' building fell silent as the clattering sewing machines stopped and the lights went off.

Although all production came to a standstill on the days when we didn't have power, a few of us in dispatch and design still went into work. We huddled round the paraffin heater and worked while the winter daylight allowed us to see, which during a grey January wasn't often past three-thirty each afternoon.

Now, you might think being allowed to skive off early two days of week was a bit of a bonus, but it wasn't when you opened your pay packet at the end of the week. And it was no better at home. Although the conservation of electricity was only supposed to apply to industry, there were regular domestic power cuts too, and being without electricity was no joke, especially in the middle of winter and with the nights drawing in at four o'clock. People panicked as they realised they were facing hours sitting in the cold and dark.

Candles quickly sold out and even though my father had managed to secure a couple of dozen, we weren't allowed to use more than one or two at any time as we had to 'make 'em last'.

With no television and often no radio – battery-powered transistor radios had a life of about three hours – the only course of action was to go to bed, lighting our way upstairs with a candle like Wee Willie Winkie. And even then you couldn't escape the effects of the dispute, because there was a freezing-cold bed awaiting you.

This state of affairs dragged on all though January. I continued to go into work for the three days when the factory had power.

The situation was resolved when an election was called in February. Ted Heath's Conservative Government was kicked out, much to my father's jubilation, after which the returning minority Labour Government under Harold Wilson immediately gave in to the National Union of Mineworkers' demands and the lights went back on.

All was well.

Well, not quite. Despite my father lauding Labour's return as 'the triumph of the working man over the system', life began to change. For a start, although we didn't know it then, the three-day week was the death knell for clothing manufacturing in the UK.

Working as a sketcher at Gold Fashions was the perfect job, and I gained experience in all aspects of the fashion industry from the first design sketch to mass production, but in the end I felt it was time for me to take what I'd learned and move from East End pastures to new West End ones.

The Star Agency, who'd found me the job at Gold's, had a branch in Wardour Street in Soho. Having worked my notice, I jumped on a 25 bus to Oxford Street and presented myself at the dingy little office squashed between a strip club and a delicatessen.

The woman sitting behind the desk, with a cigarette between her lips and a telephone receiver wedged between her shoulder and ear, signalled to me to sit down. After a few moments she finished her somewhat heated conversation and turned her attention to me.

I explained where I'd been working for the past year, the skills I had acquired during that time and then told her that I was now looking for a training post as a pattern cutter.

Although the woman in front of me was a couple of decades younger than her orange-haired East End counterpart, she had the older woman's gimlet eye and after looking me over a couple of times she flicked her way through the box of postcards on her desk before pulling out a card. She informed me that they didn't have any trainee pattern cutter posts at the moment but there was one for a grader with the prestigious tailor Jaeger, if I'd like to be put forward for that instead. She also told me the pay, which was three pounds more each week than at Gold Fashions, so I said yes, please.

She got me an interview an hour later with a smartly dressed middle-aged woman who, after waving away my GCE certificate, took me into a nearby office and gave me the rundown of what the job entailed. She also said that in addition to my basic salary I'd get fifteen pence – about the cost of a sandwich – a day luncheon vouchers, then offered me the post on a one-month trial basis if I wanted it.

Three pounds a week more than I was currently on plus luncheon vouchers? Yes, please!

I returned the following Monday, bright and early, and was again met by Mrs Wright, who ushered me through the door at the end of a short corridor and introduced me to grey-haired Olive, who was standing by the workbench at the head of the room.

Just scrapping five foot and with the same hairstyle as the Queen, Olive had worked for Jaeger for almost twenty years, starting as a sample machinist and working her way up to be in charge of the grading department.

Having made the introductions, Mrs Wright left me in Olive's charge. After quizzing me on my experience, Olive explained that, staying true to its continental origins, Jaeger used metric rather than imperial measurement. Also, instead of using rulers to make the larger-sized patterns they used a grading machine.

Making a dress in a larger size isn't just a matter of making the sides a bit wider; the block pattern needs to be adjusted everywhere, from the armhole to the neckline, so it's quite a complicated and time-consuming business. The grading machine was clamped to the bench and had four arms which you attached to the original size-twelve pattern. Using two knobs to move the arms up and down or forwards and back by however many millimetres needed, you then marked the pattern with a pencil before shifting it another few millimetres for the next calculation.

During my time in the grading room, I got very friendly with Olive and even after our lives moved on, we kept in touch. She lived in Finchley and she, like my Aunt Elaine, couldn't conceive but, like many women at that time, she'd never troubled the doctor with the problem. Having accepted they would be childless, she and her husband Fred were always off on exotic holidays. (Well, Turkey and Greece, which were counted as exotic in the seventies.)

At first I was allocated simple patterns with just half a dozen pieces to grade up and down, but as the weeks went on, I was given more complicated designs. To grade a twelve-piece size twelve pattern up to a size eighteen and down to an eight took a couple of days, unless you had a very complicated pattern.

Jaeger was a very friendly place to work, with regular workshop lunches out to celebrate birthdays, engagements, weddings, new babies, Christmas and New Year. I have to say my time there was a happy one, as I progressed from trainee to qualified grader. However, it all came to an abrupt end just over two years after I started when we were all called into the boardroom and told the workshop was being relocated to the company's factory in Burgess Hill, Sussex, and anyone not able to relocate would be made redundant. Sadly, I was one of them.

I headed back to the agency on Wardour Street, but when they couldn't find me a suitable job in the West End, I returned to the Star Agency in Aldgate.

Thankfully they did have a post for a grader in a company called T&G Clothing, which was just past Christ Church

Spitalfields in Commercial Street. Like Gold Fashions it was owned and run by a Jewish family and the company made copies of West End styles for the mass market.

However, that's where the similarities ended. Rather than a post-war factory like the one Gold's was situated in, T&G's factory was housed in an old Victorian building. It was only two storeys high and much smaller than where I'd been used to working and with limited natural light. The grading department was housed in a plywood cubicle on the upper floor opposite the owner's office. I shared the space with the company's pattern cutter, an elderly chap with greasy grey hair who looked like Captain Birdseye.

At twenty I was very much the youngest member of the team, and what with the buck-toothed, oily-haired cutter making suggestive remarks every time I came on to the factory floor, plus having to listen to the owner through the thin partition wall as he had his weekly visit from a prostitute, it wasn't long before I started looking for something else.

It wasn't easy.

Whereas a few years before there had been 'wanted' signs outside every factory, now some of those establishments were boarded up. With cheap clothing starting to pour in from the Far East, Jaeger wasn't the only fashion house packing up their London operation and heading for greener and cheaper pastures new.

I managed to get a job as a pattern cutter in an Old Street factory, but as I stood there one day unpicking a Wallis dress so I could copy the pattern, it dawned on me. I wasn't about to break into the fashion industry as the next Mary Quant or Ossie Clark; instead, I was stuck in a dead-end job in a dirty East End factory. It was time for a big change.

CHAPTER THIRTEEN

Broken Family

MY BROTHER AND I were sitting watching TV as the sound of my mother's feet running upstairs thundered above us. Father came into the lounge and took his usual chair by the fire. He told us to take no notice of our mum as she was just getting herself in a state over nothing.

We sat there for about five minutes then my mum burst in. She announced that she'd swallowed all of my father's digoxin heart tablets before collapsing on the floor. My father dialled 999 while my brother and I watched the colour drain from our mother's face as she lay on the floor.

Fortunately, the London Hospital was only a ten-minute drive away and the ambulance arrived within a few moments and, in full view of our neighbours, my mum was wheeled along the balcony and taken down.

However, shocking though this was, it didn't come completely out of the blue.

By the time I started in the sixth form at school, both my parents were working. With me and my brother 'off her hands', as my mum called it, they should have been looking forward to having some time to themselves as a couple; instead, the tensions that had been hidden beneath the surface of their marriage for many years broke through.

Because of her early life, my mum's mental health had always been precarious, but as she entered the menopause things got worse. There was not the variety of psychiatric drugs that are available today, so, after a visit to the GP, my mum was prescribed Mogadon, the drug of choice at that time for all sorts of mental health issues.

She was also put under the care of a psychiatrist in the London Hospital who offered her cognitive therapy to help get to the root cause of her ongoing depression. During those sessions she talked, probably for the first time ever, about her childhood and her relationship with my father.

She also agreed alongside the counselling sessions to receive treatment as a day patient in St Clement's Hospital in Mile End, where it was suggested by the consultant that she might benefit from electroconvulsive therapy.

My father, with his blind faith in experts in general and doctors in particular, was all for it, assuring us children that it was for the best. And so, full of hope that after her treatment my parents would become the people who had given me such a happy childhood, I waved my mum off on the day she was admitted to St Clement's Hospital for the prescribed two rounds of electroconvulsive therapy.

As she was required to stay in for observation after her treatment, I popped in to see her after school. And that visit has haunted me ever since.

St Clement's Mental Health Hospital had once been Stepney's workhouse and despite the change of name, the white tiles on the floor and the grey emulsion on the walls had the unmistakable stamp of the poor house. The smell of stale urine and disinfectant hit me square in the face as I walked in. Terrified of being attacked by one of the grubbily dressed people rocking and muttering incoherently, I made my way down the echoing corridors to my mum's ward.

I had expected the place my mum was being cared for to be like the wards in the London Hospital, with bustling nurses in lilac uniforms and starched aprons and patients propped up under clean sheets or sitting by the side of their beds. Nothing could have been further from the truth.

This place seemed to be full of elderly women in faded nightdresses who were either drooped lifelessly in chairs or screaming and thrashing about in seats that were tipped backwards. It made no sense to me as to why some were clutching dolls while others lay curled up on their beds.

Having told the nurse who was sitting smoking at the desk by the ward door that I was visiting my mum, she pointed me down the rows of beds in the Nightingale Ward towards the far end. I found my mum lying on a bed with her eyes closed. To be honest, I nearly walked past her as she was in the same shabby nightwear as the rest of the patients and without her make-up she was almost unrecognisable.

I managed to rouse her, but she was very lethargic, and her speech was slightly slurred. She rallied a bit and asked me about school. I started to tell her but then halfway through she fell back to sleep. Afraid there was something wrong, I hurried over to the nurse at the desk. She reassured me that patients were usually a bit groggy for a day or two after the procedure, but it was nothing to worry about as my mum would be as right as rain in a few days.

Walking back through the noise and mayhem of the ward, I sat by her bed, holding her hand for a few more moments then, feeling overwhelmed by it all, I gave her a quick peck goodbye and left.

I used this incident for a scene in *Call Nurse Millie,* when my heroine, Millie Sullivan, visited her mother in the same institution. I can't tell you how many emails I got from people telling me how reading it made them cry.

Thankfully, within a few days Mum was back at home but she continued under the care of the psychiatric department of the hospital and resumed the cognitive therapy. However, my mum's mental health wasn't the root of the problem between my parents.

Still crippled by a lack of confidence and haunted by his experiences of poverty in his early life, my father was very reluctant to spend money, and certainly wouldn't dream of taking out hire purchase. He didn't believe in house or life insurance either, which meant that he always felt the need to keep money in the bank. Even though he worked for Ford and would have got a hefty discount, we never had a car, which meant a long trek on public transport to see friends and relations.

Even his promotion into the office following his win at the art exhibition hadn't helped his self-esteem. I think after his early success he hoped he might be drawn into the local art fraternity, but by the time I reached secondary school that hope had long faded. He grew bitter, blaming the nebulous 'they' for keeping people like him at the bottom of the pile.

Some years later he entered one of his paintings into the Royal Academy Summer Exhibition for consideration. It was rejected, which only added to his belief that 'they', the Establishment, were against people like him, so what was the point of trying? Unsurprisingly, he never entered another.

By now, even with the lucky break that had propelled him into Ford's drawing office, my father's lack of education and the sense that he'd missed out on life's opportunities were beginning to crush him.

In contrast to my father's worsening state of mind, thanks to the counselling and medication, my mum's mental health began to stabilise. She was by now very much part of the community at St Dunstan's, and she encouraged my father to attend events instead of just staying on the periphery. He did, but always had a sour remark once we'd got home.

In an attempt to include him, the rector asked if he'd like to illustrate the front of the parish magazine. Pleased to have his talent put to use, he accepted, starting with images of the church and moving on to the chalice and old memorials. Everyone was happy to begin with, until he started drawing darker scenes that touched on poverty and social issues. People grumbled but he dismissed them, accusing them of wanting to bury their heads in the sand. However, the growing discontent came to a climax one Christmas and New Year.

Instead of depicting a Nativity scene or showing the wise men following a star, he drew a picture of a starving African mother and her baby lying next to a meths drinker on a bench. For the New Year's edition of the parish magazine, he produced a full-page spread depicting starving children, nuclear bombs, drunks, privilege and violence, topping it off by writing 'Happy New Year' beneath.

It was too much for the congregation and they complained en masse to the rector, who came around to see my father. I don't know what was said exactly, but after that he had no time for anyone in church.

Now, I'm not saying he was wrong to try to draw attention to social and political issues, but I think it is a stark illustration of how disillusioned he was feeling with life at that time.

Naturally, the whole incident upset my mum terribly. She accused him of always pushing people too far and he countered by shouting back that they were all a bunch of 'bloody hypocrites'.

There was a temporary ceasefire between my parents after that, not because they had resolved anything but because I suspect neither one of them could be bothered to talk to the other. The atmosphere around the kitchen table each night was glacial, to put it mildly.

As I was sixteen by this time, I just ate my evening meal, got changed and went out. I couldn't bear sitting with them night after night, watching TV and pretending to be a happy family when we weren't. I would go to a friend's or a boyfriend's house, returning late when I knew they would both be in bed.

My mum resumed her regular trips to the psychiatrist and surmised that her suicide attempts were linked not only to her childhood but also to her relationship with my father. He started attending the sessions with her, after which things between them deteriorated even further.

We lived in a small maisonette with thin partition walls between the rooms. Even with the TV on in the lounge or if I was upstairs in my bedroom, I could hear the shouts and accusations. There was no escape from it.

I think my father pressed for the doctors to commit my mum to hospital, arguing that he feared her erratic behaviour would have a lasting effect on me and my brother, but instead the medics offered a weekly family therapy session, which he agreed to.

Instead of going to the hospital, we had a psychiatrist, in worn corduroy trousers, an ill-fitting sports jacket and a straggly beard, turn up at our house. I can't remember all that was said, but it went on week after week, with my father often interjecting to point out to the psychiatrist how much we children were affected by my mum's 'mental' problems.

I went along with it for a bit, but I didn't like talking about personal things to this stranger who just scribbled notes and said nothing. One day I lost my temper and shouted at the psychiatrist that he didn't care about us, he was just here to write us up as a case study for his PhD. I stormed out of the room. My father followed, asking me to come back as the psychiatrist was an expert and only trying to help us. I refused.

The therapy sessions at home lasted for a bit longer but despite my father's constant cajoling, I never went to another.

Then my mum tried to kill herself again.

This time by slashing her wrist. She walked into the kitchen just after we'd finished our evening meal, covered with blood. My father wrapped her arms in towels and called 999. The ambulance arrived and again, with our neighbours and everyone else in the street watching, she was taken off to hospital. This time she was kept in and transferred to Claybury, the very same hospital her mother had been taken to over half a century before.

Although our family life lay shattered at our feet, we struggled on. With his packed lunch in his briefcase, my father went to work each day. I took over the household tasks alongside studying for my A levels and my brother, who was in the second year of his senior school at the time, returned to his class.

Over the previous couple of years my father's angina had become progressively worse but I never dreamed that one day, as I was cooking tea for me and my brother, my Aunt Martha and Uncle Wag would knock and tell me that they had just a phone call from the 'London' and that my father was on the cardiac ward in the hospital.

We ran to the hospital and found him sitting up in bed, wired to a monitor and with an oxygen mask over his nose and mouth.

I was about seventeen by then; my brother would have been just twelve. Although I'd probably escape the council taking me into care, my father knew they wouldn't hesitate to take my brother, so as well as giving me all the money in his wallet, he told me to look after my brother but not to tell his school.

So for two weeks, while my parents were both in hospital, I shopped, cooked and did the laundry, until my father – clutching a whole raft of new medication – was discharged.

When the discussion turned to my mother's return home, however, my father finally managed to wring out of one of her psychiatrists an admission that the disruption caused by her suicide attempts and her erratic behaviour might have a long-term detrimental effect on me and my brother.

That was enough for my father. He made it clear that in order to protect his children from any further harm, my mum couldn't come home.

I don't know what happened next exactly, but St Dunstan's Church must have stepped in. St Thomas's Church in Arbour Square had been obliterated during the Blitz and its assets had been incorporated into St Dunstan's Church. A small block of flats had been built on the site and St Dunstan's parish council could nominate people as tenants, which is how my mum ended up with one of the one-bedroom flats. Her friends from the church must have helped her furnish it as, other than a couple of suitcases of clothes, which someone collected for her, she took nothing else from home.

It's not unusual now for children to stay with their father after a marital break-up. However, back then it was almost unheard of. I was just seventeen when my mum left the family home for ever, and we – my father, brother and I – tried to return to some sort of semblance of normal life.

Thankfully, my father's morose mood lightened a little after my mum left, but the credit for this should rightly go to my brother. Unlike me, who'd 'wasted' my opportunities, he had gained a string of O levels, he was predicted solid A level results and planned to go to university, fulfilling my father's dream by proxy.

As my father was still several years away from being able to retire, he soldiered on, getting up each morning at six and heading off to the station with his sandwiches in his briefcase and dragging himself back home again each night.

As family life at home settled down, I re-established my relationship with my mum, going to visit her on Saturday afternoons for tea and a chat. Having found new freedom, my mum started to blossom. She made new friends and, with no meal to put on the table each evening, increased her working hours to full time. For the first time in her life she could do what she liked with her money. She didn't have much left after her rent and bills, but she was notably happier.

For my visits she would buy a cake and get out her newly acquired tea set and then, as we sat in front of the electric fire in her little flat, we chatted. She asked me what I'd been up to in the week, how my job was going, what my friends were doing and how my brother was getting on at school.

In turn, I asked her what was happening at the church and her work. Of course, she had always been very involved with St Dunstan's, but now she seemed to be at Bible study, Mothers'

Union or some other special event at least a couple of times a week, and she was always taking someone new under her wing just 'to be friendly'. She'd also made friends with people in her block of flats, doing little errands for an old couple on the ground floor if they couldn't get out.

She was always happy to see me and she'd often bought me 'a little something': a pair of tights or a fancy soap she'd seen in the market. One day she presented me with a crystal vase she'd bought, telling me that although I wasn't planning on getting married, she thought it would be a nice thing to have when I did.

Although I know my father went around there once in a while, presumably to give her some money, my mum never mentioned him, so neither did I.

Slowly, over the months, we started building the mother-daughter relationship we'd never had, and then she was gone.

We were eating our evening meal on 11 December 1975 when my father had a phone call from St Dunstan's rector telling him that if he wanted to see his wife again before she died, he'd better get to Bancroft Hospital.

We found her lying unconscious in bed with an oxygen mask. The doctor arrived and told us that she had collapsed in the street three days earlier and had been rushed into hospital, where it was discovered she had pneumonia. Despite being given penicillin, the infection had filled her lungs and now it was just a matter of time.

When asked why he hadn't been rung, my father was told they'd only found the name and telephone number of St Dunstan's rectory in her purse so they'd contacted the rector.

My father, stony-faced, walked around the bed and slumped down in the chair next to me.

Stunned, I took my mum's limp hand.

The mum who treated herself to a new hat each Easter and who sang along to the radio had been replaced by a grey, unresponsive woman struggling to breathe her last breath.

We sat there for a while in silence, then my father said she didn't know we were there and there was nothing we could do so we should go as we were only getting in the way.

I said I wanted to stay a little longer.

Half an hour or so later, he insisted we go as he didn't want to leave my brother too long by himself in the house. I bent over and gave my mum a kiss on her damp forehead and whispered 'I love you', then, walking behind my father, we left the ward.

She died an hour later.

I was just twenty-one and regret to this day that I didn't ignore my father and stay with her.

Her funeral service was in St Dunstan's Church just over a week later on 22 December. My brother and I sat at the front on the right next to my father, with my Aunt Nell, my grandfather and my Aunt Gladys in the second pew. Behind them, the Fullertons, wearing solemn faces and their deepest black, brought up the rear.

The left side of the church was packed with members of the congregation and my mum's friends from the various clubs she belonged to, as well as neighbours from her flat.

As my mum's coffin was brought in and placed before the altar, people started crying, including my grandfather and Aunt

Gladys, who just sobbed quietly behind us.

I couldn't. The wooden box on trestle legs in front of me had nothing to do with the woman who had chatted about the coach trip to see Southend's Christmas lights just a couple of weeks before.

I can't remember what the rector said or anything about the service until the end when the funeral directors came back in and shouldered the coffin.

Slowly, with me, my brother and father leading the way, we filed out after it. However, as we reached the main door, the senior undertaker stopped us and said there were a few people outside who might be a bit noisy. He told us to just keep walking and quickly get in the car.

Wondering what he could possibly mean, I carried on walking beside my father. As we emerged from the church, a crowd of women who had gathered by the railings to the right of us started screaming '*bloody hypocrite*', '*you killed her*' and other insults at my father as we scrambled into the car.

As my father had only booked one family Daimler to follow the coffin to the City of London Cemetery, my aunts Nell and Gladys and my grandfather were also travelling in the car with us. Unsurprisingly, no one spoke a word for the whole forty-minute journey.

The cremation itself was a brief affair, but as my mum's coffin rolled away and the curtains closed, I finally started crying. Not so much for my mum, who was now beyond all pain and suffering, but for myself.

My mother, who didn't buy into the whole philosophy of

allowing children free expression, gave me a sound smacking on the back of the legs more than once. But no matter how badly I behaved, and believe me I was a monster-child sometimes, she was always there with a kiss and a cuddle. She would grab me and my brother and say she could 'eat us' in the same way I did to my children.

I'm ashamed to say, for most of my teenage years I treated her arrogantly and dismissed her as unimportant.

But when she moved out and found her freedom, I believe she started to play a long game. Despite our turbulent family life, she was our mum and perhaps she knew that eventually, as I grew older, I would start to see the events of the past years and the family's break-up from a different perspective.

And she was right, but sadly, when I did, she'd been dead for almost a decade.

When we cleared out her effects there was no sign of her three-stone engagement or wedding ring; however, we did find a pawn ticket with just two days until it expired.

My father was going to throw it away with the rest of the rubbish, but I went to the pawnbroker's. After handing over the five pounds required, he gave me her wedding ring, which is on the third finger of my right hands as I type these words.

CHAPTER FOURTEEN

The Times They Are a-Changing

FROM AN EARLY age children today are given books describing how babies are conceived and born. The subject of sex and relationships, in terms of both biology and psychology, is discussed quite openly in most families. But when I was young, parents were not so forthcoming as to the whys and wherefores of reproduction.

Partly, this was because many of them were unsure of it themselves; during my nursing career I met women of my parents' generation who'd had no idea what to expect on their wedding night or exactly where babies appeared from.

Sex was something that you didn't talk about. It was right and proper if you were married but if you weren't it was shameful. When I was a teenager, anyone who had sex with the lights on was considered daring.

Of course, I'm sure all sorts of things went on behind closed doors, as they have since the world began, but when I was a child my understanding of what went on between men and women was – well, nothing because the subject was never mentioned.

I remember a tiny child with light-red hair and freckles called Susan, who was the leader of a little gang who all lived on the same housing estate and hung around in the playground together. I don't know why she was so popular, but I suppose that's the mystery of group dynamics.

I was on the periphery of the group – they would pick me if they wanted someone to turn the skipping rope but they'd give me the cold shoulder if they were organising a little ballet routine amongst themselves for the next drama lesson. I wasn't too bothered as I had other friends who, like me, weren't part of the popular bubble, but at some point during fourth year, I suddenly found myself the focus of their attention and not always in a good way.

The trouble was that despite being the youngest in my class, by the time I got to the top year at school, I was almost five foot tall with a burgeoning bust, whereas my classmates still looked like little girls.

The first upshot of my new towering stature was being assigned the position of permanent goalkeeper in the netball team; the second was that I received a certain amount of sharp-eyed envy from the popular gang, the members of whom, like their diminutive leader Susan, all had chests like two peas on a breadboard.

Back then, only physical assault counted as bullying, so sly remarks about my home-made clothes, giggling about my gawky size and my pointed exclusion from playground games were regarded as a normal part of growing up. I told my mum, but her answer was, 'That's what kids are like.' She also added, completely falsely, that, 'Sticks and stone will break your bones but names will never hurt you' and advised me to 'just to ignore them'.

I held my own, until one day I wandered into a huddle of girls surrounding Susan as she told everyone, with the voice of an acknowledged expert, the facts of life. She explained what her sister had told her.

'One day you'll ask your boyfriend to zip up your dress or something,' said the ginger wee know-all, 'and he'll push you on the bed then pull your knickers down. Then he'll put his sausage between your legs and into the hole where your wee comes out and that's how you have a baby.'

The pigtailed audience was agog, until I pitched in and said, 'Babies come from God, who leaves them at the hospital so the mums can go and get them.'

Quite a few of the schoolchildren around us started nodding, as this was the story told to children considered too young to know the truth. Susan, however, went the colour of her hair and she rounded on me. She marched over and hit me. I shoved her and she staggered back.

'It's the daddy puts the baby in the mummy's tummy,' yelled Susan, springing back into action. 'And they come out of the belly button. That's what my sister said and she knows because she's grown up and wears a brassiere.'

The carroty conqueror then ran off to inform the boys in the class what I'd said and so all afternoon I had classmates looking slyly across at me, sniggering.

Red-faced and smarting with humiliation, I dashed out of the gates after school. On arriving home, I asked my mum where babies really came from to which she replied, 'I'll tell you when you're older.'

Not satisfied with that, when my father returned from work three hours later, I asked him the same question. Knowing that the human reproductive system was one of the few topics not covered in the Books of Knowledge, he squirmed with embarrassment. However, desperate to be an enlightened modern parent, he told me he didn't have time to explain now but he promised to do so the next day when he had more time.

The next day duly arrived and I waited patiently for him to finish his evening meal. While my mum was getting my brother ready for bed, I asked him the question again. This time, instead of giving me a full and frank explanation about conception and birth, he delved into his briefcase and pulled out a slim green book.

'There you are,' he said, handing it to me. 'This book will tell you everything you need to know because it's written by an expert doctor.'

With that, he picked up his cup of tea and left the kitchen to watch the news on the TV.

Although the little book did cover menstruation, conception and birth, probably being too embarrassed to stand in WH Smith in Stratford for any length of time looking at a sex education book, my father had bought one written for boys. Of course, after I'd read it, I stopped worrying about waking up with an erection or having a wet dream!

For as long as I can remember I've been a hopeless romantic, imagining myself as Maid Marian to Richard Greene's Robin Hood or as one of the doe-eyed Spanish ladies who'd 'gone a roving' with swashbuckling Captain Dan Tempest in *The Buccaneers,* and *Heidi* was my favourite book because of the childish romance between Heidi and Peter the goat herder.

I'd fallen in love with Micky Dolenz who played Corky in the *Elephant Boy* at about six – and I'd fall in love with him all over again when he returned in *The Monkees* when I was thirteen – so I was no stranger to love, but this time, instead of a historic figure or a character from a book or on TV, I'd fallen in love with Peter Kemp, he of the angelic voice in school carol concerts fame, an eleven-year-old boy who sat across the classroom from me.

Truthfully, I don't know why because with uneven yellow teeth and unruly mousy hair, he didn't have much to set a young girl's heart aflutter. However, he must have had something because there were a handful of other girls in my year who had taken a fancy to him, one of them being the ginger gangster Popular Susan.

They were a bit of a couple in the class, if such a thing could be, as she always nabbed him as her partner for country dancing and if she was the starring role in a play, she always coerced him into being the hero, but this didn't stop me from casting him as my own romantic lead.

The sausage discussion wasn't an isolated incident, as boys and what you were supposed to do with them was an ongoing topic in the top year of junior school. Although some children were still very much pre-pubescent, there were a few who, like me, had started to bloom. A few of the boys, too, had darkening top lips and ridiculously long legs sprouting from their school shorts.

Play changed, too, as games like kiss chase started between the older children, with certain girls being cornered and subjected to inept sloppy kisses. I've got to say, towering over most of the boys in my class and with a layer of puppy fat, I wasn't much pursued. However, although they were very much about courtship rather than any under-the-bedcovers stuff, I'd been making up romantic stories in my head for as long as I could remember, so I was definitely interested in the grubbier sex. Judging from the way the boys skulked in corners secretly giggling at girly magazines, I have a pretty good idea what the boys were interested in, but for us girls it was all about getting a boyfriend. And was it any wonder, when we had Snow White and Cinderella as our role models and songs like 'Bobby's Girl' blaring out of the radio?

Now, for those of you who don't know this little ditty, it's about a girl who just wants to be some chap called Bobby's girlfriend. During the course of the song she states this is all she wants to be and if she were ever lucky enough to be 'Bobby's Girl' she'd be grateful and thankful. Appalling, I know!

However, even though the boys and girls in my year had started to eye each other with new interest, unless you wanted to endure days of mickey-taking and classmates taunting 'kiss, kiss, kiss' as they shoved the two of you together, you kept any romantic feelings very quiet.

Sadly, for me, and much to my eternal humiliation, while we were on the fourth-year school trip to Bexhill my secret love for the decidedly average Pete Kemp was wheedled out of me one day.

Popular Susan was informed and, surrounded by her posse, confronted me about it during one of our afternoon nature rambles. I denied it, of course, but I clearly wasn't very convincing.

Almost in tears, she asked what I was playing at as everyone knew she liked him. Then, without waiting for an answer, she grabbed my arm, and with her fluttering minions scurrying behind us, dragged me across the field to Pete Kemp.

During our earlier visit to the museum, the guide showing us around had explained how the contents of an egg could be blown out through pinholes in the shell to preserve them for display. Unfortunately, Pete Kemp was at that very moment trying this technique out for himself using an egg he'd found in a hedge. Startled by our sudden arrival, he forgot what he was doing and sucked in the snotty contents.

Ignoring his spluttering and gagging, Susan told him of my secret and asked him if he loved me too. Cornered by a group of girls and with a face the colour of a beetroot, Pete Kemp fell back on the killer 'I like you as a friend' line.

'Because you like someone else, don't you?' prompted Popular Susan.

Still spitting egg from his mouth, Pete nodded.

'See, Jean, I told you,' she shouted, then, leaving me standing in the field, she and her entourage stormed off.

Wishing the ground would open beneath me, I looked across at the object of my affection. I stared at him for a moment and then fled back to my friends.

We both endured days of ribbing from our classmates, with Susan making sure she was always near Pete when we lined up for at lunch. To be honest, my interest in Pete Kemp waned almost immediately my secret was out.

Having only just turned eleven a month before, I was surprised that a few weeks after I arrived at secondary school, I had my first period.

Thanks to that natty little book my father had given me the year before, I knew what the smear of blood on my knickers meant as I prepared to go to school. Hopeful for a day off school, I bounced down the stairs in our maisonette and informed my mother, who was washing up in the kitchen, that I'd 'come on'.

Leaving her task, she marched me back upstairs. After fumbling around in her top drawer, she gave me a small box and what looked like a slab of cotton wool and imparted her one and only piece of sex education by informing me that I 'was a woman now'.

The box my mum had given me contained an elastic belt with a couple of hooks dangling from it which attached to the loops at either end of the towel. Young women today should be very grateful for the slimline towels and tampons that are available now because, believe me, Dr White's, the only brand of sanitary towel available then, felt like you were wearing a pillow between your legs. If that wasn't uncomfortable enough, after a few hours of wear they solidified into a mass that made you feel as if you were sitting on a narrow, triangular beam.

As Ignorance was one of the Five Giants that needed slaying, the powers that be in the council's education department deemed it their duty to enlighten pupils on the facts of life when we got to senior school.

Towards the end of the first year in St Trinian's, I mean Redcoat Secondary Modern, we arrived at our cookery lesson one afternoon to find our teacher at her usual place at the front of the class, but with a district nurse who looked like an all-in wrestler standing beside her.

Once we'd settled on our stools, our cookery teacher announced that this afternoon, instead of pummelling grey pastry or getting covered in raw egg, Sister Whoever-she-was would be talking to us about a very important subject: the facts of life.

What followed was an hour and a half of hand-drawn diagrams showing us the reproductive parts of the female and the male, which made us squirm and giggle in equal measure. The session concluded with the nurse showing us what a Dr White's sanitary towel was and how to wear it, something probably half of us had already mastered.

Of course, Sister Whoever-she-was made a big mistake by asking if we had any questions, as she then had to explain that 'no, you couldn't get pregnant just wearing a pair of boys' pyjamas' and 'no, you didn't become a virgin again if you didn't have sex for a year'.

Of course, they weren't real questions but just designed to wind her up. Anyone who had a real query certainly wouldn't air it in front of their mates. Well, not unless they wanted to have the mickey mercilessly taken out of them for the rest of their school life.

Finally, having handed out several leaflets on menstruation and hygiene, our domestic science teacher thanked Sister Whoever-she-was for her informative talk and the nurse departed.

'Well, I hope you found that interesting, girls,' our cookery teacher said, as the door closed.

'Yes, miss,' we chanted.

'Good, but there's one bit of advice I'd like to add,' she said. Crossing her arms over her ample bosom, her eyes ran over us. 'Keep your legs together until you've got a wedding ring on your finger.'

Obviously, on the cusp of our teen years and in the middle of the Swinging Sixties, it wasn't a piece of advice most of us would follow.

Thanks to that little book my father had given me, I was pretty much up to speed with the mechanics of sex. However, as a couple of girls in the class later found themselves in the family way because they believed you couldn't get pregnant the first time, I guess this attempt at enlightening us was well meant.

It's also worth noting that other than our cookery teacher's words of advice at the end of the talk, there was no reference to any sort of contraception during the whole afternoon.

Inconvenient though periods were, they did confer on me a bit of status among my peers, as they signalled that I'd moved from childhood to, if not full womanhood, certainly teenagerdom. This rite of passage also coincided with the start of a new school, and the added bonus that there was a whole new crop of boys to ogle. I wasn't sure how you went about attracting boys, but I decided that perhaps it was time to find out.

My first step in this process was that I started shaving my legs, secretly using my father's razor. I then concluded that, as the school's policy on uniform was non-existent, I would ditch the sensible skirts and blouses and go straight into miniskirts and cropped jumpers, like every other girl in the school. Also, as I'd never been allowed to have long hair because 'it was too much trouble and attracted nits', I announced that henceforth I was growing my hair, and I have worn it long ever since.

Sixties make-up was nothing if not bold. The baby-doll look, as popularised by Twiggy, was what we were aiming for so after liberally applying panstick (foundation that came in a short, black tube), you added blue or green eyeshadow before sweeping a thick line of black eyeliner along both upper and lower lids. The next step was to apply mascara as thickly as possible, again to both sets of lashes. Thankfully, as the cylinder-and-brush configuration had just come out, I no longer had to apply my mascara by spitting on a block of black pigment, as my mother did, and then working it into a paste with a small brush. The look was finished off with a liberal application of either very pale-pink or white lipstick.

I must have looked totally ridiculous, but with my face on and my skirt hitched halfway up my thighs, I was ready to hone my boyfriend-getting skills. To be honest, it was a bit like trying to learn how to be a bronco rider on a herd of Friesians, as the boys in A1 were a pretty mixed bunch.

Many were still very much boys and although some were developing deeper voices and bristles, I can't remember any that got my newly awakened heart fluttering. Still, you have to work with what you've got, so I practised flirting and batting my eyelashes as I'd seen Emma Peel do on *The Avengers*. I probably looked more like a demented Mama doll than Mata Hari, but well, you know…

Even with a new crop of boys when we amalgamated with Sir John Cass the following year, things didn't improve. In fact, I had to wait another two years before things started to look up on the girl-meets-boy side of things.

As you've probably gathered by now, I absolutely loathed PE and games at school, and even the state-of-the-art swimming pool and gymnasium in the new school didn't alter that.

However, towards the end of the Summer term in the fourth year, our whistle-blowing, jolly-hockey-sticks PE mistress gathered the class together at the end of a sweaty PE session and told us there would be an opportunity for some of us to do horse riding when we moved into the fifth year that September as part of our weekly Games afternoon.

In order that everyone had the chance to take part, we would be able to go for only one term and anyone interested would be put on a waiting list.

Thankfully, as the boys in my year considered ponies and horses a bit girly, plus the afternoon included mucking out and grooming, none of them put their names down. This doubled my chances and after a swift drawing of names out of a hat I found myself allocated a place in the autumn term. In the end there were eight or nine of us who were chosen.

Naturally, my big concern was having the right attire but as luck would have it there had been a jumble sale at the church a few weeks before we were to start our riding and I managed to pick up a pair of cream M&S slacks with an underfoot stap that looked as near as damn it to a pair of jodhpurs, plus a russet-coloured corduroy hacking jacket.

It was a bit scuffed around the cuffs, but that didn't matter as rather than looking like I'd bought the outfit specially, my second-hand get-up gave the impression that I'd been in the saddle for years. Add to this the thick hairnet and I reckoned I looked the bee's knees.

We were also told that we wouldn't be the only school at the stables: boys from both Stepney Green and the Coopers' Company schools would be joining us.

Like Redcoats, Stepney Green Boys was a secondary modern school and was so close to our school that you could see its whitewashed main block from the top of our playground. In contrast, Coopers' was a grammar school situated a couple of miles away in Mile End.

On the first Thursday of our new venture, me and the eight or nine other girls who had been chosen piled on to the coach and took up the front seats. Within a moment or two the boys from Stepney Green clambered aboard.

Naturally, as this new crop of lads passed between the seats, we girls gave them the once-over. I wasn't overly impressed until one of them, a tall lad with fair hair, caught my eye. We shared a long look before he joined his friends at the back.

Thinking this broadening of the physical education curriculum might be even more interesting than I'd first thought, we set off for Aldborough Hatch Stables, picking up the grammar school boys on the way. On arrival we were split into two groups and while one half had their hour's riding lesson in the covered training paddock, the other group were taught stable management and horse care. We learned to clean out and replenish the stables and to groom and saddle a horse, along with how to tack up and use the different bridles. I have to say, whether ankle deep in manure or mastering the rhythm of the rising trot, I absolutely loved every single minute of it.

In fact, although I was only supposed to have one term of horse riding before returning to the horrors of cross-country running and hockey, many of my school friends who had initially put their name down dropped out so when we returned after Christmas, I stayed on the programme through to Easter and beyond.

Whoever it was in the council's education department who dreamed up this out-of-the-box addition to the physical education programme has my eternal gratitude. Unlike algebra, logarithms and making puff pastry, the skills I learned each Thursday afternoon have come in useful ever since. Thanks to those horse riding lessons, I've ridden over the green hills in Ireland, across lava flows in Iceland and through the rain forest of Costa Rica. However, apart from improving my equestrian ability, another area of my education was broadened, too.

The Stepney Green boy who'd I'd spotted as he boarded the coach happened to be in my group and pretty soon we were circling around each other to gauge how serious each of us were.

Back then the onus was very much on the boy to make the first move, so after a couple of weeks of mucking about and flirting, he asked me if I'd like to go to the pictures one night. Naturally, I said yes.

We met outside the ABC in Mile Road the following Friday. The man was also expected to pay for everything, so after he'd bought the tickets and the popcorn, we went in. Although we were both very inexperienced, we sort of knew what was required for a successful first date. Having ticked off casually draping his arm across the back of my seat before placing a tentative hand on my knee in the dark, we moved on to the big one: the first kiss.

After a bit of misalignment on both our parts, we did manage something akin to what we'd seen on television, so we had passed the first hurdle and arranged to meet again.

Like almost everyone I knew, his family lived in a council maisonette. He was the youngest of three children and both his elder brother, who was married, and his engaged sister also lived at home, which was on the newly built estate behind our school.

One of the problems youngsters had back then was that even if you were lucky enough to have a bedroom of your own, you weren't allowed to take a member of the opposite sex up there. The logic for this, I suppose, was that the sight of a bed might give teenagers ideas.

To be honest, with every girls' magazine talking about how to get a boyfriend and boys thumbing through girly magazines, fourteen-year-olds with hormones pumping though their bodies didn't need any help getting all sorts of ideas. Well, that was certainly my experience.

Courting couples had to practise their adolescent fumbling tucked in a doorway with people strolling by or in the stairwell of flats with the wind whistling around them. The cinema was the only other option but that was too expensive to visit more than once a week, especially if you were at school and your only income was pocket money or a paper round. Of course, there were graveyards, but rolling about on a slab of granite wasn't very appealing at the best of times, never mind in the middle of winter.

Of a weekend, if you were lucky and someone's parents were out at a party or up West for any length of time, a gang of you might seek refuge in their front room, snuggling up together on settees or armchairs for long snogging sessions, but most of the time you ended up smooching in the kitchen with constant interruptions as family members came in and out.

Over the coming months we started seeing each other and although I brought him home a couple of times, because my parents had their own troubles most evenings saw us in his kitchen or lounge.

Now, his sister was engaged to some chap and although they were older, they had the same problem finding somewhere private as we did. They got around this by doing most of their courting in the lounge with the lights out, and after a couple of weeks we joined them.

However, in order to ensure we stayed on the moral straight and narrow, each evening when his father went to bed at nine, his mother brought a chair in from the kitchen and placed it in front of the TV. Stoney-faced, she sat down and stared unwaveringly at the telly for an hour while we indulged in French kisses and heavy petting on either side of her.

Anyway, although there wasn't much wrong with the way he looked, as the months went by it became obvious that we were poles apart in our ideas and aspirations. I was focused on getting my O and A levels and he'd already decided to leave school the following year to get a post with his brother on the Gas Board. He saw his future as having a steady job and a nice little house in Dagenham, while mine was college and a West End fashion house.

Frankly, by the time Christmas came that year, the spark had gone. With all the parties and excitement of the festive season our relationship had a bit of a second wind, but it came a cropper just after New Year.

My parents were out at work and my brother's school had gone back a day or two earlier than mine. My boyfriend came around and with no one in the house we went up to my bedroom. We started kissing and cuddling and the inevitable happened.

It was the first time for both of us. It was totally unspectacular and over in a matter of minutes.

I was just fourteen and a half at the time and, mercifully, four days later I had a period, after which he broke up with me. I remember the occasion with no special fondness or embarrassment. In fact, looking back he'd done me a favour because I didn't have to worry about my virginity ever again.

In a world of Tinder and friends with benefits, it might seem laughable to know that when I was starting my sexual life, girls were still debating if it was too forward to let a boy kiss you on your first date. Flower power and free love might have been all over the papers and magazines, but they certainly hadn't reached the good folk of East London.

Girls had it drummed into them that no man would respect them if they let a man have his way. If you were stupid enough to give in, you'd be ruined because no man wanted 'second-hand goods'.

The pill had been approved for use in 1961, but only for married women. Although the NHS Family Planning Act in 1967 allowed for birth control to be made available to women regardless of marital status, in practice, most clinics and GPs would only prescribe it to married women, often insisting on their husband's consent before they did.

This meant that unmarried women were blocked from managing their own fertility and forced to rely on their sexual partners having a condom when needed, withdrawing before ejaculation or just taking a chance.

There were also myths around the process of conception that many girls believed. One of the most common was that you couldn't get pregnant the first time, or you could only get pregnant if you had an orgasm. Some girls, probably based on a half-understood whisper about the Catholic rhythm method, believed that you couldn't get pregnant during the week after a period.

Although girls were given dire warnings about being thrown out of the house if they 'bought trouble home', sadly, due to the limited ways in which women could access contraception, many of them did find themselves in trouble and were banished from their homes for bringing shame on the family.

If you found yourself pregnant, your boyfriend might do the right thing and marry you. Or, as happened to one of my school friends, he could say the baby wasn't his, and if you tried to take him to court, he'd get a handful of his friends to say you'd slept with them too. After that you were left with very few choices.

I knew a couple of girls who, having missed two periods, tried the old remedy of a hot bath and gin but with no effect other than having a splitting headache and a scalded rear end to add to their troubles.

After which, prior to the Abortion Act in 1967, if you were determined to get rid of the baby, you had to try and find yourself a back-street abortionist.

If girls opted to keep their babies, their choices still weren't clear cut.

Often young girls were sent away to bleak mothers' homes where once they'd had the baby they were encouraged to put it up for adoption, the argument being that it would be selfish of them to deny their child a better chance in life with a loving family. With their parents' shame raw in their minds, many girls chose this path, especially as to return home as an unmarried mother would make them little short of pariahs.

Sadly, there were stories in newspapers almost every week about desperate young women who, having been made to give up their own baby, sunk into post-natal depression which led them to take someone else's unattended infant from outside a shop.

Perhaps the best option was a very old one, whereby the girl's mother took the baby and raised it as her own child, relegating the actual mother to the role of the child's older sister. I knew at least three friends who this happened to, and thanks to the recent availability of family records online, I've met countless people who have discovered that the person they thought of as their older sister was actually their mother. I even had a boyfriend whose younger brother was, in fact, his older sister's child.

Being a wife and mother was held up as being the pinnacle of any woman's achievement, so everything to do with sex was looked at from a man's point of view.

For example, a few years later, one of the girls I worked with recounted how she'd put her hands down the front of her fiancé's trousers and grabbed his erection. Rather than him accepting her sexual needs, he'd told her, 'Get off me, you dirty bitch.' She cited this outburst as evidence of how much he respected her and that she was a lucky girl because she was marrying such a man.

Men were largely ignorant of women's sexual feelings and while women were supposed to dress sexily to please men, displaying their overt desires was considered less than wholesome.

One time when we girls in the lower sixth form were discussing the merits of going braless under a T-shirt as a way of catching a boy's interest, Prissy Brenda, who was always a font of wisdom on such things, announced that she wore her bra even in bed as her mother had told her it kept her perky. When one of our number – it could have even been me – appeared with a poorly disguised love-bite, she informed us that her mother had once told her that a love-bite was the way prostitutes marked their men. After overhearing a discussion about how far we should let our boyfriend's hands wander, she gave us another of her mother's pearls of wisdom by informing us that boys tried to take advantage to test us but if we actually gave in they'd never respect us.

Obviously, she had more interesting conversations with her mother than I did with mine.

Of course, like thousands of other young women of my generation, I found ways around the prohibition on single women accessing the pill. As might be expected when a group of teenage girls gathered together, the main topic of conversation amongst the Saturday girls in Woolworth's was the opposite sex. One of the snippets of useful information I discovered from sitting at a table in the staff canteen was that there was a private family planning clinic at Moorgate who would prescribe the pill to unmarried girls over the age of sixteen, no questions asked.

Having found out the address, one evening after school, I changed out of my uniform and jumped on a Metropolitan line train at Whitechapel station for the thirty-five-minute journey to Moorgate.

I was a month or two over fifteen but when I arrived at the clinic and was shown into the waiting room, with my false eyelashes and pink lipstick, I looked as old as any of the other nervous young women sitting there.

Having been called through to her office by a middle-aged, grey-haired woman wearing a white coat, I gave my details – remembering to subtract a year from my date of birth – and she went through my medical history, which other than my tonsillectomy wasn't very much. She then questioned me about my periods and weighed me, after which she went through how the pills worked, how to take them and what to do if I missed one. Then she gave me a prescription, which I took to the reception desk.

I handed the note over along with three pounds, which was a day and a half of my Saturday wage in Woolworth's, and was given three small pale-blue packets of pills and told to come back two weeks before they ran out for another prescription.

At least if you were an unmarried woman who was on the pill and sleeping with men you could keep it quiet, but what happened if you wanted to take your relationship further?

Today, the vast majority of people live together for many years before finally tying the knot, but when I was a teenager 'living in sin', as it was called, was very much frowned upon and a woman who moved in with a man without a ring on her finger was regarded as having loose morals.

My good friend Audrey, much to her parents' disgust, had fallen in love and so had abandoned her plan to become a nurse in order to get married. Of course, even though she'd turned eighteen a few months after I had my seventeenth birthday, she couldn't just run away and get hitched – in 1971 you still had to have parental consent until you were twenty-one. Having failed to squeeze her parents' permission out of them, she announced that if they wouldn't let her marry her fiancé, then she'd move in with him and they would live together until she could. To avoid the scandal of having a daughter living in sin, her mother grudgingly agreed, but refused to attend the wedding.

However, that's not to say that people didn't live together. In fact, it wasn't so much my friends who were co-habiting with a man who wasn't their husband, but my friends' parents. I knew at least three of their mothers living with a long-term partner who wasn't the father of their children. The mother of one senior school friend was actually the 'other woman', as her father lived a few streets away with his wife and other family.

In my family, apart from my Aunt Nell passing herself off as my grandfather's wife for almost twenty years before they finally married, there were whispers that my Aunt Millie had refused to grant her first husband a divorce even after the woman he was living with – and their three children – turned up on Aunt Millie's doorstep to persuade her.

Because of the Suez crises in the late 1940s, the army issued the Z call-up to men who'd served in the Second World War and my father got pally with a chap called Gordon, who lived on the newly built council estate in Dagenham. He was married with one daughter, and they were one of the few people outside the family we visited regularly. However, his wife was always out when we called and although my father's friend would make up some excuse or another, it was clear they were having marital problems. Somewhere along the line, Gordon met a woman who he brought to our maisonette many times for tea. They were obviously having an affair. However, my parents went to great lengths to emphasis to me and my brother that Gordon and his lady were just friends and it was all respectable.

The widely accepted attitude was that boys could sow their wild oats but if a girl slept with a man or, God forbid, several, she was a slag.

Now, given the prevailing social norms and the moral imperative of the time on young girls to 'save themselves for their husband', you might think my attitude towards my lost virginity was somewhat odd. And you're right. It was. But there was a reason for that.

Unlike my friends, I had never had a lecture about keeping myself until I got married. Other than my mother telling me that getting pregnant at my age – I was about fifteen – would 'ruin my life', neither of my parents ever threatened that I'd be thrown out of the house if I did.

Even though the message of chastity and purity was a common theme in the church youth club, my father dismissed this as an out-of-date delusion. I even remember as a fifteen year old that when I went to confession – we were High Church – I didn't confess I was sleeping with my boyfriend as I didn't consider it a sin.

When I was sixteen or so and my father knew I was having sex, he never said a thing. In fact, looking back now, I realise he studiously avoided the subject completely. It was only a few years later when I was at work and wanted my then boyfriends to stay in my bedroom with me that my father finally acknowledged that he knew I'd been sexually active for a while.

While going through a few things for this book with my brother I brought this point up and asked him why he thought that our parents – in particular our father – were so lax in giving us any moral guidance. He summed it up perfectly by saying our father liked to think of himself as a sort of 1950s beat poet and an avant-garde thinker.

Thanks to my father's view of himself as part of the fifties and sixties anti-Establishment counterculture and passing on those beliefs to us, I never agonised over my decision.

Good Times, Wild Times

By the time I left school at eighteen, I'd had several serious boyfriends, but then with a wage packet in my pocket each week I set about the task of enjoying myself.

I was with the chap from Bermondsey who worked in the cigarette wholesalers then, so we would pack into the Fort on

Old Kent Road. And I mean pack: not only did you have to fight to get into the bar, but the noise was such that you had to shout yourself hoarse just so the barmaid could hear your order over the blare of Motown and Reggae.

My drink then – as it is to this day – was black rum and coke and I used to knock back half a dozen each night while my Bermondsey boy supped his pint of brown.

The weekends in the Fort were wild with a capital W. After hours of drinking and singing, the evening inevitably ended with a fight, either in the pub itself or on the pavement outside. Usually, they were just drunken scuffles with boys squaring up at each other while their mates pulled them back. However, sometimes it ended with a full-blown bust-up, with girls screaming and dashing for safety as boys slashed at each other with knives or broken bottles.

I got caught in one such fight and got separated from my boyfriend and his friends. As the route to the door was blocked and chairs and glasses were flying past me, I dived behind the sound system to find the DJ already crouching there under the turntables. After what seemed like an eternity but was probably only twenty minutes or so, the police turned up and started wading into the melee, smashing heads and shoulders with their truncheons. Finally, after they'd cleared the pub and with my block-heel shoes crunching over glass, I made my way outside. The sight that greeted me was total carnage: young men splattered with blood were being helped into ambulances while others in handcuffs were loaded into the back of a police vans.

Thankfully, my boyfriend wasn't in either group and he looked mighty relieved when I walked through the bar door with a few others who had hidden inside.

I have to confess I was almost always very drunk by the time I got home on Fridays and Saturdays. It was rarely before midnight and often later. After the pub we would hang around the Elephant and Castle shopping centre for a while before wending our way to Rotherhithe station to catch the last train home, or, if we missed it, we'd walk through the road tunnel to Limehouse. He always took me home or, if he couldn't, he paid for a taxi, which was very gallant.

Now, although I started going to pubs when I was sixteen – two years below the legal drinking age – it was never a problem. Even when the police were called, unless you were causing trouble, they didn't bother who or how old you were. The publicans knew that, so they served anyone who had the money to pay for a drink without fear of prosecution.

Having managed to sober up by midday on Sunday I would head off south again for our regular date at the Elephant and Castle for the matinee showing at either the ABC or the Odeon cinema. It didn't matter what was on; we paid our money, got our coke and popcorn and went in regardless.

They often showed films that had already been released so I saw *The Good, The Bad and The Ugly* trilogy, all the Hammer House of Horror Draculas with Christopher Lee, plus *Bonnie and Clyde, M.A.S.H., Catch 22* and loads of others I've completely forgotten, after which we adjourned to the Wimpy opposite for burger and chips.

His parents also had a caravan on a site on Romney Marsh, so I went down there with them for the weekend quite a bit, too. Instead of going to the onsite clubhouse, a gang of us would walk along the seawall to invade the village pub.

With me following the path to A levels and my Bermondsey boy following Charlton Athletic, we didn't have much of a future, so when I moved into the working world we parted company and I started hanging around with other groups of friends.

The first gang of girls I fell in with outside school were eight or nine girls who worked full time in the boutique in Kensington High Street. Most of my fellow shop girls came from Wembley and Fulham, along with two Irish girls from Ladbroke Grove. For the most part they had left school at fifteen and had been doing shop work of some kind ever since.

Although they were my age or slightly older, some of the things they'd been through made my problems with my parents sound like a picnic. One girl, who was in her early twenties, had found herself pregnant at fourteen and been forced to put the child up for adoption. Another, who originally came from somewhere up north, had run away to London to escape from a drunken, violent father.

They were all serious party girls, often arriving to work even on a weekday morning with their eyes still dilated from whatever they'd taken in a club the night before. In fact, if they'd come in without having gone to bed at all they often popped a couple of pills – amphetamines, I guess – to keep them going.

They invited me to join them and I did on a couple of occasions. The parties were usually miles away, in Hammersmith or south of the river, and held in squats occupied by artists and self-styled anarchists who had all the banter about liberating yourself from class oppression, although their only real objective was to get you drunk and screw you. Having your drink spiked or finding yourself in a situation with a bloke you couldn't get out of was a real danger, so after a few months I made my excuses. Also, the whole drug-taking scene they were into wasn't something I wanted to get involved in.

Having moved back to East London when I took my job in Whitechapel Library, Suzie – she of the Bunny Girl audition – and I started meeting up after work for an evening in the pub. She lived just off Green Street in Bethnal Green, so we had plenty of local watering holes to choose from.

At that time pubs went through phases of being very popular and then falling out of favour. One week the Rose and Punchbowl, which was just up the street from me, would be so popular you could barely squeeze through the door, but then a month later the Black Boy, just along from Stepney Green station, would be the place to go. The Green Gate, which was on a corner halfway down Bethnal Green Road, had us all fighting to get in for a few months before we headed back to the Angel and Crown next to the London Hospital.

Sometimes we ventured further afield – to the Tiger Tavern at Tower Hill or the Three Rabbits at Manor Park. Wherever you went there was music blaring out, making it impossible to hold a conversation, and when you stumbled out at closing time you were temporarily deaf.

I remember hotpants were all the fashion and I had several pairs, both in tartan and in denim, and a silver satin pair with bib and braces, all of which I made and wore until they practically fell apart. I teamed them with my other creations: fitted blouses with extravagant bishop's sleeves, over which I wore a faux-fur waist-length jacket with box shoulders. Add the green eyeshadow, thick eyeliner, massive false eyelashes and pink lipstick and you'll have a pretty good idea what I looked like teetering out of the house on my platform shoes.

However, sometimes, instead of squeezing ourselves into a local pub on a Saturday night, we'd jump on the train to Ilford for a visit to its legendary Palais. No matter what night you went it was always busy, but Saturday was the best night to go as there was a band. It didn't matter who was playing, either, as we took to the floor and danced around our handbags regardless of who was on the stage. With a huge dance floor, twinkling lights high in the ceiling and a bar, it was the perfect place for a girls' night out.

The Palais was a lot stricter on underage drinkers than most of the pubs, and some people used to talk to the doorman and slip out to a pub during the evenings, but as I was then eighteen looking twenty, I had no trouble. Not so the diminutive Suzie, who often had to show her birth certificate before getting her tipple.

Although boys were always offering to 'buy you girls a drink', we usually bought our own because if you accepted a drink or two then the next question was, 'Do you fancy nipping outside for a bit?' You were expected to agree, plus you couldn't trust them not to add a vodka or two to the requested rum and coke.

There were always fights but usually the Palais bouncers stepped in pretty quickly to break things up and clear up any broken glass. To be honest, by the time I was a regular there, the Ilford Palais' heydays of the fifties and sixties were behind it, but even though some of the glitz had worn thin and the big acts were playing in clubs up West, I still smile when I think of the evenings I spent knocking back rum and cokes, jumping up and down on the dance floor and singing along to the band.

I'd stayed friendly with one of the Woolworth's Saturday girls called Linda, who lived in Shoreditch. She had a regular boyfriend who was in the Army and as I wasn't seeing anyone seriously, we started hanging together on Friday and Saturday nights. I would often bring a change of clothes to her house and after having applied our false eyelashes and put on our hippy glad rags we'd jump on the train and head off West for a night on the town.

We usually started the evening by having a couple of drinks in a pub somewhere in Soho while we decided which club to go to. One of our favourites was the Whiskey a Go Go in Wardour Street. Although a decade later it was the place to be seen if you were a New Romantic, when we went in the early seventies it was still very much a Mod place.

It was in the basement and like every club in Soho it was deafeningly loud, claustrophobically packed and pitch black, but after a few rum and cokes you didn't care. It was quite sleazy, too, with older blokes always trying to buy you a drink and chat to you.

Another favourite that we often went to was the Marquee, which was also in Wardour Street. If there was a big name like The Move or Status Quo playing that night, you'd never get in but otherwise you were fine. The Marquee was also packed but it had a decent-sized dance floor so it didn't feel so suffocating. It had ultra-violet lights over the dance area, too, which made your teeth looked brilliantly white and showed your bra through your clothes, assuming, that is, you were wearing one.

There were always drugs on offer for a couple of quid – usually amphetamines and weed – and although many people took them, I never did.

We normally spilled out of there just before midnight and just in time to catch the Central Line train back to Bethnal Green or if we missed that, the night bus outside Bourne & Hollingsworth in Oxford Street.

Staggering through my front door at some time around 1 a.m., I would collapse into bed very much the worse for wear and spend all Sunday drinking milk to get over a hangover.

They were bloody great times. Well, I think they were. After a dozen rum and cokes, a tour of a sewage works would look like a bloody great time. To be honest, when I think of me and my friends at the tender age of seventeen and eighteen, fighting off men who kept offering to give us a lift home or just wanted to take us down an alley and show us something, I shudder.

Being a young woman and drunk in Soho is not a good idea today but back then it was more than just dangerous, it was plain stupid. And if you were assaulted or raped then the police would have viewed it as your own fault because, as everyone knows, if you're wearing a skimpy dress and high heels, you're asking for it.

One Sunday after I'd sobered up, and for reasons that escape me now, I found myself watching a football match in Coram's Fields, where I met Geraldine. She was a paid-up member of the Westminster Scouts and after standing on the touchline all afternoon, Gerry and I started a decade-long friendship that only faded after I had my first child.

She lived on the Churchill Estate in Pimlico and, on hearing I was foot loose and fancy free, she invited me to meet her fellow Scouts down the pub for a drink.

Now, I have to say, up until that point in my life, my experience of uniformed brigades hadn't been positive, having been kicked out of the Brownies for getting into a fight and destroying the troop's toadstool. So I jumped on to the District line heading west to Victoria and then went one stop south on the newly opened extension of the Victoria line, thinking I was in for an evening full of woggle and sheaf-knot talk. However, when I arrived at the Pride of Pimlico pub and was introduced to Gerry's friends, I was pleasantly surprised. Most of the young men, about a dozen of them in total, had known each other from school and were not the badge-obsessed short-wearing group I'd expected.

Pretty soon I was part of the crowd and when it was suggested I went on one of their camping weekends I readily agreed. So we bundled our belongings into the back of a beaten-up green Ford transit and set off for somewhere in Surrey for the weekend, after which I hooked up with a chap who was an environmental health officer.

I was still working in the Dickensian clothing factory at this time, but among Gerry's friends was Sally, who was engaged to a handsome chap called Eddie, a police officer in the mounted branch. And meeting Eddie changed my life.

CHAPTER FIFTEEN

East End Girl Goes West

AFTER COMING TO the realisation that I was going nowhere fast in the fashion trade, I'd started looking around for other options. I still didn't fancy an office job or going back to shop work. I toyed with nursing, but the pay was too low. My father still wanted money for housekeeping, so I was caught in the same trap I had been in when I'd been offered the apprentice job at the costumier.

However, after getting to know Eddie a bit better, it occurred to me that applying to the Metropolitan Police to become a woman police officer might be the way forward. In addition, although the day-to-day situation with my father had improved, joining the police force would also offer me a chance to finally leave home.

After I mentioned this to Eddie, he pitched up at the next of our pub nights with swathes of literature about the career opportunities offered by the Met and information about how to join the police.

Finally, my hard-earned GCEs could be put to good use and so, early in 1976, I sent in my application to become a woman police constable in the Metropolitan Police Force.

After a bobby from Arbour Square police station had visited our home to check out my family circumstances, I was invited to an interview at Paddington Green police station. It was a modern concrete-and-glass building, towering up some ten floors, and after I'd had my name ticked off at the reception desk, I was directed via the lift to one of the floors above. Having reached the spacious classroom with tall windows, I found it filled with rows of desks where half a dozen young hopefuls, mainly men, already sat. Finding a free table, I took a seat and waited.

By the time a well-stuffed and pugnacious sergeant who had more than a passing resemblance to Jimmy Edwards marched in, nearly every other seat was taken. However, other than myself, there were only four other women in the room. Accompanying the sergeant was an officer with a small crown pinned on each epaulette. His cap with braid around the peak was tucked under his arm.

The officer gave us a mind-numbing twenty-minute talk about the modern police force and all it had to offer as a career. He then informed us that today was about sorting the wheat from the chaff and that Sergeant Whatever-his-name-was would guide us through the process, starting with an English and maths test.

The papers were handed out and once the time allotted was up they were collected and taken away for marking. While this was being done, we were sent for a ten-minute coffee break. Once we were all seated back at our desks, the sergeant called out a handful names and instructed those people to go out of the room where someone would be waiting to tell them what to do next.

That turned out to be 'go home', as they were the candidates who hadn't passed the written paper. Thankfully, I wasn't one of them, and the rest of us were told that after lunch the next stage would be individual interviews, which would be conducted alphabetically.

Ordering us to stand up, the sergeant then marched us down to the police canteen a few floors below and ushered us over to a couple of long tables in the corner that had been reserved for us. Instructing us to be back at our desks on the dot of one-thirty, we were left to it.

Trying to ignore the police officers lolling about with their jackets open and ties off, hoovering up plates of food, I joined the queue with the rest of the interviewees. After grabbing a cup of tea and something that looked faintly edible, I returned to the table.

Having provided plenty of comic relief for the old sweats enjoying their midday break, we headed back to the classroom. The sergeant was already there, so we resumed our seats and waited. There were obviously two panels interviewing people as names were called out in pairs.

Thankfully, with a surname beginning with F I didn't have to wait too long and after the usual round of 'why do you want to be…?' and 'what qualities do you think you…?' questions, I was directed upstairs to see the medical panel.

I was shown into a small room by a woman police constable and found one of the other girls already there. We were instructed to strip off to our knickers and wait.

Thankful that I'd put on my sensible Marks and Sparks knickers rather than my skimpy Dorothy Perkins ones, I did as instructed, resting my folded clothes on my lap to retain what little dignity I could.

The woman police officer then told us that when we were called through into the next room, we had to place our feet on the markers on the floor and do as the doctor requested.

The door opened and one of other girls, a blonde with a short bob, came out, red-faced, her arms across her bare chest.

Someone through the open door barked, 'Fullerton.'

I stood up and walked in to be confronted by two men and a woman sitting behind a long desk with their back to the windows. Feeling totally exposed, I told myself that they were doctors and probably spent all day sizing up near-naked twenty-two-year-olds. Waking gently so as not to jiggle or bounce, I made my way to the middle of the room and stood on the white-soled imprint marks as instructed.

As I fixed my eyes on a point just above their heads, the panel of three looked me over for a few seconds then asked me to turn. Thankful for the change of position, I did.

There was a pause for a moment or so then one of the men behind me told me to touch my toes. Having satisfied themselves I wasn't a hunchback and had a spine that worked, they instructed me to get dressed and return to the classroom.

When I did, I found the sergeant waiting. He congratulated me on passing the interview and assessment and said I'd be sent a letter in a week or so with my start date.

I know. You're aghast. So am I now!

And they'd never get away with it these days but back then, well…you had to play their games.

Although several members of the Pimlico gang had started pairing up and getting engaged, Environmental Health Man showed no inclination to follow their example. However, after I got my acceptance letter from the Met he suddenly proposed. Naturally, as we'd been going out for some time, I agreed.

We went and told my father, who congratulated us with the news we'd have to pay for the wedding ourselves.

We bought a second-hand engagement ring from an unredeemed pledge at Fish & Brothers pawnbrokers on Commercial Road and then booked the church, hall and caterers for April the following year.

We met up with the rest of the gang on the Sunday night before I started my training. Eddie was there and asked me how I felt.

I replied, 'Nervous.'

He smiled and told me not to worry, reassuring me that I'd soon realise it was the best thing I'd ever done.

And do you know? He was right!

With my suitcase clutched in my hand, I arrived at Paddington Green police station at eight-thirty on 5 April 1976. I was greeted this time by another sergeant, who after ticking my name off on his clipboard pointed me towards one of the three green coaches chugging out fumes as it idled in front of the station. Having deposited my suitcase with the driver,

I clambered on board and found a seat beside another young woman called June, who I later learned came from Croydon.

Having loaded us on the bus, the sergeant made sure we were all present and correct and then we set off in convoy for the half-hour journey to New Scotland Yard.

After alighting, we were told to pair up and then we were marched through the front door, past the police officers and civilians milling around in the foyer, and into a lecture theatre where again we were told to find a seat while the other trainees filed in.

We were each passed a card upon which was written the oath that we would all be required to take before being sworn in as police officers.

Once we were settled, one of the three senior officers on the stage in front of us stepped forward. After introducing himself he asked us to all stand up, raise our right hands and read the words on the card out loud as we made our attestation, promising to serve queen and country without fear or favour, and to act with integrity and diligence.

With one of the sergeant's booming voice keeping the pace, the hundred or so other world-be constables and I recited the words in unison, apart from where we were required to state our own names in full.

Once we'd each handed back our card, the senior officer explained that we would now be bussed to Hendon, where we would be issued with our uniform and warrant card, after which we would all have to sign the Official Secrets Act. He wished us the best of luck in our careers and then, after everyone on the stage had saluted their fellow officers, our sergeants ushered us back out to the waiting coaches, and we sped off northwards.

At Hendon we were allocated our rooms in one of the tower blocks used for housing trainee recruits, and after finding our luggage amongst the pile deposited from the coaches, we took our suitcases up to our rooms before being marched off to have our first taste of 'force feeding'. Thankfully, this didn't entail having a tube rammed down our throats Suffragette-style.

Sometimes when large cohorts of officers are sent to police football matches, demonstrations or events, hundreds of police officers need to be fed in double-quick time. To do this the police canteen operated a system called force feeding, which was much like a grown-up version of school dinners.

After lunch our names were called again, and we were assembled into four groups. My group was called A class and we were told that we would stay together through the duration of our sixteen-week training.

I found myself in the same group as June, and we were joined by another young woman called Maggie who came from Islington. We were the only three women in a class of thirty-three.

Having sorted us into our cohorts, we were marched off to the massive uniform store to be kitted out. For men that was the familiar uniform of the British bobby, but for women the uniform consisted of a navy skirt and single-breasted jacket, topcoat, white shirt with clip-on black-and-white tie and a sort of white plastic-covered pill-box hat with a black-and-white chequered band and a two-inch navy brim.

In fact, the only things we had to buy ourselves were tights and shoes, the latter of which had to be flat, black lace-ups with no decoration. In addition, we were given a chain with a key attached to it that would open any police callbox, and a metal whistle, which still dangles from my keyring.

We were also issued with a black leather handbag in which to carry our lady's truncheon. And no, that isn't a euphemism – women were issued with a miniature version of the fourteen-inch wooden stick our male colleagues carried. These smaller truncheons fitted into the handbag and made us the butt of many very unfunny and predicable jokes among our male colleagues.

Having been loaded up with our clobber, the men were then taken off by the sergeants to the barbers for a short back and side. Thankfully, the powers that be in the Met had decided to let the female contingent sort out their own hair, so we were taken to collect our warrant cards – which then was a stiff card hinged with bookbinding fabric with just our name and warrant number on it but no picture.

Having had our names entered into the constable register, thereby officially becoming police officers subject to passing our training, we had to sign the Official Secrets Act. Admin finally complete, we were allowed to retire to our rooms.

For obvious reasons, the women were all housed in the same block. The rooms were very like those in university student accommodation with just a single bed, a built-in wardrobe and a sink with a mirror fixed to the wall above it. There was also a small desk and chair.

If I remember rightly, there were about ten or so rooms on each floor with a small kitchen supposedly for making tea and coffee, although the fridge was always filled with booze.

June, Maggie and I were the newbies, as the other women on our floor were all ahead of us in their training. We said our hellos and then trooped back down to the canteen, which could be described as 'son of holiday camp dining', for our evening meal.

Hendon Training School canteen food, filling and stodgy, was served, or rather plonked, on to our plates by women who looked as if they'd just lost a pound and found a penny.

The three of us ate our meal and chatted about the day's events and then, after clearing away our plates, we made our way through to the bar, which was next to the canteen. After a couple of rum and cokes I queued up at one of the payphones in the lobby. After calling my father to let him know I'd arrived, and Environmental Health Man to tell him the same, I headed off to bed so I'd be fresh for my first day as a woman police constable.

The sixteen-week training course designed to turn you from a jelly-kneed civilian into an iron-spined police constable ready to do your duty without fear or favour consisted of three five-week blocks of training, with week eleven spent with the division where you were destined to be stationed.

Each day started with the whole school taking part in a military-style parade in front of the bronze statue of Sir Robert Peel. One of the inspectors, accompanied by your class sergeant, would pass down the rows to check that your shoes were bulled (achieved by applying layer upon layer of shoe polish then buffing vigorously until you could see your face in them) and to make sure your buttons sparkled in the sun and that your hat was on straight. If you passed muster, then you were marched off to your classroom. If you didn't, and were found to have less than blindingly white plimsolls or were repeatedly late for class, then you were put on early parade, at the crack of dawn with other miscreants, where you were bawled out colourfully and roundly for letting the service down.

The days consisted of tedious hours sitting at a desk attempting to cram chapter and verse of the Road Traffic Act or the difference between common and aggravated assault, ABH (actual bodily harm) and GBH (grievous bodily harm) into our numb brains.

We were taught the history and structure of the Met, the meaning of the different combinations of crown, pips and wreath insignias, which indicated an officer's rank so we wouldn't embarrass ourselves by addressing a commander as chief inspector. We were led step by step through the vagaries of the judiciary and, as this was prior to the CPS, when police officers still prosecuted their own cases, the laws of evidence.

We had specialists from the various police departments, such as the Criminal Investigation Department (or the Creeping

Insect Department as the uniform branch preferred to call them), the Traffic Division and the Diplomatic Protection, who brightened up a dull afternoon when they brought their guns with them.

There was some relief each day, if you can call it that, when we spent an hour or so marching back and forth on the parade ground, learning to coordinate our arms and legs in time with the rest of the class, while being bawled at by Drill Sergeant Butcher.

There was also physical training, of course, which might be the dreaded old-style PE in the gym or running around the rugby fields or swimming, but sometimes we'd have something a bit more exciting like learning how to wrestle a knife from a suspect before pinning him to the ground.

Every Friday we had a written exam on that week's subject; if you failed two weeks in a row you were out.

Although today promotion in the Met can be achieved through a variety of channels such as degree direct entry, in the early 1970s the two hurdles you had to overcome if you wanted to move up the ranks were the sergeants' and the inspectors' exams, after which you were promoted by a selection board. However, both exams were competitive. The pass bar shifted each year according to how many posts were available, so obviously the better your score the more chance you had of getting a senior job.

One of the best ways of ensuring you passed your exam with flying colours was to spend all day long teaching the acts and procedures you would be tested on, which was why the great majority of our classroom instructors were men – and they were predominantly men – in their early thirties who were all keen to progress.

In contrast, the officers employed at the training school were a different matter. The top ranks – inspectors, chief inspectors and superintendents – were often old sweats in the last few years of their service who had, in the best tradition of the Met, found themselves a nice little number to see out their professional twilight years.

The instructors in charge of the physical side of training, while often also in the final years of their service, were a different kettle of fish altogether, as many of them had joined the Met after a stint in the army and were, to use a lay term, bonkers.

One such instructor was Sergeant Butcher, a string bean of a man, with uneven teeth and a voice like a foghorn, who was straight off any army training camp parade ground. The PE instructors, meanwhile, with their whistles and relentless verbal abuse, would have made battle-hardened paratroopers run up the white flag.

However, somehow, despite my aversion to all things sporty, I managed to scrape through the physical training element of the ongoing assessment.

The first few weeks at Hendon were a blur of late nights studying legislation and police procedures, days in the classroom and hurried meals. However, after completing the first five weeks things got more interesting.

Having absorbed reams of acts and sections of English

criminal law, and lost a couple of colleagues along the way, our class breathed a collective sigh of relief when we were handed over to our second-phase instructor.

Sergeant Burrows, a thin, dark-haired Liverpudlian with an accent straight off the Anfield terraces, marched in on the Monday and, swivelling on the balls of his feet to face us, spent five minutes telling us what a shambles we were. Even though it was a 'bloody hopeless' task, he said he'd turn us into proper police officers if it was the last thing he did.

Actually, he was a good bloke. I met him on several occasions over the years and he would always put his hand in his pocket and buy you a drink.

With our new sergeant we were allowed out of our classrooms to start learning the practical skills of being a police officer. It was then we discovered that as well as having their eyes fixed on promotion, our instructors were also frustrated actors.

After being marched out of the classroom and down either to the wide road in front of the teaching block or to the car park, we would be lined up in a semicircle. One victim would be drawn from our ranks before a sergeant or two, loosely disguised as ordinary members of the public, burst on the scene calling for the police!

What followed could be anything from a staged drunken fight that you had to break up to someone catching a thief that you were expected to apprehend, or the aftermath of a road traffic accident with an injured pedestrian. The most provincial am-dram company had nothing on our instructors, who would ham it up, throwing in a curve ball by suddenly clutching their chest and keeling over or, having provided you with a completely rational explanation about the event in question, giving their name and address as the King of England, Buckingham Palace, then doing a little dance.

If confronted with the victim of an assault or two collided cars, you had to shout, 'Did anyone see what happened?' a phrase only every used in the confines of the police college because in real life, even in the middle of Oxford Circus during the rush hour, no one ever saw anything.

Hats and, in my case, handbags would fly, and uniform buttons popped as we scuffled with the pretend felons in our attempts to arrest them.

The stock reply to any WPC cautioning the arrestee that 'anything they said would be taken down' was always 'knickers'. Very tedious. Of course, you had to pretend it was funny to show you could take a joke.

Sometimes they tried to provoke trainees into losing their temper by calling them pigs and scum and swearing at them. The other way they tried to rile them was by nicking their police hat and running off across the rugby pitch.

However, one day one of our frustrated thespians picked on the wrong man. One of our number was a winger for a county champion rugby club. After being provoked one too many times, he tackled an instructor mid-fight, putting him in hospital for two days with concussion.

The practicals were a real free-for-all, but working through problems and assisting each other to untangle an incident or to protect each other in a confrontation did promote an *esprit de corps* amongst our class. You wanted to be seen as part of the crew, and there was a real pressure to keep up with work and stay fit. If you missed two days' instruction in a week you were in danger of being back grouped into the class behind.

After an early-morning exercise-induced migraine, I sat through the whole day with zigzags dancing in my eyes and my head cleaved in two just so I wouldn't have to be sent to the medical facility. Thankfully, other than the odd hangover, for the rest of my time at Hendon I was a hundred per cent fit.

By this stage in our training we had started to form ourselves into social groups. Although there were a couple of trainees in their very late thirties who after completing their twenty years in the army had joined the Met, the rest of the class were more or less evenly divided between trainees in their thirties who were married with a couple of kids and the rest of us who were in our twenties, with a handful of seventeen-year-olds who as they were approaching their eighteenth birthday could join the service proper.

One of the army chaps, Sid, who knew the score regarding marching, bulling your boots and keeping his nose clean, was made class captain. Another member of our class, based on the fact he looked uncannily like John Cleese, but without the brains or humour, tried to take on the role of class clown but he was beaten at every turn by a quiet Irishman from Belfast whose arid wit and Ian Paisley tone had us rocking with laughter.

Although we had very little in common, we three girls got on well enough but, truthfully, most of my time off duty was spent hanging around with the young men in the class and that's where things started to go awry.

Now don't judge me. I know I was engaged but, well…what girl can resist a man in uniform?

And I was surrounded by dozens of them. Most of them fit in both the traditional and the modern sense of the word. In my defence, I wasn't the only one running wild. There were plenty of my twenty-something male colleagues with wedding plans who were chasing after and bedding a handful of women on campus.

In my defence, I have to confess that, although we were engaged, things with my environmental health officer weren't entirely rosy. Although outwardly my respectable, professional fiancé with his regular salary seemed everything a girl could want, as time went on there were a few things that gave me pause for thought.

Firstly, although at the start of our romance he would gallantly escort me home from Pimlico, after we'd been going out for a while he would only take me as far as Victoria, leaving me to travel on the underground alone at night. Today, if you travel on any of the tube lines at midnight, you'll find them as busy as they are during the rush hour, but in the early seventies when people were able to park their cars on almost any road in Central London, the underground trains after ten o'clock at night were filled with drunks and gangs of yobs. I tell you, it couldn't have been much scarier walking around Spitalfields with Jack the Ripper on the prowl than waiting for the doors of the eastbound District line train to close at the ghost-like Mansion House station. And even when I got to Stepney Green, the ten-minute walk home had its dangers, as a girl alone was fair game for gangs of young men who'd just tipped out of the pub.

However, this wasn't the most unsettling thing about Environmental Health Man. When I was twenty-one, my bras, if I wore one, comprised of little more than a pair of elasticated fabric triangles held in place with thin straps. I mention this because one day, after a year or so of going out with Environmental Health Man, I discovered him wearing them.

He laughed it off as a prank, but then I noticed that whenever we went to a fancy-dress party, which were all the rage in those days, he always chose to go as a woman – Marlene Dietrich, complete with stockings and suspender, sticks in my mind. He also started shaving his legs.

I had, of course, come across men dressed as women and vice versa before; there was a supervisor at Woolworth's who was clearly a man, five o'clock shadow and all, who presented himself as a woman. There were also a couple of women at church who lived together, who had very short hair and dressed 'mannishly', as my mum described it – the word lesbian never once, to my knowledge, crossed her lips. They were just regarded as a bit unusual. And, to be honest, I didn't think much more about it.

Now, you're probably laughing at my naivety, but although all manner of sexual orientations and lifestyle choices are openly talked about now, back then they weren't even whispered about. Trans anything wasn't even in our vocabulary, let alone binary and non-binary. On their billing, drag acts Danny La Rue and Barry Humphries aka Dame Edna Everage were described as female impersonators.

Anyway, putting my confusion about his inclination to don my underwear aside, the growing problem between us was that after we'd been going out for a year or so, he suggested that we should partner swap with a couple of friends for a bit of variety.

I was shocked at the suggestion, and not just for the obvious reason. Despite being a fit young man in his mid-twenties, Environmental Health Man was a once-a-week man, and then only if he hadn't had a tiring day!

I said no to his suggestion, adding that if I ever did sleep with someone else then it would indicate there was something very wrong with our relationship. A prophetic statement as it turned out.

Hendon Police Training School was a watershed moment for me. It gave me confidence and made me look at myself. It was the classic 'it's not you it's me!'

And it was.

I'd changed and I knew, even as Environmental Health Man stood alongside my father watching me at my passing-out parade, that I'd never be walking down the aisle as his wife.

Weekly tests came and went, then at week ten we were told which division we were going to be sent to. Although you were told from the word go you wouldn't be sent to your home area, you could request a division, which many of the married and soon-to-be married officers did.

The rest of us, who didn't have a preference, had to take pot luck, so when our class instructor read out my name and said I'd be going to C Division, I could have run up to the front of the class and kissed him, as it was the top of my wish list for posting. Away from home to be independent, but in the centre of London.

After spending the week with our future division, we returned to Hendon and progressed through the final weeks of our training. Having survived sixteen gruelling weeks together we were now a tight-knit team, strutting around with confidence. Our last night together was spent celebrating, and then it was time to say goodbye. Saluting the training-school staff, we marched past the loved ones who had come to see us pass out on our final parade. Then, swearing we'd stay in touch, we departed Hendon, fully fledged Metropolitan Police constables, ready to keep the queen's peace and make the streets of the capital safe.

CHAPTER SIXTEEN

West End Plonk

A FTER A WELL-EARNED week's holiday on the south coast, I pitched up at Trenchard House, the police section house in Broadwick Street, on the Sunday before I was to report for duty. Having unloaded my luggage from the back of Environmental Health Man's car and carrying a suitcase each, we struggled up half a dozen stairs from the marble-clad lobby to the warden's office.

I found myself staring up at Sergeant Perriman, an enormous barrel-chested sergeant with heavy features and a full head of steel-grey hair. After checking my name off on his list, he told me my room was on the second floor and handed me a key. He then informed me in a voice as hard as the granite of his native Cornwall that although members of the opposite sex weren't allowed in officers' rooms, Environmental Health Man could take my suitcases up with me as long as he came down within half an hour.

Having been directed to the lift, and wondering if I'd slipped back in time to the 1950s, I trudged to the second floor.

The room I'd been allocated was directly in front of the lift doors and probably no more than fifteen foot by twelve. It had a single bed, a built-in wardrobe with drawers, a sink with a mirror over it and a non descript rectangular rug on the floor.

Not wanting to blot my copybook with the ferocious-looking Perriman on my first day, I ushered Environmental Health Man back to the lobby, waving him off with a promise to ring the next day. Returning to my room, I unpacked my suitcases then set about exploring.

The officers' accommodation block was probably fifty or so years old and had seven floors. Although originally the building was designed solely for male occupants, after the Metropolitan Police amalgamated the Women's Police Division into the main body of officers in 1973, the whole of the second floor was given over to female colleagues.

All of the corridors had bare concrete floors and shoulder-height wooden panelling, which meant every conversation, slammed door, too-loud radio and even footsteps echoed down the entire length of the corridor.

Making my way back downstairs, I didn't have to ask directions to the canteen – the smell of fried food and boiled cabbage drew you to it as soon as you entered the lobby. Although there was a larger eating area at the very back of the canteen, the place where most of us had our meals overlooked the front of the building. It was filled with the standard six-seater Formica tables surrounded by an assortment of chairs. At the far end of the canteen was the serving counter with the kitchen behind.

Having gathered my supper of greasy shepherd's pie and assorted grey vegetables, I found a table, and after eating the less than inspiring meal I returned to my room, intent on getting an early night to be ready for my first day of walking the beat.

I was up bright and early the following morning and, after locating the shower room at the other end of the corridor, I washed then donned the still very new police uniform I'd acquired at training school. This comprised of a straight navy knee-length skirt, the same colour jacket with silver buttons, white shirt with black-and-white checked bowtie, which attached to the top shirt button, a narrow-brimmed felt hat with a detachable plastic crown and the same black-and-white check band as the bowtie.

With my heart thumping in my chest, just a week after my twenty-second birthday, I stepped out of the front door of Trenchard House.

Praying as I made my way through Carnaby Street to Regent Street and then across to Savile Row that I wouldn't encounter a car accident, a fight or an armed robbery, I walked to West End Central police station.

Although C Division's art-deco-style headquarters looked straight out of the 1930s, it had in fact been built two years after the war. The building sat like a squat sandstone toad among the elegant Regency townhouses that lined Savile Row.

Half a dozen steps led up to a large set of glass doors which took you into the lobby. In front of you was a door that led into the main part of the station, which could only be opened from the other side. Behind it was a tall wooden cabinet with files stacked on it and a striped mirror above, concealing the radio control area behind it.

Here the clerk, a wizened-looking officer in an ill-fitting uniform, told me I'd been assigned to D Relief – the twenty- to thirty-strong team that I would be attached to – and that my divisional number was 585. He then gave me the silver digits to attach to my epaulettes.

I was then taken to meet Inspector Smith, the relief inspector, who, after a brief pep talk, welcomed me to the division and introduced me to Geordie Buxton, explaining that the dour, fair-haired constable with a Pancho Villa moustache would be taking me out on 'learning beats' for the next couple of weeks.

My mentor was from the north-east and as one of the longest-serving officers at West End Central he was one of the PCs chosen to show newbie constables the ropes. He took me on a little tour of the CID office; the male and female cell blocks, where he introduced me to the hard-bitten matron responsible for the welfare of female prisoners, and the canteen via the station's backyard.

With a male-to-female ratio of approximately twenty to one, you can imagine that the appearance of a new girl in the station caused a great deal of interest. With dozens of pairs of eyes watching me, and feeling acutely self-conscious, I followed Geordie over to a table where he introduced me briefly to my new colleagues before we headed back to the front office. Picking up our radios, we headed out.

C Division's northern boundary was Oxford Street while its southern boundary skimmed the top of Trafalgar Square.

It covered the opulence of Mayfair, the seediness of Soho, the then run-down area of Covent Garden, the Piccadilly 'meat rack' (the place where male prostitutes solicited for clients), and the glitz of Leicester Square.

In addition to West End Central, this part of London was served by two other police stations: Bow Street, alongside the famous court, and Vine Street, tucked behind a shop at the bottom end of Regent Street's west side.

The area covered by your station was divided into certain streets and, other than refreshment breaks, you were expected to patrol your 'patch' on foot for the duration of your time on duty.

On C Division, each beat wasn't particularly large – less than three miles in circumference in most cases – but given the number of casinos, strip clubs, pubs and brothels within it, you had very little chance of being idle while on duty.

If I needed to call for assistance, I had a personal radio, the size and weight of a house brick, which just about fitted into my Met-issue handbag. Of course, this was assuming that a) the battery hadn't lost all power and b) I had reception, which a good part of Mayfair didn't.

Although I didn't know every road and alley covered by West End Central, having been working and shopping in the very same streets for the past half a decade, I did know which end of Oxford Street Selfridges was and how to get to Covent Garden from Piccadilly, which was more than a lot of the new recruits did.

I arrived on the ground in August during one of the hottest summers on record, so we were often in shirtsleeve-order, which meant jacketless with our cuffs rolled up. It was also prime holiday season, so the whole area was swarming with tourists peering at maps as they tried to make sense of the underground system. If we had a spare hour before our meal break, Geordie would wander up to Oxford Circus to meet visitors to London.

Although he was no Adonis, women of all nationalities swarmed around him, all wanting to have their photo taken with a 'real London bobby'. The Americans, in particular, were fascinated by the whole funny-shaped hat and truncheon thing rather than the gun they were used to seeing their police officers carry.

In fact, young female tourists were keen on policemen for other reasons, and there was an unofficial competition amongst some officers to see how many nationalities they could sleep with in a month.

They had other competitions amongst themselves, too, like who could wear the same shirt without washing it. Legend has it that someone managed thirty days. However, given that the uniform shirts the male police officer wore were made from non-breathable nylon, I'm thankful this was before my time.

Of course, there was always rivalry among the more experienced officers for the best arrest, be it for uncovering a con-artist or intercepting a cat burglar, and this was particularly true for uniformed officers hoping to move into CID. Well, that, or making sure you sent the detective chief inspector a bottle of his favourite tipple each Friday.

My time patrolling the streets around Oxford Circus with Geordie brought him up short because although I was one of the more junior officers on C Division, London was my home town and so, unlike other newbies, I knew my way around. I didn't have to take out my Nicholson Streetfinder to know which tube line went to Waterloo or how long it would take to walk to the British Museum.

I have to say, though, that over the next few weeks, through bleary-eyed early turns and wild late-night duties, Geordie taught me well.

As a probationer you were expected to be eager to get stuck in and bring in 'a body' a day. Now, I don't want to put you off fair London Town, but I have to tell you, making an arrest in the West End is very, very easy. There are the big department stores and shops for a start, with their constant stream of shoplifters. Then there's the illegal street traders, selling tat from open cases, not to mention the drunks and vagrants loitering in doorways. Then at night there were the prostitutes, drug dealers, burglaries and break-ins, which the CID or specialist squads stepped in to investigate.

Before long I was giving cautions, arguing the toss with street traders and tussling with felons like I'd been born to it. I started to learn how to judge if those I arrested would come quietly or if I needed to call for assistance.

And although the first time I stood up to give evidence in the dock at Marlborough Street Magistrates Court I shook like a leaf, within a few weeks of having a prisoner up before the magistrate every other day, I was soon taking it in my stride.

Geordie taught me other things, too, that weren't in any police training manual.

There's a common expression among officers that 'a good policeman always knows where a kettle has just boiled', and that was certainly true on C Division. Geordie introduced me to all the plush hotel kitchens on our patch where we'd be given a full meal, day or night.

He also told me to make sure I always arrested someone while on night duty, even a drunk, so I could go to court the following morning, thereby incurring overtime. In the same way, he taught me that the best time for arresting a foreign national shoplifter when you were on early shift was after midday because it always took hours to get an interpreter, so you'd have at least four hours' overtime out of it.

And finally, if your suspect was released on police bail, then make sure their return date was within the month and on your rest day – day off – so you got double time plus the day back in lieu.

To be honest, even as a very new officer you didn't have to be too inventive to work the system, as some days the charge rooms and cells were heaving with prisoners waiting to be processed, which meant there was always overtime to be had. Many a time on a Saturday, you'd only just finished dealing with one shoplifter before you were sent off to arrest another.

In addition to criminal offences, you were also expected to deal with traffic infringements. Often this was just things like obstructive parking or a double yellow line violation but sometimes, before the shops were open and store detectives started calling, if your traffic-processing tally needed topping up, you and a colleague could catch a few red-light jumpers.

The best place for this was Park Lane, so, concealing yourself with a clear view of a set of traffic lights, you'd wait until a car sped through a red light then quickly shout the colour and make of the offending car down the radio.

Your colleague, who was waiting a few yards down the road on the other side of the traffic lights, would leap out in front of the oncoming traffic and, raising their hand, bring the speeding vehicle to a screeching halt. Hopefully! Although to my certain knowledge no officer was ever knocked over while dashing out into four lanes of oncoming traffic, it wasn't for the faint hearted.

You had to learn the lingo, too.

'The ground' was the area covered by your police station. A 'collar' was an arrest and a 'body' was the prisoner, while prostitutes were 'toms'. 'A shout' was a call for assistance but if you were 'captured' it meant you'd been caught out doing something you shouldn't be. Getting a 'one six three' was having a complaint made against you. Being 'stuck on' was being found guilty of some other misdemeanour against Police Regulations and having it formally recorded on your record. Being 'over the side' was committing adultery, a common pastime for some officers.

'Spinning a drum' was an expression used by probationers who'd watched too many episodes of *The Sweeney,* meaning to search premises; and if you wanted to find the CID or Crime Squad during opening hours they'd be at the 'back door' – the nearest pub to the police station.

A 'governor' was an inspector or above, and you were very quickly instructed to avoid telling them anything about anything, particularly a fellow officer.

However, I don't want to give you the impression that being posted to West End Central was all laughs or that becoming an accepted member of the workforce there was plain sailing. Because it most certainly wasn't. Certainly not if you were a woman.

I joined the Met in 1976 just after the Metropolitan Police Force subsumed A Division into the main force, and some on both sides hadn't yet come to terms with the change.

Like many men who'd grown up in the fifties and sixties, the prevailing attitude among the majority male officers, although not necessarily vocalised, was that women just weren't cut out to be police officers. Women were 'too emotional', 'not tough enough'. They lacked common sense and were a liability in a fight. They were also either tarts or lesbians.

For a start, the nickname applied to all WPCs (woman police constables, to give them their proper title) was Plonks. It was common to hear even senior officers tell the PC taking calls from the public to allocate 'a plonk' to a trivial matter rather than waste a 'proper officer'.

Some of the older WPCs, who'd spent all their service dealing exclusively with women and children, now became involved in things like traffic, licensing laws and raids on clubs – areas of the law they'd never dealt with before.

There was an attitude among some of the men that you'd be better off patrolling alone than with a plonk because if there was trouble, you'd have to look after them as well as yourself. On top of this, you had to put up with all sorts of innuendoes and smutty talk, as well as male officers trying to see if you were wearing stockings by pinging your suspenders through your skirt. If you objected, you were brushed off for being too touchy and told they were just having a laugh.

However, the worst thing that happened to some WPCs, thankfully never to me, was being station stamped. Usually instigated by one of the older officers, a WPC who they regarded as being a bit stroppy, stuck up or not pulling their weight would be bent over a desk, her skirt pulled up and knickers down before having the rubber stamp with the police station official crest pressed on to her bare flesh.

Thankfully, it wasn't widespread, but I did meet a couple of WPCs who had been assaulted in that way.

There was another WPC on D Relief called Denise, and although she was a few classes in front of me, I'd met her at training school. She, like me, was a native Londoner, from south of the river, and she was already living in Trenchard when I arrived.

We got on from the start and now we were on the same relief we started to walk to and from work together and formed a friendship that has held true through life's trials and tribulations to this very day.

Despite being one of only a few women in a very male world, with all the disadvantages that entailed, there were some massive advantages as well. Although male probationary officers were often included as part of the team when the Clubs unit or Vice squads were going on a raid, they were forced to take female probationers with them, because a WPC was needed to search women and act as chaperones, so we were often seconded.

Today the streets of Soho are full of fashionable restaurants, bar and pubs packed with tourists, theatre-goers and office workers, but back in the mid-seventies Old Compton Street, Beak Street, Dean Street and Greek Street were renowned for their strip clubs and bookshops selling all manner of explicit literature, along with peep shows and cinemas showing what were described as 'continental' films.

In addition to the sex trade, the other lucrative industry in Soho was drugs, both soft and hard, and the paraphernalia associated with drug-taking – needles, scorched spoons and silver foil – were easily spotted discarded in the gutters. Sadly, we also found drug-addicted casualties in the same gutters, or collapsed in doorways or behind dustbins.

Consequently the Vice and Drug squads frequently raided the clubs and brothels in Soho, so almost every night duty either me or Dee, or often both of us, would be called back to the station at midnight and told to report to the detective sergeant or inspector leading the raid.

There were many times Dee and I followed the male officers into Soho dives thick with smoke and reeking of cannabis as they searched for drugs, and we often ended up spending the night in an interview room with half a dozen prostitutes who'd been picked up in a raid on a Piccadilly gambling den.

It's easy to imagine that women who work in the sex trade are a breed apart, but they're not. Truthfully, there but for the grace of God and all that...

Most women I met who worked the streets and alleyways of Soho and Piccadilly were single parents with a couple of children to provide for.

There was a strong feeling that if WPCs were getting paid the same as their male counterparts then they should be treated the same, which in practical terms meant that we were sent out on patrol alone. During the day this wasn't a problem as there was always something to do and people to talk to, so the time passed swiftly. However, at night, especially if you were posted to one of the tedious Mayfair beats where you could walk for hours without seeing a soul, minutes passed like hours.

It was pointless, too, because as a probationer you were told in no uncertain terms that if you discovered a burglary, came across a person who'd been assaulted in the street or were called to break up a fight, you had to call for another PC to assist for safety.

However, on a night duty the relief governor often turned a blind eye to PCs on adjoining beats patrolling their assigned areas together. Probationers, myself included, often felt happier patrolling with someone, even if it was only for a few hours or so.

Dee and I would often do this, walking along chatting while we checked premises on our ground for break-ins and directing people to the all-night bus stops if they'd missed the last train. We also teamed up successfully from time to time to catch street traders selling out of suitcases in Oxford Street – because of our diminutive stature even with our white hats the look-outs couldn't see us among the shoppers.

Once I walked right up to a trader who was bellowing 'Where's the rozzer?' as he scanned the crowd above my head. I had the pleasure of smiling up at him and saying, 'Boo.'

Now, I'm sorry to say that it wasn't only our fellow officers who didn't take women police officers seriously, but also some members of the public, especially drunken ones. In my experience, drunks fall into two main categories: happy and friendly or aggressive and belligerent.

Friday and Saturday nights were the worst and it was almost routine to come across gangs of young men who'd just tipped out of strip clubs and drinking holes careering along the streets screaming, fighting, peeing in corners and generally making a nuisance of themselves.

Usually, after a bit of argy-bargy and 'words of advice' from us, they would think better of it and go on their way. However, sometimes things got completely out of hand, as it did one night for me and Dee in the middle of Oxford Street.

We were strolling along towards Tottenham Court Road when a couple of very drunk young men stumbled towards us shouting at passers-by. They spotted us and turned their attention our way, blocking our path. Wheeling about in front of us they started making indecent suggestions, so we told them to push off home. One of them shouted about not being told what to do by a 'bit of skirt' as they tried to back us into a doorway.

Warning them that if they didn't watch themselves, they'd be spending the night in a police cell, we told them to stand aside. Predictably they refused and grabbed our hats, which they offered to return if we gave them a kiss.

At this stage we grabbed them and arrested them.

Then it all hit the fan as, giving us another torrent of abuse, they tried to break free, but Dee managed to get hold of her radio and shout for urgent assistance. Despite being shoved against a brick wall, we held on to them for what seemed like an hour but was probably just a few minutes before the area car, with its blue light flashing and siren blazing, screeched to a halt beside us and four burly policemen jumped out.

Barrelling forward, they grabbed the two young men in a rugby tackle and then sailed through the plate-glass shop window in a shower of glass.

The two men who had assaulted me and Dee were taken into custody and charged with drunk and disorderly behaviour. They were kept in custody overnight and hauled up in front of the magistrate at Marlborough Street the following morning. They pleaded not guilty, stating that they were only having a laugh with us. After listening to my and Dee's evidence, the beak failed to see the joke and fined them thirty pounds.

As well as taking part in ad-hoc CID raids and long hours of beat duties, there was fierce competition to be attached to one of the specialist squads.

This was one of the times that being a female police officer worked in our favour. Because there were so few women among the probationers and the top brass had to be seen to be giving us equal treatment, just a few months after I'd started at West End Central, I was asked if I'd like to undertake a three-month attachment to the Juvenile Squad.

The unit was headed up by Woman Police Sergeant Barbara Wilding, who had transferred to the Met from Jersey. She was one of the new breed of career policewomen who, after holding various posts in the Met and other police forces, retired as the longest-serving Chief Constable of South Wales. She was not only friendly and supportive but knew her stuff.

For the Met, most of the work in the Juvenile Squad entailed dealing with children who had been caught shoplifting, and I'm sure that would be true of any urban police force charged with policing the country's main shopping areas, especially leading up to Christmas.

However, it's a sad truth that the criminal gangs who ran prostitutes and drugs also needed a constant supply of fresh meat to keep the money rolling in; therefore, our main focus was not on petty crime but on exploitation.

While no one believes the streets of the capital are actually paved with gold, like Dick Wittington, people from all four corners of the realm were and still are drawn to London. Alongside the actors, writers and entrepreneurs heading for the capital to make their fortunes, many youngsters also headed for London's streets. Some were just bunking off from school, others were escaping much darker conditions, but regardless of their circumstances all gravitated to the capital and to the West End in particular.

Unlike the CID, and the specialist squads like Crime, Vice and Clubs, who all operated at night, the Juvenile Squad was a uniformed unit that patrolled during the day. Their remit was to search out juveniles (children under the age of sixteen) wandering around Soho and Piccadilly and take them into custody in an attempt to protect them from the less savoury aspects of London's streets.

Mostly this entailed returning children to their very shocked and distressed parents, who had thought their little Johnny or Jane was studying hard in school, not playing the one-arm bandits in a dimly lit arcade in China Town.

However, sometimes when we took youngsters into protective custody, we uncovered stories of children running away from social services care or abusive households and one such a case sticks in my mind.

While checking among the backstreet arcades off Piccadilly with a male colleague, I came across a young lad of about ten shoving money into a slot machine. It wasn't just his young age that caught our eye but the fact that although he was wearing what was obviously a private school uniform, he and it were very grubby.

We took him back to the station. He answered all our questions about his school and his sister, but when asked about his parents we found out he lived with his father. We also discovered that despite the fact his mother had left the family home some time ago he didn't know where she was.

He was a bright, articulate lad and he gave perfectly reasonable replies to all our questions, but something didn't feel right.

Although it was usual practice to ask parents to attend the station to collect their wayward offspring, after consultation with our sergeant she commandeered a patrol car and the three of us set off with the young lad.

The address was an ordinary street of semi-detached, well-maintained houses in a prosperous area of North London. The door was opened by the boy's fourteen-year-old sister, who reluctantly let us in, and as I stepped in, I understood why she wasn't keen for us to enter the house.

Later, during my time as a district nurse in the East End, I went into some squalid and chaotic places, but in all my twenty years of going in and out of houses in East London I have never been to anywhere quite as appalling as the one those two children called home. The whole place was utterly filthy, and I mean back-of-a-rubbish-truck filthy. On top of which there was an eye-watering, stomach-wrenching smell that would have made the antelope house at London Zoo seem like a bunch of violets.

And every room in the house was the same. The kitchen had greasy plates and pots piled high in the sink, there was barely any food in the cupboards and only curdled, green-moulded milk in the fridge. Unwashed clothes were strewn everywhere, none of the beds had a sheet and the blankets were almost threadbare.

The young girl explained that she'd managed to do some washing and tidying when her father was at work, but he'd told her off when he found out as he said her mother would do it when she got home.

While we were there their father returned and was naturally surprised to see three police officers standing in his front room. It turned out he was a chief engineer at an aeronautical company and was noticeably less shabbily dressed than his children. He was pleasant enough and agreed that the domestic side of family life had got away from him a bit, but it would all be back to normal once his wife came back.

Back from where? we enquired.

Then he started to prevaricate about where she actually was, first saying she was with a relative, then a friend, before admitting he didn't seem to know when she was coming back. That was enough for Sergeant Wilding, who informed him she was going to contact social services with a view to taking the children into care, after which he would be charged with child neglect. She also told him that she was calling in the local CID.

Somehow, between the ensuing shouting and screaming, we managed to keep the situation under control until social services and a couple of CID officers arrived some twenty minutes later.

Thankfully, by the time CID found their mother hanging from one of the eaves in the loft and arrested their father on suspicion of murder, social services had already removed the two children to a place of safety. After extensive inquiries and an autopsy, it was found that the father hadn't murdered his wife, but on discovering she'd committed suicide, he'd had a mental breakdown which had resulted in the scene that we'd uncovered following the routine investigation of a vulnerable child.

There were other instances, too, that stick out – like the very scruffy teacher who ran into the station in a panic having 'lost' six teenagers with learning difficulties somewhere among the strip clubs and bars in Soho – but mostly we dealt with children and teenagers who had run away from social services.

Children who habitually ran away from what was considered to be a safe environment or what appeared to be a loving family would be repeatedly returned to goodness only knows what horror. The prevailing attitude of the courts, social workers and many senior officers was that the children were misfits and troublemakers rather than vulnerable youngsters screaming for help.

Of course, this was the time when Jimmy Savile was still regarded as a national treasure not a predatory abuser and Cyril Smith was considered one of England's eccentrics and a philanthropist who gave up his time to befriend boys in care homes. It's only with hindsight, now that all the physical and mental abuse perpetrated on innocent and defenceless children by those who were supposed to be protecting them has come to light, that I realise, sadly, we on the thin blue frontline were part of the problem.

Now, being a police officer was an all-encompassing role and, unlike every other job I'd ever had, I was never truly off duty. As a serving police officer, all my actions were subject to police rules and regulations. This sense of *being* an officer rather than *working* as an officer was further reinforced by the fact that many of us not only worked together but also lived in the section house together.

Accommodation for officers became available when the Metropolitan Police Force was established in the mid-1800s as a way of making sure officers weren't living cheek by jowl with criminals. Also, as it meant you lived rent free, it was an added incentive for men to join.

When I was growing up there were blocks of police flats between the maisonette where I lived and my school, and my mum was friendly with a few of the police wives who attended St Dunstan's Church.

This policy remained right through to the 1980s that any police officer who was getting married could apply for free police accommodation. If you did decide to buy your own property, then the force would give you a rent allowance to compensate. However, single officers were housed in a section house.

Trenchard House, where I'd been given accommodation, was completely self-contained, and along with the twenty-four-hour canteen there was a laundry area with washing machines, drying racks and half a dozen ironing boards in the basement. There were two TV lounges on the first floor, one each for BBC1 and ITV, plus a smaller one in the basement assigned to BBC2. There was also a games room with a snooker table.

Other than the second floor, where the women's rooms were, the rest of the building was set aside as accommodation for any male officer who wanted it.

Although most of us in the section house were probationers under the age of thirty, there were twenty or so older male officers who could best be described as professional bachelors. They had been on C Division 'ground' for a number of years and had settled into a comfortable niche. Oddly, however, despite the fact that these men didn't seem to want to settle down, many of them were engaged to WPCs who also lived in the section house.

I was puzzled by this until I noticed that whenever I met these WPC fiancées in the laundry room, they were either washing or ironing a pile of their intended's police shirts.

In addition, these engaged PCs benefited from this arrangement in other ways apart from the obvious conjugal one.

Those desperate to move into the CID felt one way of increasing their chances of selection was to get the swagger, slang and attitude off pat. And the best way of perfecting this was to study the experts: Inspector Jack Regan and Sergeant George Carter in the cult TV show *The Sweeney*. Although the ITV lounge could comfortably accommodate three dozen people, the seats in front of the twenty-two-inch screen were much prized. Each week for up to two hours prior to the programme starting, the front row was occupied by a handful of engaged women, who were keeping the seats warm for their PC fiancés.

Of course, eventually, the WPC would realise that they were in fact little more than a skivvy with benefits. Once the penny dropped so were their insincere fiancés, but lo and behold a month or two later, when a new WPC moved into the section house, these professional bachelors became engaged all over again.

Even though many of the other women at the section house were based at other stations and reliefs throughout London, I soon got to know them all as there were only twenty or so or us living at Trenchard House. The kitchen became a bit of a meeting place as we made ourselves a hot drink or did our ironing.

Also, despite Sergeant Perriman's assertion that members of the opposite sex weren't allowed in officers' rooms, nearly all of my fellow WPCs had boyfriends who slept in their rooms. In the good old days, when he had only the male officers' moral welfare to worry about, the warden would patrol the corridor, key in hand, ready to burst into the room if he heard female giggling or gasps of ecstasy, but even the chauvinistic top brass realised that allowing a male warden to enter young women's rooms at any time he felt the rules were being infringed was asking for a heap of trouble.

To be fair to the beleaguered sergeant, the section house was in the middle of Soho with half a dozen strip clubs visible from the front door and prostitutes pinning up their cards in every telephone box, so trying to keep a hundred-plus healthy young men from being led into deep trouble by their cods was a nightmare posting. And once women were actually in the building rather than having to be sneaked past the front desk, then poor Perriman was fighting a losing battle.

Within a few weeks of moving into Trenchard House I felt like I'd been there for ever. I'd quickly settled in but as my room, which was opposite the lift and main entrance to the stairs, with people opening and shutting the door at all hours, wasn't exactly conducive to getting a good night's sleep, I asked to move to another room around the corner and further down the corridor.

My new room was slightly larger and over the kitchen, which meant, even with the draft from the ill-fitting Crittall windows, it was lovely and warm. After my first payday as a proper policewoman, I strolled up to John Lewis and bought myself a new duvet and bed linen, a pair of flowery curtains, a set of shelves to put the books I'd brought from home on and a fluffy rug.

All in all, with my room snug and cosy and an exciting new job, life was brilliant, but there was something important missing. However, about a week or so after I started at West End Central, I found it.

CHAPTER SEVENTEEN

Finding my Anchor

N OW YOU MAY have noticed that I haven't mentioned
Environmental Health Man for a while but perhaps
that's not so surprising given the antics at training school.

When I started at West End Central at the beginning of
August we were still engaged, with a church and wedding
reception booked for the following April, but while I was
working up the courage to tell him it was over between us,
fate stepped in.

For those living in the section house, if you were on the
same relief, the usual practice was to meet for breakfast in the
canteen and then stroll across to the station. However, on my
first Sunday I was late down so everyone had already set off.
Knowing that my first stop with Geordie would be Claridge's
kitchens I wasn't too put out, but as I started down the stairs
a deep voice called wait.

I turned to see one of the probationers on D Relief who
was walking past the warden's office.

Although I hadn't spoken to him before, I had noticed him
on parade that week as being tall, dark-haired and well-built

with sideburns and a moustache, as well as having a bit of the young Elvis about him, he was very much my type.

Happy to have a good-looking man in uniform accompany me on the ten-minute stroll to the station, I found out he had the unusual name of Kelvin and that he was just a few months from finishing his probation. He also spotted my engagement ring and I told him I was getting married the following year.

Having reached the station, we headed to the parade room where we parted company. I can't say I gave him too much thought until he appeared again one evening in the games room. I was playing snooker with one of the other probationers when he strolled in, and after loitering about for a bit, he came over. I'd like to think it was my dazzling beauty that drew him to me but, as he later confessed, it was the fact that I wasn't wearing a bra under my T-shirt that caught his eye!

After the game finished, he asked if I fancied joining a couple of the others from the relief down at the St Moritz Club, a stone's throw away in Wardour Street. We decamped there and after a couple of dances and a few rum and cokes and beers we made our way back to Trenchard House.

Well, what can I say? One thing led to another and suffice to say, we woke up the next morning in the single bed in my room. Now, although I was no innocent, I was no good-time girl either, and finding myself suddenly having what I thought was a one-night stand made me stop.

However, although, it was clear that Kelvin wanted to take things further, he didn't push or crowd me, but he made it clear that he was waiting for me to make a decision.

I visited Environmental Health Man to see if the old happily engaged me was still there, but it wasn't; there was no going back.

The whole thing came to a head one night when, stupidly, in an attempt to be 'one of the lads' Dee and I went to a relief stag do somewhere. After several hours of drinking and riotous rugby songs, in true stag-night tradition, the prospective groom was de-bagged. Waving his trousers in the air, the others were dragging him over, half-naked, to where Dee and I were standing, shouting for us to have a look. At that point Kelvin stepped in and drew me away from the tussle, and he stayed beside me for the rest of the evening.

I woke up in my own bed the next morning, alone and with a sore head, and came to a decision.

That evening I went down to the floor below and knocked on Kelvin's door.

My husband often says he fell in love with me at first sight. I have to admit it took me a bit longer, but although I knew next to nothing about him, after only a few weeks, I knew he was the one for me.

I made one last trip to Pimlico and told Environmental Health Man I'd met someone else and that I was cancelling the wedding.

At a dance a week later Kelvin told me he was going to marry me and, as he always tells people, it was the one time in our life together I didn't argue. We got engaged three weeks later and Kelvin moved into my room, bringing his TV with him. Somehow we slept quite comfortably in a single bed until we got married just over a year later.

I knew I'd chosen well when, after I passed my driving test a few weeks later, he agreed to get a mini as I'd learned to drive in one. Quite an act of love for a six-foot man with the physique of a rugby player.

As the only people I knew who had more than three children were Catholics, I was surprised to find out that although he was one of seven children, his family didn't belong to this religious persuasion. His family also lived in St Albans and as I knew only the High Street and the olde-worlde Georgian houses around the cathedral I thought perhaps he came from a well-to-do family. However, when he took me home to meet his family a few weeks later I realised that the old cathedral city had council estates, too. His mother hated me on sight; despite me having a cockney accent that could cut glass, for some unfathomable reason she considered me posh!

In contrast to the reception I received from my future mother-in-law, the Fullertons took Kelvin to their bosom like a long-lost son. My father, in particular, thought he was the best thing since sliced bread.

When Kelvin formally asked him for my hand he assured him that he would look after me, to which my father replied, 'Good, cause she'll need some looking after.'

My father was now a regular at the Friday-night visits to the pub with the rest of the Fullertons and a handful of old family friends, all of whom had known each other since they ran barefooted through the streets fifty years before. When not on duty, my intended and I, in our little mustard mini, drove over to join them at the Duke of Norfolk.

The pub, a short walk from Martha's house, was one of the last proper East End family-run pubs, with an out-of-tune upright piano and a pitted dartboard with an oche – the rubber mat in front of the dartboard – so worn, the distance marks were barely visible.

Along with the drinkers there were some other Friday-night regulars in the Duke of Norfolk. The Salvation Army, or Sally Army as they were affectionately known, in their peaked caps and straw bonnets were often at the pub selling copies of *War Cry*.

Another familiar face was the shellfish man, lugging a wicker basket over his arm filled with the cockney delights of cockles, winkles, jellied eels and shrimps. With a splash of vinegar on them, they were a must for any pub singalong.

Of course, being an East End pub there were other regulars too, usually offering you stuff that had fallen off the back of a lorry. After a quiet word from the landlady, they usually slipped out the other door without bothering us.

We decided on a date, and set about organising our wedding, pitching up at St Dunstan's to book ourselves a slot. Having booked the church, we thought we should treat ourselves to a proper honeymoon. We considered the Isle of Wight but plumped instead for a week in Benidorm as it was cheaper – £63 each, all-inclusive. Neither of us held passports and back then you could have a passport issued in your married name before the wedding, so when mine came back, for the first time ever I was officially a Mrs.

Despite the IRA planting two dozen letter bombs up and down Regent Street and Oxford Street the night before our engagement party, which meant we'd been called back to the station, we still made it to our party in St Albans.

As my friend and partner in crime Dee was also getting married a few months before us, she and I spent a lot of time flipping through bridal magazines and planning for our big days. However, I was only looking for ideas because I'd already decided to make the dress for my special day.

For weeks I trotted back and forth to my father's maisonette and, using my mum's old Singer sewing machine, I made fifteen yards of ivory moire satin into a medieval-style wedding dress with a three-foot train. I bought my veil mail order but made the orange-blossom comb headdress with wax flowers and silver cake decoration leaves.

My Aunt Martha kindly made all six of the bridesmaid dresses, including poke bonnets for four little ones, while I bought white hats for the two adults, one of whom was my old school friend Audrey.

Having been allocated our two-bedroom police flat only a few weeks before the big day, it was a bit of a scramble to get everything ready in time, but we managed to decorate, get the carpets down and the furniture in.

In time-honoured tradition, the lads on D Relief insisted on organising Kelvin's stag do in the King of Corsica, the pub that was for all intents and purposes an annexe of Trenchard House.

I did insist that he have it on Thursday rather than the day before the wedding as some police stag dos ended up with the groom tied naked to a lamp-post or waking up on the night train to Glasgow.

Finally, a year and a month after we'd first met, the big day arrived.

Unlike today, when you can have a make-up artist and hairdresser turn up at the crack of dawn to make the bride and all the other women in the bridal party look like film stars, I had to go to the hairdresser and put my own face on. I have dead straight hair that would defy curling with a blowtorch, so within minutes of leaving the hairdresser my bob had fallen out, but thankfully, after a couple of goes, I managed to get my false eyelashes to stick.

As the wedding service was at three-thirty we had all morning to get ourselves ready, so, with my Aunt Martha standing in as mother-of-the bride, the dresses were removed from their protective wrappers and hats steamed as the neighbours popped in throughout the morning to wish me luck. My Uncle Wag collected the flowers from the florist and after we'd set our buttonholes and bouquets aside someone took the rest to the church for the guests.

My Uncle Bob took the bridesmaids and my aunt to the church, leaving me and my father to wait for the Rolls-Royce to turn up. I imagine he said something to me as we sat there in the lounge waiting for the car to arrive, but it was clearly nothing memorable as I can't remember what it was. The driver knocked on the door within a few moments and we sped off to the church. With his stick to steady him, my father walked me down the aisle and I happily swapped my Miss status for Mrs.

We emerged from the church under an arch of police truncheons formed by our relief, who were standing outside. After the usual round of photos we climbed back into to the Rolls-Royce and headed to the reception. As it was in Dame Collet House, which backs on to the churchyard, this was the shortest journey ever. Even so, as we'd had another round of photos in the car, by the time we reached the hall, our guests were already there waiting for us, many of them up at the bar ordering their first pint.

We had a three-course sit-down meal of soup, roast beef followed by apple pie and ice cream, plus a glass of sparkling white wine, all for the princely sum of £1.50 a head.

As my father wasn't well enough to make a speech, my Uncle Bob stood in for him. As always, Bobby went at it with gusto and soon everyone was laughing. The meal over, the caterers cleared away the tables and the evening reception began. The disc jockey took his place behind the turntable on the stage and put on the Carpenters 'We've Only Just Begun'.

Cheesy. I know!

Holding the train of my dress so as not to have us both fall flat on our faces, we managed to stumble around the dance floor a couple of times before others joined us.

As the music faded Kelvin's mother came over and announced that as it was getting late – it was about six-thirty in the evening – they would all have to go. We said our goodbyes, and after gathering themselves together, two dozen family members from the groom's side left.

As the door closed behind them my Uncle Wag shouted, 'Thank gawd they've gone, we can all enjoy ourselves now.'

And we did.

My father, in an uncharacteristic burst of generosity, put fifty pounds behind the bar and everyone got the drinks in. Bob and Elaine tripped the light fantastic around the dancefloor while after a bit of cajoling my Aunt Martha and Wag did the same.

Despite being lifelong thorns in each other's side, my aunts Millie and Nell were up there doing some formation dance they'd both learned called the Slosh.

Between hits from Steve Wonder and Abba, we all put various limbs in and out for 'The Hokey Cokey', then after a bit of communal air guitar along to Status Quo, we swaggered around with our thumbs in imaginary braces for 'The Lambeth Walk'.

Sometime around nine-thirty, we said our goodbyes and headed off through the old streets that I'd played in as a child, past the stall in the markets where I'd squandered my Saturday-girl wages buying Mary Quant knock-off, my old senior school and away from East London and on to our new life together.

Epilogue

SADLY, FOR THE older generation of Fullertons, whose lives stretched back to the dawn of the twentieth century, our wedding was the last hurrah.

My Aunt Millie developed dementia a few years later and spent her final months in a mental hospital. Uncle Wag died of a heart attack and Martha, who never got over the loss, moved to Southampton to be with his sister. Nell lived long enough to see my first two daughters born, but after a lifetime of maintaining 'just a little bit of something' her diabetes finally caught up with her and she died of kidney failure three days after having a necrotic toe removed.

As for my father.

He lived long enough for me to be able to tell him just before Christmas 1980 that I was expecting a baby. He died of a massive heart attack six weeks later.

Although I moved out of Stepney, I stayed in East London rather than moving into Essex like so many other of East Enders: first to Wanstead in our police flat and then to Romford where the East End spirit lives on.

But although many of us who knew the old streets and ways have shifted to pastures new, thanks to its proximity to the City and the regeneration of the Docklands in the 1980s, the East End has done what it has always done and reinvented itself.

The old Victorian and Edwardian houses have now been renovated as the whole area has been gentrified. The Jewish bakers have been replaced by specialist coffee bars and the high windows of the old weavers' houses in Spitalfields are now the homes of artists. The markets are still there, but sari fabric has replaced Carnaby Street knock-offs and the stalls sell avocados instead of turnips, but that's fine. Some old East Enders shake their heads and say East London's not the same. And in some ways it's true.

The London Hospital, which treated East Londoners' ailment for almost three hundred years, is now being converted into a new town hall. Thanks to its association with the Krays, the Blind Beggar is now a tourist stop, and Brick Lane now has a worldwide reputation for its curry houses. Club Row, which used to be an open-air pet shop each Sunday morning, has long gone. There's a massive flyover spanning Mile End Road at its junction with Burdett Road, which joins the greenery on either side.

Watney Street is almost unrecognisable as the old street I knew as a child and most of the Chapman Estate, where my family first settled and lived for a hundred-plus years, is beneath the concrete edifice and playground of Mulberry School for Girls, but in all the ways that it matters, East London is just the same.

It is now what it's always been: a melting pot of people, like my Huguenot ancestors who fled to this country because of persecution or my Irish ones who came to escape starvation, or my Scottish family who travelled south for work and my Somerset forebears who left rural poverty behind.

Whereas a hundred years ago those born within the sound of Bow Bells had Irish or Jewish heritage, today most cockneys trace their families back to the Middle or Far East, but they are still part of that robust heritage of grafters and survivors.

Although the large Fullerton family who left an indelible mark on me have shuffled off this mortal coil, the world they knew and their indomitable spirit spring back to glorious life as I weave countless threads of their lives into my East End stories.

I no longer live in East London but am a frequent visitor to the old streets, and wandering around I feel just as at home as I did when I was a child. But that's no surprise because as I said in my introduction, East London is a place in your heart, not on a map.

Acknowledgements

Following on from my personal dedication I'd like to thank my brother Andrew who helped me remember something about our shared childhood I'd forgotten. A few friends of my tribe. Janet Gover, Carole Matthews, Fenella Miller, Lynda Stacy, Rachel Summerson who have walked with me alongside me on this very personal journey and supported me in their own unique way.

I'd like to thank my agent Kate Burke, from Blake Friedmann Literary Agents for her steadfast support, encouragement and editorial skills. A big thanks goes to Sarah de Souza for her detailed and insightful edits. I'd like to extend that thanks to the wonderful team at Atlantic Books, Karen Duffy, Jamie Forrest, Sophie Walker, Harry O'Sullivan and Hanna Kenne for all their support and innovation.